Kicked a Building Lately?

By the Same Author

CLASSICAL NEW YORK
PIER LUIGI NERVI
WILL THEY EVER FINISH BRUCKNER BOULEVARD?

Kicked a Building Lately?

ADA LOUISE HUXTABLE

QUADRANGLE/THE NEW YORK TIMES BOOK CO.

Book design: Beth Tondreau

Library of Congress Cataloging in Publication Data
Huxtable, Ada Louise.
KICKED A BUILDING LATELY?

Includes index.
1. Architecture—Addresses, essays, lectures.
2. Architecture, Modern—20th century—Addresses,
essays, lectures. I. Title.
NA2563.H88 1976   720   75-36276
ISBN 0-8129-0630-6

To Garth

Contents

CONTENTS

THE PRESENT—CITIES

CONTENTS

CONTENTS

Introduction

It is five years since my first group of essays on architecture and the urban scene appeared as *Will They Ever Finish Bruckner Boulevard?* In case anyone wants to know, Slattery Associates claims that they have, indeed, finished Bruckner Boulevard; they were stung enough by the inquiry to issue a release on the subject.

Well, it depends on what you mean by finished. And how you read the question in the first place. It was intended as an ironic comment on technology, bureaucracy, illusory solutions that exacerbate problems, the relative qualities of bottlenecks, and almost anything else that turns the environment into the world of the absurd. That was meant, in fact, to be the theme of the book.

The theme is intact. The expressway brontosaurus whose bones lay strewn and half-attached for what seemed like fifty years and was definitely twenty, is now in place; concrete has supplanted mud. The expressway landscape offers its soulless and scaleless limbo with a trompe l'oeil efficiency. For anyone following an ordained route to suburbia, it functions. But if you happen to come by way of the Hutchinson River Parkway and try to head for that magnet of civilization, Manhattan, be prepared for the death-defying squeeze-dance that shunts you to the service roads, or right back onto familiar old, unchanged Bruckner Boulevard, past Joe and Joe's bar and the little row houses with headaches, before you can get to the Expressway again. In summer, there are amazing roses and zinnias in those concrete-girdled pocket-handkerchief front yards, a vista the Expressway bypasses.

There is also the problem now of inadequate and frequently choked connectors to the new expressway. The suggestion of the ultimate solution (how optimistically we pursue the ultimate solution) is a self-deception. Obviously, it all works on paper and is all balled up in reality—perhaps the definitive comment on our times. Nothing is finished, nothing is solved. But then, nothing ever is. History, after all, is a continuing state of flux. And Utopia is a recurring nightmare.

I prefer the nightmare of reality. In fact, I have developed a certain attachment to it. Reality, as I write this, is New York in extremis, approaching bankruptcy, a situation that may or may not have changed radically when this book appears. What will not have changed is the new and awful necessity that increasing city, state, and even federal financing problems are pressing upon us: the reexamination of our social and democratic doctrines and our system of government to find out how to make the world we believe in work, or whether that world is irrevocably lost.

Right now, with default in the air, garbage in the streets and New Yorkers not knowing where their next 50 cent carfare is coming from, the situation is desperate indeed. The question seems to be whether there is going to be a New York at all, and refinements on that particular theme in terms of the environmental quality of the holocaust appear foolishly beside the point. First things first, like existence. Others can wait, like a city worth living in. That is considered a frivolity under the circumstances, something in the luxury category.

And yet the city, close to failure and facing depression-level stringencies and deprivations, has never seemed richer. Layers of ground-in soil and vintage litter dim its luster, but New York is like impoverished aristocracy—shabbily elegant to the end. Not at City Hall, where the tragedy is enacted like comedy by bit players, but in the still-beautiful side streets of the East Sixties with their intimate, throw-away palaces, in the maze of Lower Manhattan with its drop-dead skyscrapers, in the superb shops and boutiques which prosper in direct relationship to their stratospheric prices, in the creative electricity that poverty does not seem to touch. If this is catastrophe, it comes with class.

It is an irony that apocalypse coincides with a triumph for environmental values, which now seem emblazoned on everyone's consciousness—at a time when no one can afford to do much about them. Outside of New York, where the money crunch is bad but has not yet reached the bottom line, a great deal of attention is being paid to those preoccupations of place, from far-ranging, critical court decisions on whether a city can control its growth and the quality of its destiny (Petaluma, California) to a record amount of creative preservation of a once undervalued and marvelously motley heritage.

Let me say that the satisfactions of the urban critic's job are few, but they are monumental. If some of these essays seem mellower, if the tone seems a little less desperate, if the thread is no longer a sustained wail, it is not because there are any fewer battles to be fought; it is because they are taking place on different ground. The situation has changed. The campaigns are now being waged with the backing of an unprecedented public commitment and a vastly increased public knowledge. It is proving difficult for even an unenlightened political leadership to retreat on the environment.

What has happened is that there is a far more sophisticated sense of architecture and a deeper response to the built world today than ever before in history. And this comprehension is developing an almost universal constituency. The voice-in-the-wilderness role has passed. In these years, a kind of wisdom has emerged. People have learned to see and feel the city; they are consciously involved in the technology and esthetics and human effects of its buildings, spaces, and styles. These considerations have become—true test of relevance —political issues.

We have been through the total rejection of the free-standing monument as irrelevant to society; we have survived the pendulum swing to advocacy architecture which set social needs as the sole criterion of practice. The truth is somewhere between art for art's sake and art for society's sake; but art is the eternal constant. We are finally beginning to understand its true role.

We know now that the art of architecture is extremely sensitive, sophisticated, and complex; that it is the art of solitude and of the total city; of esthetic absolutes and urban synthesis; that both body and soul must be satisfied. We are only beginning to understand why, and how. But we are setting higher standards for the form and quality of cities and the kind of life that they produce. The challenge, even without an uncooperative economy, is staggering.

This is actually a period of transition between knowledge and practice, comprehension and effect, and these writings reflect that state of the world and the art. It would have been tempting to weight the score with small triumphs—there is really a rather remarkable list— but that would be misleading in the face of the dimensions of the problems that remain. We are dealing with a large victory of attitude and perception laced with a lot of small defeats.

On the plus side, there has been a near-total reversal of attitudes toward the past. Preservation, the woolly, sentimental cause of those little old ladies in tennis shoes, is now endorsed by astute developers everywhere in an avalanche of imaginative recycling of old structures of diversity and dignity. This is being done with taste, wit, educated

Garth Huxtable

judgment, and a firm grasp of such esoterica as historical and cultural relevance and urban variety and enrichment. It isn't just a movement; it's a mild stampede. (I've just thrown my tennis shoes away.)

Neighborhood conservation has become a priority in cities everywhere, based on a growing recognition of the values of community and its roots in the history and amenity of the physical setting. In a complex and still-evolving national about-face, bulldozer speculation has been slowed less by recession than by the concept of neighborhood, an idea and reality evolving through the innovative use of a variety of legal, government, and architectural tools that never existed before.

The level of architectural design has risen significantly across the country (although I will be the first to admit that you won't find a masterpiece on every corner), along with the frequency of professional response to the human and urban condition. To take the most unpromising indicator, one need only look at that traditional slough of mediocrity, public and institutional construction. There is, of course, no moratorium yet on instantly disintegrating courthouses and county seats and expressions of fallible vanity, and Washington remains a disaster area. But Boston's handsome Government Center, or the recent buildings of New York's Civic Center, with far-above average structures and open-space treatment, are clear demonstrations that the standard of official construction has been raised light years beyond that of a generation ago, when the norm was unadulterated hack.

One finds that the infrastructure of the city is also responding to design. New Yorkers have quietly celebrated a small explosion of plazas, passageways, greenery, and places to sit (we need much, much more). Carefully reworked zoning regulations have transformed sterile spaces into increasingly pleasant and knowing demonstrations of urban design expertise. Other cities have successful pedestrian malls and revitalized Main Streets.

There are brilliant exercises in design and urbanism in such places as Atlanta and Minneapolis. For every inevitable atrocity in America's largely rebuilt cities, there is at least one distinguished performance or redemptive architectural act that was inconceivable a few years ago. And in the best commercial work, professionalism has quietly married art.

Any country that can build like this, and that has developed the sensitivities to past and present and a wise, sympathetic awareness of identity and place, can't be all bad. But the paradoxes are baffling and tragic. We can do some things almost too well, and other, essential things, not at all.

INTRODUCTION

We can create masterworks of technology, but we cannot house our poor or keep open our schools and libraries, or make simple commitments to basic human needs, just as we are beginning to understand what those needs are. We have made no impression on the city's worst pathology, the ghetto slum.

Still, we are developing a kind of social, cultural, and esthetic consciousness unparalleled in history, based on a growing knowledge of the nature, effects, and components of the built world. At the same time we have a government renouncing that vision and retrenching on those values at the moment of their most spectacular flowering, and an economy that cannot support them at all. And there is never any moratorium on the four urban horsemen: expediency, obstructionism, stupidity, and greed.

This is an extremely troubling and uncertain time, but I would not swap it for any other. It is a source of extraordinary gratification that I have seen the environmental and architectural climate change substantially, and the level of public concern and comprehension rise meteorically, even though there has been no discernible progress toward a dubious Utopia. In fact, this selection of essays starts with a few classic kicks. They are aimed at those monumental structures of high visibility and high aspirations that should represent the American architectural genius at its best and have failed to do so. Our most conspicuous disasters are in the two essential areas of cultural symbolism and the provision of housing. But there are many successes and pleasures to celebrate as well, in new and old buildings and in a burgeoning sensibility to the built environment. I measure success by the street-corner. My obsessions are now shared and my co-conspirators are everywhere. Assuming survival, the battle for the future is well-joined. I'll still be kicking buildings for a while.

The Present—Buildings

The Monumental
Muddle

THE KENNEDY CENTER, I*

The capital city specializes in ballooning monuments and endless corridors. It uses marble like cotton wool. It is the home of government
of, for, and by the people, and of taste for the people—the big, the
bland, and the banal. The John F. Kennedy Center for the Performing
Arts does not break the rule. The style of the Kennedy Center is
Washington superscale, but just a little bit bigger. Albert Speer would
have approved.

It has apotheosized the corridor in the 600-foot-long, 60-foot-high
grand foyer (the length of three New York City blockfronts), one of
the biggest rooms in the world, into which the Hall of Mirrors at
Versailles could be cozily nested. It would be a super-tunnel without
its saving Belgian gift of mirrors.

The corridor is "dressed up," in the words of the architect Edward
Durell Stone, by 18 of the world's biggest crystal chandeliers. There
is enough red carpet for a total environment.

There are two other flag-hung, polished marble-walled, red-car-
peted, 250-foot-long and 60-foot-high corridors called the Hall of
States and the Hall of Nations. They are disquietingly reminiscent of
the overscaled vacuity of Soviet palaces of culture. They would be
great for drag racing.

The two halls separate the three theaters that are the structure's

* This review was written for the opening of the Kennedy Center on September
6, 1971. It is followed by a piece that examines it in greater detail.

3

raison d'être: the Opera House, the Concert Hall, and the Eisenhower Theater. The grand foyer is the entrance to them all.

The building itself is a superbunker, 100 feet high, 630 feet long, and 300 feet wide, on the Potomac. One more like this and the city will sink.

Because it is a national landmark, there is only one way to judge the Kennedy Center—against the established standard of progressive and innovative excellence in architectural design that this country is known and admired for internationally.

Unfortunately, the Kennedy Center not only does not achieve this standard of innovative excellence; it also did not seek it. The architect opted for something ambiguously called "timelessness" and produced meaninglessness. It is to the Washington manner born. Too bad, since there is so much of it.

The center sets still another record—for architectural default. What it has in size, it lacks in distinction. Its character is aggrandized posh. It is an embarrassment to have it stand as a symbol of American artistic achievement before the nation and the world. The interiors aim for conventional, comfortable, gargantuan grand luxe. This is gemütlich Speer.

The Opera House, a 2,200-seat hall with superior sightlines and equipment, looks like one of those passé, red-padded drugstore candy valentines. Its dark red fabric walls are buttoned down with rows of gold knobs and its Austrian crystal lights suggest nothing so much as department store Christmas displays.

The 2,575-seat Concert Hall, its acoustic wood walls painted white, has red seats and carpet and is buttoned down with Norwegian crystal fixtures. It suggests 1920s modern. Restaurants on the top terrace floor are in expense-account French by way of Austria, or they are near-Scandinavian. They are all red.

There are two ways of defending the center's design. One, already popular, is to say that it doesn't really matter and that the only things that count are those badly needed performance halls and how they work. But nothing justifies wrapping those halls in nearly $70-million of timid corn and 17,000 tons of steel—all a conscious design decision —and ignoring it. If you could ignore it, which is hard.

To say that everything else about a landmark structure of this stupefying size is irrelevant is nonsense. The emperor, unfortunately, is wearing clothes. And the world is looking.

The second defense is simply to accept the fact that the center probably represents the norm of American taste. But it is a fallacy to equate the great middle common denominator of popular taste with the country's actual and potential level of creative achievement.

From this point of view, however, it is almost an interesting building. If Mr. Stone has been aiming for an architecture that all America can love, he has found it. This is architectural populism. He has produced a conventional crowd pleaser, a safe, familiar blend of theoretical glamour and showroom Castro Convertible. It is a genuine people's palace.

For the more architecturally sophisticated, it is hard to admire a failure of vision and art. The center was probably wrong from the start. It was conceived as a giant economy three-in-one package. If it hasn't cost more than three separate buildings, it certainly hasn't cost less, and it has had formidable construction problems as a result of the "simple" concept.

The three houses have had to be separated and insulated from each other for vibration and sound inside and jets outside, and from other floors and functions. Suspension and soundproofing have been achieved through incredibly complex and expensive concrete and steelwork that belies the apparent logic of the plan. Structurally, the achievement is considerable. The giant steel trusses hidden behind the scenes are far more impressive than the truly awful, gold-epoxy-painted steel columns that run visibly through the building, which add decorative aluminum fins along the facades.

Environmentally, the center has been severely criticized for its setting and isolation from city life. But many Washingtonians like the idea of driving to a "safe" bastion of culture. Again, it's what people really want.

As completed, the center's plusses include its public amenities—its entrance plaza, riverfront promenade, eating facilities and outdoor terraces with views. And credit as well as sympathy must go to the dedicated and hardworking sponsors who have actually brought three major performance halls to Washington.

May all the performing arts flourish. Because the building is a national tragedy. It is a cross between a concrete candy box and a marble sarcophagus in which the art of architecture lies buried.

September 7, 1971

THE KENNEDY CENTER, II

It seems like simple sense to understand that housing the arts is also an act of art, and how they are housed is terribly revealing of the state of the arts, or at least, of the state of mind of the sponsors.

What the Kennedy Center implicitly says about both is that they are consummately conventional, totally lackluster, distrustful of creativity and fearful of greatness. The building flatly declares the ordinary.

It is worth examining why. First, however, it must be noted that it could easily have been better. The current plans for the National Gallery extension are bold and brilliant, and no Washington institution carries a greater inhibiting burden of tradition and orthodoxy.

One Washington tradition is that large architectural decisions are made by committees. These committees, set up for worthwhile purposes such as the Kennedy Center, tend to be heavy with people of position, wealth, leverage, and national reputation and light on people who might have professional knowledge of the arts of building, design, and environment.

The Kennedy Center committee was notoriously light in those areas in the decision-making stage. This means that a lot of fine, well-intentioned people, experienced in business, diplomacy, and other prestigious but largely irrelevant pursuits to the task at hand except for fund-raising connections, decide what shall be built and where, and who will design it. They follow their personal taste. They may not know if it's architecture, but they know what they like.

In the case of the Kennedy Center, that taste led directly to Edward Durell Stone. Now the case of Edward Durell Stone is a touchy one. Mr. Stone is a man of great charm and talent, with a reputation made originally in experimental works of the early modern movement, the buildings of which were admittedly full of innovative glory and grievous error. Then he slipped out of the limelight until recent years when he resurfaced with great fanfare and a completely revamped design philosophy and became enormously successful.

Mr. Stone had developed a package that any businessman, layman, or committee could buy. He told them that "modern" didn't have to be austere or difficult. He said there was no reason why it couldn't offer traditional luxuries served up in a "timeless" style. If red and gold, for example, made good traditional interiors, they should make good modern ones. (Interestingly enough, in his redundantly red and gold

6

The Kennedy Center, a marble box in which the art of architecture lies buried. *The New York Times/George Tames*

buildings, they don't. They look cheap, dull, or gaudy, because they cannot approximate the traditional arts and crafts that were intrinsic to those traditional decorative effects.)

This formula, he said, would outlast more daring or temporal designs. This is exactly what the amateur sponsor, unequipped to judge "daring" designs, wanted to hear. He could have his fancy cake as long as the cake could be called contemporary, and the result would cause neither intellectual nor emotional angst. Somewhere along the line Mr. Stone sold himself on this theory as thoroughly as he sold his clients.

The test of the theory is in the buildings, and the final proof of failure is the safe and sanitary kitsch that is the Kennedy Center. The demonstrable fault is in Mr. Stone's architectural philosophy.

The fallacy is that you can't deliberately aim for "timelessness" without falling on your face. A great building grows naturally out of a confluence of conditions intrinsic to a particular moment in history. All great buildings are inescapably of their own moment in time; they are the signposts of civilization. They become "timeless" in relation to their greatness—later.

A great building is so magnificently of its period and so perfectly expressive of the creative genius as conditioned by existing uses, beliefs, and technologies, that it transcends its time to become one of those historical signposts. Thus Chartres, Sant'Ivo, Ronchamps.

Therefore, when Mr. Stone says, "I did not want to build a 1970s building," he is already crossing up history and the muse. Bernini built 1670s buildings. They express everything of the immediate baroque world. The level of genius by which this particularism becomes a specific esthetic makes them timeless. To aim for something untouched by, or that sidesteps, the moment, is to miss both history and art. The moment contains the stuff of immortality.

Mr. Stone's approach has brought a plague of dreadful buildings. (There are exceptions: the somewhat Wrightian National Geographic Building in Washington keeps within the stream of architectural development, albeit in the backward-leaning way that seems to suit Washington best; it has not abdicated totally to the formula.) But it is time to see this package of philosophical and esthetic pablum for what it is: a client-pacifier guaranteed to produce non-architecture. In the resulting pastiche of decorative adaptations there is nothing to elevate, ennoble, enlighten, or enlarge the esthetic experience or sensibilities of the user in the way that great buildings have always expanded and enriched the spatial and sensuous awareness of man. Decorative recall is no substitute for a creative act. Good architecture is considerably harder to achieve. The Kennedy Center makes one sad, angry, and considerably ashamed to see art and architecture so short-changed.

September 19, 1971

THE HIRSHHORN MUSEUM

It is hard to know whether Washington does something to architects or architects do something to Washington. Perfectly respectable practitioners fall on their faces with alarming regularity, unstrung by the Capital's overblown scale and frequently overwrought grandeur. Even in the case of the most secure talent, something seems to go awry.

The last architect in the world it would be expected to go awry for is

THE MONUMENTAL MUDDLE

Gordon Bunshaft of Skidmore, Owings and Merrill, designer of the new $16-million Hirshhorn Museum and Sculpture Garden, the well-publicized concrete cylinder added to the Smithsonian's public museums in 1974, a collection that lines and encloses the Mall like a brontosaurian marble boneyard. Mr. Bunshaft is known for a kind of monumental absolutism so unyielding that the environment crumbles before it. He is not guilty of excessive humility or false modesty. He would therefore seem more than a match for the Capital's jinx.

But in the case of the Hirshhorn he has fought the Capital and the Mall to a draw, and alas, nobody wins. The result is a maimed monument and a maimed Mall, and saddest of all, even a major part of the collection that it has been built for is maimed. The sculpture garden or court that is one of the museum's principal features fights the large-scale sculpture; the pieces seem to do battle with the hard, bleak geometry of their setting, losing scale and power. This garden is so lacking in grace that it will not close the controversy over whether it should have been permitted to extend into the open green of the Mall.

One therefore questions the nature, no matter how good the intention, of the architectural design. And since Mr. Bunshaft is a known aficionado and collector of twentieth-century art, one tends to ask anew, must each man kill the thing he loves? If architecture is the weapon, something is very wrong indeed.

On the positive side, the building contains generous galleries that display painting and smaller sculpture well and work pleasantly for the visitor. The exhibition space consists of a large underground area, the ground level with its outdoor extensions, and two upper floors. (A top floor is for administration.)

The galleries have paintings on a windowless outer ring and small sculptures on a windowed inner ring; the two make up the building's hollow circular shape. The inner ring provides seats and a daylit view of an open court in its center. There is no sense of being thrown off balance, as at the Guggenheim, with its ramp and open well and total floor-to-roof view. But there is also no particular source of orientation as one goes in circles.

According to Mr. Bunshaft, deliberate architectural anonymity has been sought for these interiors. The intent is to display art so that it can be seen without "architectural distractions." But the architect makes no such claims of anonymity for the exterior, or for the building as a whole, referring to it as "a large piece of functional sculpture." The Hirshhorn publicity goes further to call it "an innovative and elegant architectural statement on the Mall."

Unfortunately, it is none of these things. Already famous, or notorious, for its circular shape and windowless bulk and labeled a marble doughnut by preconstruction publicity (high costs have substituted concrete aggregate for marble), it is known around Washington as the bunker or gas tank, lacking only gun emplacements or an Exxon sign. Its blind mass is broken by a Mussolini-style balcony on the Mall side. But jokes are too easy a dismissal of the undismissable. There are serious reasons why the museum and sculpture court fail as architecture.

To start, there is a heavy, lifeless brutality about this building. But it totally lacks the essential factors of esthetic strength and provocative vitality that make genuine "brutalism" a positive and rewarding style. This is born-dead, neo-penitentiary modern. It offers a rigid resistance to everything around it or part of it that should properly interact with it. Neither a sympathetic background nor an enriching balance of esthetic tensions is created. Its mass is not so much aggressive or overpowering as merely leaden.

Needless to say, these failures are writ large: the building is a hollow cylinder 231 feet in diameter and 82 feet high, with a 115-foot diameter inner court. This court is an eccentric circle, four feet off

The Hirshhorn Museum, where nobody wins. *Dennis Brack/Black Star*

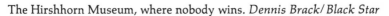

center. In the court, also off-center, is a bronze fountain 60 feet in diameter; by its size, position, water movement, and lighting it is clearly meant to upstage everything else in the place.

The round structure is raised 14 feet off the ground on four immense piers, and the bottom surface of the building, under which the visitor walks, has massive nine-foot-deep coffers with recessed lighting. Within the glass-enclosed entrance lobby, escalators slash through the coffers to the upper floors.

The fact that there is a dramatic structural rationale does not help the end result. The system of segmental ring girders and piers and columns that raises the building above the ground and carries its curved walls is a daring and ingenious one. (It's good they didn't run out of reinforcing rods in the piers.) But the structure does not lend itself to any kind of architectural presence beyond sheer bulk.

Big as this all is for anywhere else, however, on the Mall where buildings measure in thousands rather than in hundreds of feet, and with the neighboring Air and Space Museum being built to what seems like marble infinity, the Hirshhorn's round design is clearly meant to command attention through form if not size. But the lesser size cannot be mistaken for intimacy.

Due to budgetary problems, the extravagant materials and details usually characteristic of the architect's work are missing. It is rumored that Mr. Bunshaft has removed more travertine from Roman quarries than the Eternal City has used since Imperial days, and his way with a stainless steel joint is pure panache. And while the difference here does not bespeak modesty so much as economics, it does considerably dull the impact of an excruciatingly tastefully overstated richness that is his trademark. Without this luxury, the building is about as interesting as a bomb shelter.

A particularly questionable aspect of the design is the device of enclosing the site with a wall. Baldly stated, it is a disaster. This is clearly meant to isolate the Hirshhorn from everything around it—a dubious objective in the first place. Certainly the monumental sculpture could have held its own nicely against the richly coloristic Victorian Smithsonian on one side, or the ultimate blankness of the Air Museum on the other side. But it does not hold its own against that overpowering wall that not only cuts the Smithsonian but also the U.S. Capitol in half, with a similarly disturbing line running through some of the pieces. The Mall does not love a wall. It becomes an act of environmental effrontery.

In response to critical protest and design review, the sculpture garden was lowered 14 feet. However, it would have been an act of civility beyond this change if some gesture had been made toward the immediate surroundings, either in simple recognition or in character of design. The unbending rigidity of this open space design is surprisingly insensitive to anything except its own didactic aspirations. (One reaches the sculpture garden from the building either by tunnel under Jefferson Drive or by walking across the street.) It has not only been lowered; the original plan called for it to intrude twice as far into the Mall.

Why have the subtle, sensuous lessons of paving and planting and procession of spaces of the Museum of Modern Art sculpture garden never been learned? And how has it escaped notice that a first-rate piece of sculpture looks great on a simple swath of green, or in a field, or anywhere as part of something, not in *resistance* to it?

At best, this architecture is a male chauvinist marriage of building and art. And it raises a crucial point about container and contained that the design never addresses. To what degree can, and should, a museum building be a work of art in itself, and what kind of balance can be struck between the structure and the objects it serves?

Not only has Mr. Bunshaft apparently given a better answer at the Albright-Knox in Buffalo (which is almost universally admired although this writer has not seen it), but one senses an answer at the Everson Museum in Syracuse by I. M. Pei. A bold and beautiful sequence of related spaces, illuminated by passages of outdoor light and scenery, still preserves the painting and sculpture inviolate. In fact, the building offers complex and sensitive relationships that make the art come even more alive. The architecture gives skillful homage and support and enrichment to the other arts, and the mutual experience bespeaks the totality, greatness, and uniqueness of the esthetic achievement of the twentieth century.

Maybe the Pei-designed, massively expensive new East Wing of the National Gallery, currently under construction, will bring this revelation to Washington. Or maybe Mr. Pei, too, will take the Washington pratfall. The Capital has gained an important collection, but it has yet to have the appropriate expression of modern art and container that the national collections deserve.

October 6, 1974

THE LEHMAN WING
OF THE METROPOLITAN MUSEUM

The Lehman Wing of The Metropolitan Museum of Art, open to the public after a stormy five-year course from concept to reality including a trip through the courts, is now a fait accompli and a tour de force. Fait accompli, because construction is complete, making all of the heated controversy about the Lehman collection's disposition and housing, including pressures for museum decentralization and a lawsuit to prevent expansion in the park, almost—but not quite—academic. Tour de force, because it carries out a highly questionable program with consummate ingenuity, artistry, and skill.

What the Met and architects Kevin Roche, John Dinkaloo and Associates have produced is a coolly impersonal and quite exquisite small museum dedicated to the myth of the perpetuation of the personal stamp of the donor, through a stipulation of the bequest that seven rooms from Robert Lehman's 54th Street house be re-created as they were in his lifetime, as part of the building and its installation.

If one can, as a start, accept as desirable the reproduction of a 1959 Paris decorator's version of how to turn 1905 rooms designed by the architect of Grant's Tomb into an "appropriate" background for Renaissance art—the rooms laid end-to-end in the park (buried and blind) instead of top-to-bottom on a city street—then one will have no ambivalent feelings about the building.

If it seems a little ludicrous or less than ideal for the art—then this handsome building falls down, conceptually, like a pack of elegant cards. But if the premise is accepted, the talented agility with which this curious handicap is metamorphosed into a structure of considerable esthetic drama can only be admired. It is a neat trick, superbly executed. On these terms, it is a classy job.

Let me make my own feelings clear. I am split right down the middle. I believe that the Met has done the wrong thing impeccably. The architects have designed their way out of the trap set by the terms of the gift—and it is a trap no matter how glossed over by smooth rationalizations—with taste and expertise. The quality of the collection and the pleasant way the building functions for the viewer are, in the end, the all-important factors. It is my personal feeling, however, that the pavilion vastly overcelebrates the collection and the donor. Having said this, let me describe how well a dubious thing can be done.

13

The Lehman wing, which cost $7,100,000 and is completely paid for by Lehman funds, is set like the jewel of the Met's crown, on the building's main axis at the west, or park side. It is approached through the entrance wall of the original museum building, an 1880 Ruskinian Gothic remnant by Calvert Vaux and Jacob Wrey Mould, preserved by order of the Landmarks Commission.

The addition is a near-square set at 45 degrees to the central structure, topped by a pyramidal glass roof. This roof covers an 82-foot-high open court at the heart of the building, treated like an orangerie, with trees and movable chairs. The lovely moods and mutations of daylight and sunlight, so long banished from so many artificially lit modern structures, are rediscovered and celebrated here.

The walls are of solid masonry construction, of the same buff Indiana limestone quarried for the old Vaux and Mould building. Paralleling the four court walls are wing walls that screen stairs to a lower level, where there are drawing galleries and a library and offices. As these walls rise to upper gallery level, they become open frames, offering views of the painting galleries beyond the court that add elaborate planes to the visual space. These spatial effects are calculated with the greatest care, at once dramatic and subtle, simple and complex.

Surrounding the court are two rings of galleries. The skylight continues, sloping, over the first ring, the natural light reinforced by tubes of artificial light shielded by louvers. The second ring contains the "period" rooms. There are, of course, superb study and storage facilities. The museum's director, Thomas P. F. Hoving, and his architectural administrator, Arthur Rosenblatt, have been model clients.

Ordinarily, I love museum period rooms. I grew up in them, as a solitary city child exploring art and history; and the peculiar timelessness of the soft, gray false light through false windows leading to no real world, sealed in a silent, strange serenity, has always been a magic way of capturing another century or style. For me, they are discovery and nostalgia.

These are not great rooms; they are just elaborate rooms filled with great things. This is a trip to nowhere, unless one is curious about the ideas of *richesse* and suitability with which the collection was housed by its owner—hardly a sufficient reason to go to all this trouble. (But getting the collection was obviously good and sufficient reason.) Balanced against the stairway with no destination and the windows with no views is the advantage of a continuous, horizontal traffic pattern over a tight, vertical town house, now that the collection has "gone public." But even with that change, the museum anticipates "show-

ings" or "ticketings" for the small rooms to accommodate the crowds that have become its way of life.

If crowds permit, there are some fine effects to be enjoyed. The architects have not underplayed their hand. The impact is strongly architectural; the visitor gets the court, not the collection, as his first impression. Although the building is actually not large, the style is monumental. There is a moment of uneasiness, in fact, in the transition from the strength and scale of the court to the much smaller scale of the paintings on the surrounding walls. It succeeds in part because the process is eased by some brilliant, almost sleight-of-hand installation: museum theatrics of placement and lighting knowingly underplayed.

Ingres's striking portrait of the Princesse de Broglie is directly on axis across the building as one enters; an outstanding Balthus nude is luminously focused at the end of a long vista between stair walls; large and stunning tapestries emphasize the faceted gallery space between the period rooms. The small, movable gallery chairs (by Ward Bennett) and the passage of people on two levels and in the court below serve to humanize the monumentality and bring the building to life. The drawing galleries on the court floor level, opening onto that light and leafy oasis, add a sense of intimacy to the pleasure of the contents.

But the best view of all was not created; it was there. Facing that marvelous 1880 wall from the far side of the court, one blesses the resolve of the Landmarks Commission. Vaux and Mould upstage Roche and Dinkaloo. The tactility and proportions, the bold style and texture, the strong coloristic effects of striped buff stone and red brick lunettes in the five pointed "Gothic" arches of boldly contrasting buff and gray blocks, the soft salmon brick, make the new structure seem limited in range and somewhat pallid. Past and present together are a knockout esthetic. The new building is a cool, beautiful statement; but there is more real sense of architecture in that one old wall.

Outside, Coffey, Levine and Blumberg's landscaping is a curious blend of bucolic illusion and covert security. Tons of earth are piled up against the structure, almost covering the galleries and leaving the glass roof exposed, for a steeply inclined hill rising from an elevated walk at the edge of the East Drive. This mound is being gentled with flowering magnolias and a carpet of ivy. Again, neither money nor taste is being spared to make it beautiful, and although there is less usable land for the public (the museum promises more later), it is about as successful a compromise with non-park use as could be effected. It is not going to make park conservationists happy.

The questions that remain unresolved are large ones about a museum's proper urban and environmental role. The Lehman Wing is the first addition of an estimated $50-million expansion that will increase the museum's collections enormously and enlarge its space by almost a third, upping the present overwhelming 950,000 square feet by another 350,000. The recent gifts of museum-size collections such as the Lehman pictures, the Rockefeller Collection of Primitive Art and the Temple of Dendur—construction for all is in progress—become a kind of museum overkill or engorgement with no viewer able to see or absorb more than a small fraction of the whole.

The Met is a champion acquirer; for a while the Cooper-Hewitt decorative arts also seemed slated for absorption. Instead, the city has gained the Carnegie House for a Cooper-Hewitt Museum where the fine, small-scale possessions will not have to compete with overwhelming grandeur. Some years ago there were plans to annex the Whitney Museum; in its own distinctive building now, it provides another kind of museum-going experience.

Infinite possibilities exist for museum-size collections to provide a diversity of resources and pleasures to other neighborhoods. The small museum is a nucleus of development, a generator and reinforcer of values, an incentive to community activity, a diversifier of function, an unparalleled social and urban asset. There are threatened landmarks, such as the Villard Houses in midtown and the Custom House downtown, crying for this role.

The Metropolitan has chosen to interpret decentralization as the provision of aid and loans to community facilities. That misses the point. The museum as neighborhood anchor goes beyond such generous gestures. It is a city-strengthening physical resource; it can stabilize, enrich and renew to tremendous urban advantage.

That is why this superbuilding venture for more and more supercollections in the mother lode in the park disheartens the thoughtful urban critic. There is no doubt that the city's loss is the Metropolitan's gain. But if the critic counts among his finest memories the unique impact and joys of the encompassable small museum, associated with special parts of cities, often with its own style, subject, beauties and eccentricities, the reaction to the Met's program is depression and alarm. Numbness and numbers are no substitute for the intimate esthetic experience. And the Lehman wing, for all of its splendor, is a suave and seductive exercise in some of the less admirable aspects of the world of art and museology.

May 25, 1975

THE KENNEDY LIBRARY

The provision of presidential archives has turned into the promotional manufacture of questionable presidential monuments. The Presidential Library started out as a rational, scholarly depository for documents and has grown into a public-relations monster. Propaganda has replaced appropriate purpose. Scholarship has taken a back seat to masterful image-selling.

This is all fairly clearcut; where the moral quicksand comes in is at the point where scholars and architects capable of giving the stamp of credibility and taste to these increasingly peculiar enterprises lend their names to them, affected, perhaps, by equal dreams of glory. They package the dubious product with high expertise. Then it is handed over to tourism and head counts. A whole false thing has grown up, icon-conscious and publicity-wise, supersold, with a skillful eye cocked at the masses. At what moment, one wonders, did American presidents get into the competitive pantheon business?

These ostensibly above-politics buildings are highly political and partisan. Set up as foundations manned by a president's friends and political associates, they are funded largely by his supporters, aided by a general patriotic appeal. Once built by private funds, the increasingly enormous and elaborate structures are then paid for in maintenance and operation by the General Services Administration of the federal government. The expenses have gotten bigger with the buildings, and they are, of course, open-ended for the duration of the Republic.

So now you have a library, a museum, a monument, and a memorial, with each element inflated for maximum impressiveness, and with each president being his own image-maker and all of them playing can-you-top-this. It has evolved into architectural hard sell. Place it at a university, add a school of government or public affairs, and size and status increase immeasurably. It doesn't matter that researchers, usually people with limited funds, have to hop across the country from monument to monument for presidential papers. It is not important that this extravagant exercise in ego-gratification becomes ludicrous, redundant, and gross.

There may be some poetic or philosophical justice in the fact that the Johnson Library is cracking up shortly after it was built, suggesting both the vulnerability of an overblown concept and the morality of contractors, which is no better or worse than anyone else's today.

THE MONUMENTAL MUDDLE

Here is a building whose joints we personally admired, notable for a Pharaonic air of permanance, falling apart at the seams. No one seems sure who should sue whom. Can you sue an American value system?

One of the most interesting things about the Johnson Library is that the architect, Gordon Bunshaft, has translated that value system into a truly effective edifice, a paradoxical achievement, if there ever was one. That great travertine hall and stairs, the soaring sweep of scarlet-boxed papers behind glass, holding what the shredder didn't get (one assumes that there were shredders and bugs before the Nixon administration) is great architectural drama and calculated symbolism. Nagging doubts keep raising their heads as to the purpose and meaning of the drama. Who is glorifying what and whom for what purpose? Researchers will just want to know where they keep the tapes.

The trend is toward something that is part Hollywood, part hokum, and part Grand Old Flag. How far to the Taj Mahal and Forest Lawn? No one has come up with a "Presidentland" yet, because it is all being done on a very high plane, but there are links. At what point did the archive become instant memorial and did instant memorial become consummate ballyhoo? The ball is rolling, and it obviously will not be stopped.

It is rolling right now in Cambridge, Massachusetts, where plans for the Kennedy Library—and museum—and school of public affairs —are in process.*

I. M. Pei is one of the country's best practitioners, and he admits to considerable soul-searching about the impact and implications of the job. He has even used the word "anguish." What first came out of that anguish was an 85-foot-high truncated glass pyramid for the public museum and memorabilia, connected by an open plaza to a long, wrap-around, five-story building for an Institute of Politics for Study in Government and Public Affairs, part of Harvard's renamed JFK School of Government. It had a Harvard Square site, adjacent to the university. The second version was a radically scaled-down modification.

The project started as something much simpler, but it soon became clear that it would attract many more tourists than scholars, and the program changed to emphasize "imagery" and memorial functions. "Library" has become a thorough misnomer.

As a nation, we are creating a most curious set of presidential shrines.

September 30, 1973

* After two versions of the design, and sustained protest from the Cambridge community, the entire project has been moved to the University of Massachusetts.

19

The Hospitality Industry

The new American landscape is made of plastic pretensions and false dreams. The unfulfilled promise is the American way of life, from the oversize restaurant menu suggesting farm-fresh succulence and delivering dreary precooked fare, to the die-stamped motel with its celebrated plumbing that is already beginning to fail and synthetic Elizabethan pubs with styrofoam beams and food.

The big sell leads to the big letdown. For some reason the American public is unable to realize that it is being had. This is not necessarily because people like schlock that pretends to be what it isn't—some do and some don't—but because each of these essentially downgraded products is part of a game plan in which the environment is the loser and the consumer is the sucker. The process is "merchandising" and the results are achieved through assiduous corner-cutting shrewdly calculated to get the biggest return.

Caveat emptor, as they used to say, only the buyer is no longer in the position to beware. He takes what he gets. What he gets in hotels and motels illustrates the point. The modern hotel-motel is an almost symbolic American product. Exported all over the world, it has created super-millionaires, and has the sanctity of success.

And yet I never approach a trip requiring an overnight stay without a sinking heart. It's not that I won't be reasonably comfortable— basic things like beds and baths and ice and Coke machines are the preoccupation of the American "hospitality" industry—it's that I will

20

be so depressed. It is not the impersonality or anonymity of a hotel room, which is not always an unwelcome thing. It is that one is forced into a banal, standardized, multi-billion-dollar world of bad colors, bad fabrics, bad prints, bad pictures, bad furniture, bad lamps, bad ice-buckets, and bad wastebaskets of such totally uniform and cheap consistency of taste and manufacture that borax or camp would be an exhilarating change of pace.

All this is arranged in identical, predictable layouts smelling of stale smoke and air-conditioned at a temperature suggesting preservation of the dead no matter what the climate outside. Like the roads leading to airports everywhere, you never really know where you are. It is complete loss of identity—both personal and place. Ask any psychiatrist about that.

The alternatives are grimmer. You can have seedy grandeur with creaky mock room service and tarnished silver or small town hotel horrors. One takes the standard hotel-motel almost in relief—you know what you're getting—but not through any process of legitimate choice.

That may come as a surprise to the geniuses of the hospitality field —as much as the falling occupancy rate as their prices rise. This might even suggest that the plastic esthetic of tacky assembly-line lookalikes is not universally considered the promised land, no matter how great the operational expertise. But there is no pride like Holiday Inn, Sheraton, Howard Johnson, or Ramada pride, to name a few at the top, and no one can infer that their populist designs are less than divinely inspired. The cash in the till has to be the Almighty word.

It's as if it had all come out of a not-very-bright computer, and it probably has. The basic question is, why can't the computer come up with anything better? Why does the vaunted American hotel-motel never deviate from mediocrity? Whatever happened to American know-how? When did it turn into know-nothingness?

The accusation of elitist critical bias, or subjective judgment, just won't wash. Schlock is schlock. You can make it amusing and pregnant with social innuendo, as in Miami, or you can make it utilitarian. But there is absolutely no proof that the great washed American masses would be significantly less happy with something less hack, that causes less distress among those with greater experience with the design process and its products. It doesn't all have to be plastic orange trees, Mediterranean modern, pseudo-Buffet, and costume comedy in the Olde Shakespeare Grille.

Even the English critic and historian Reyner Banham, long the delighted devotee of "pop" American motel art and culture (reverse elitism?) now writes rather edgily of the "trashbuilt" environment. The hotel-motel is a conspicuous part of that scene. It isn't that there's anything wrong with the basic idea of the quick, efficient accommodation, any more than there's anything wrong with quick feeding; they are both, in principle, good, essential, and satisfactory solutions to modern life. Quality need not be automatically excluded from the equation. But in America the pendulum swings from cheap expediency to cheap pretense; there is nothing, for example, between fast food and foolish flambé.

Who can argue with 1,549 Holiday Inns with 237,936 rooms (as of last July) from Kyoto, Japan, to Yeehaw Junction, Florida? Or with predictable Hiltons around the world, with a few notable exceptions such as the Istanbul Hilton and the Tel Aviv Hilton by architects Skidmore, Owings and Merrill and Jakov Rechter, respectively? The difference is in design, which leads to amenity, and to genuine ambience, and to pleasure, which is what travel used to be about.

One searches for reasons for the undeviating pattern. I have found two in particular: the Holiday Inn products division and the Cornell Hotel School.

The Holiday Inn system's level of plastic taste is for sale to all the other hotelmen of the world. According to an article by Marilyn Bender in *The Times* last August, the Holiday Inn products division's Innkeepers Supply Company, through its design department and the Institutional Mart of America, offers "a one-stop supermarket for commercial properties" with three regional showrooms. "In them are displayed acres of motel front desks and lounges with fake rustic beams. . . . It takes 4,000 items to furnish a motel and the Innkeepers Supply Company sells them all." In a sense, they not only sell, they propagandize the system's taste.

An overnight stay at the Cornell Hotel School's endowed model hotel wing revealed an interesting fact. The existing formula is enshrined here, and no future hotelkeeper is going to learn anything else. The training sample includes every cliché to the stale air.

A request for a place for a simple, quick supper to a charming young man at the desk practicing Miami polish resulted in directions to a hermetically sealed box in a vacant field, miles away. It was a soft spring country evening with a lovely glow, but inside the inspiration was either Aga or Khubla Khan. Metallic flocked wallpaper and ornate silver flatware that stretched a foot on either side of the plate gleamed dimly in candlelight. The accoutrements, as they like to call them in the hospitality business, included tastevin type rows of heroic empty glasses, unused by nice Norman Rockwell families. The suggestion was debauchery and great burgundies. The menu was steak and steak and steak. The "format," as it is known in the business, is the universal alternative to Elizabethan.

There is almost no way out, anywhere. London has had a new hotel boom as the result of government subsidies and there are now American chains and American formulas rampant. There is nothing wrong with standardization as a rational instrument of design. It's how you do it, and London has been done.

Simon Jenkins, commenting in an article on the new hotels in *New Society*, says he has a "numb sense of having been transported right out of London in a great supranational package up there in the sky, with a celestial choir of developers' architects and moulded plastic manufacturers."

Oh well, you can't stay home. Gertrude Lawrence traveled with her silver knickknacks and blue satin sheets. But for the rest of us, it's an awfully familiar trip. There is no longer any choice at all.

October 14, 1973

EVERY LITTLE ROOM IS LAPIDUS IN BLOOM

I had a much better time at the Morris Lapidus show at the Architectural League than I've ever had at a Lapidus hotel. "The Architecture of Joy," a tribute of sorts to the High Priest of High Kitsch who virtually invented the Florida hotel (somebody had to), made an absolutely dandy little exhibition, compactly and impeccably installed in the League's tiny exhibition space at 41 East 65th Street.

The exhibition was conceived and coordinated with a straight face by John S. Margolies, who made the selections with Billy Adler and Robert Jensen. The installation, with some killing critical quotes and text by Mr. Margolies, was the work of John Bowstead and Alan

Some of the best esthetic sight gags in the world.
Morris Lapidus, Architect

Lapidus. It was accompanied by the strains of Muzak and the outraged cries of those League members who felt that the show was an unpardonable breach of standards.

The show was presented as an exercise in mid-American, mid-twentieth-century popular taste and art, and what 90 percent of the American people really likes and wants. (If three people say you're drunk, lie down, says Mr. Lapidus; if 90 percent of the American people like these buildings they're right, says Mr. Margolies. Will the real American architecture please stand up?)

The architect credits his use of curves to the influence of Mies van der Rohe's Tugendhat House. Other influences are Louis XIV, XV, and XVI. From Fortunoff's rather than Versailles. Plus every movie of mythical high life that ever graced the silver screen.

Several bland, tanned manikins in Lapidus-designed uniforms, with a token display of hotel plates and matches, indicated with wax museum impassivity the stunning lengths to which the architect goes for consistency of style. I regret that the purple and gold uniform of the

Miami Americana bellboys is not included. The effect on arrival, still vivid after seven years, was like being hit by an exploding gilded eggplant. Unreality was reinforced in the scaleless, relentlessly adorned lobby, where two sluggish alligators dozed beneath a giant terrarium that burst through the roof with tropical chutzpah.

Beyond the uniforms a simultaneous projection of stills and movies documented some of the 68 hotels and 18,000 hotel rooms that Mr. Lapidus has designed. These pictures detailed every remarkable excess with a wickedly knowledgeable and sophisticated and—let us admit it—aristocratic eye. So much for the intellectually fashionable claim of democratic suspension of taste on which the endorsement of this work rests. Come off it, boys; you haven't dumped your cultural baggage. You've only dropped a few sterile taboos. Your value judgments are showing.

Every little room is Lapidus in bloom, as they sang at the Upstairs at the Downstairs or vice versa. I must confess that I did not follow the Lapidus-designed carpet (striped, in accordance with Lapidus design principle No. 1, never leave anything alone) to the color photo of the main entrance of the Eden Roc. The label tells you that you have gone right to it in response to Lapidus design principle No. 2, the moth principle, which takes the viewer immediately to the brightest thing in the room.

I was too distracted by such true documents of American art and architectural history—and don't think they aren't—as those nonpareil cultural quickies: the polystyrene Venus next to the slot machines, the sweeping stairs going nowhere, the galleries of $300 familiar great oil paintings commissioned from copyists in European museums.

However, one man's joy is another man's hell. I have never felt more joyless than in Miami in the midst of all that joy. I was depressed in direct ratio of esthetic illiteracy and hokey pretensions to the shoddiness of the execution. I got a terrible case of the Fountainblues.

Undeniably, Mr. Lapidus has elevated a kind of taste to a kind of art, even if it is made of plastic, mirrors, and spit. He is something of a genius, and how he does it fascinates. It also instructs. His work is often wonderfully, pratfall funny—these are the best esthetic sight gags in the world—and its intimate revelations of the pop mentality are mind-blowingly fine. He can teach taste-straitjacketed architects a lot about human needs and responses to environment and design for public pleasure.

To those who have always loved what he does, it is superglamour. To the young and older professionals who have recently come to love it, it is supercamp. They savor every nuance of legitimate psychology and outrageous parody and translate it into homilies about the pop scene that are sincere but not without the scent of patronage.

The current vogue is for turning an appreciation of the lessons of Lapidusland into a canonization of the results, elevating them to some kind of esthetic pantheon. That is intellectual baloney. It is still inspired superschlock.

October 15, 1970

Housing the
American Dream

MEASURING THE DREAM

Earnest study follows earnest study, and nowhere are they more earnest than in the housing field. "America's Housing Needs: 1970–1980," produced by the Joint Center for Urban Studies of the Massachusetts Institute of Technology and Harvard University, while not exactly *The Story of O*, is intriguing literature for housing study buffs. It is, in its earnest and institutional way, a fascinating document.

What I look for in such reports are insights through the statistics, revealing flashes about American life and society, occasional blinding basic human truths derived from the depths of demographic analysis. These nuggets of societal wisdom usually have got to be dug out, but they are there for the connoisseur.

Each study has its own style. The Kaiser Report, prepared by The President's Committee on Urban Housing in 1968, is a solid, nuts and bolts document with heavy emphasis on financial machinery and operational procedures. It is also the document on which the federal government's housing programs, now largely abandoned, were based.

The Douglas Report of the same year, "Building the American City," is the official record of the National Commission on Urban Problems. This one is more abstract, more richly philosophical, with occasional soul-searching about the quality of life (1968 was a good year, as they say about wines, for urbanology; the Johnson administration was as committed to cities and housing as the Nixon and Ford administrations were uncommitted, to put it delicately).

These reports rarely, if ever, give answers to anything. Each, in its own way, simply states the problem. That problem, disguised and dulled by data, is a mix of bruising tragedy—housing deprivation and stoic suffering at extraordinary numerical levels—and for those who can afford it, the unending pursuit of the American Dream. There usually are wishful recommendations at the end, stated ringingly and consistently full of holes.

The Joint Center report goes considerably farther toward relating human aspiration to statistical abstraction than any of its predecessors. There is a significant reason for this: the work draws as much on behavioral science as on conventional data extrapolation. That departure extends the data dramatically by providing new kinds of interpretation for the figures.

What emerges is a portrait of American social values that has barely been suggested inferentially before, and is now shown as a prime determinant of housing needs and desires in this country. It becomes clear that the realities of housing need—the study projects 23 million units for the next 10 years—are as concerned with people's hopes and fears as with construction and dollar investment.

This may sound a little like discovering the umbrella. But the reliance on relatively new behavioral research makes this study a sociological, as well as a statistical document. Because the research has also been able to take advantage of the 1970 census finding, it is automatically one up on earlier efforts, which relied on much outdated material. The results sometimes startle by their obviousness (the truth, like the umbrella, was always there) or their occasional unexpectedness.

The man in the street knows, for example, that he is having a harder time paying for housing and is getting less for what he pays; the report now puts cost high under the heading of "housing deprivation." This category has been traditionally limited to definition by substandard physical condition. In a conspicuous change in emphasis, the Joint Center stresses financial factors in determining deprivation. "Housing deprived" families, in fact, have just about doubled from the six to eight million of the 1968 Kaiser count to 13.1 million today.

These new figures are shocking. They are due in part to the fact that the Joint Center definition of deprivation is broadened from measurement by substandard physical dwellings to include factors of crowding, financial burden, and neighborhood environment. It is also noted that much more attention needs to be paid to the social and environmental context of housing—a truth that has come conveniently with hindsight.

HOUSING THE AMERICAN DREAM

Perhaps the report's most extraordinary conclusion is that any assessment of housing need in this country depends to a remarkable degree on what the study calls "neighborhood dissatisfaction." People look for neighborhood first, housing second. Whether it is the under-privileged dreaming of health and safety and basic amenities or the overprivileged "trading up," the name of the housing game is the quality and stability of the neighborhood. And everyone is bailing out, not just the rich.

Another name is class. Basic standards and values must be alike, even more than income, and the pattern of housing need is closely linked with the desire to be with one's own kind, away from the dis-comforts and dangers of the inner city. Variety, often cited by resi-dents as desirable, apparently means having a doctor, or journalist, or management type as a neighbor, as long as he shares similar styles and convictions. Neighborhood threats are considered to be the influx of an alien class or group with "different" standards, or deterioration of municipal services. A good neighborhood, as defined by one respond-ent, has "no bars or buses."

Although the Douglas report established the tie between housing and neighborhood, it remained for the Joint Center study to hold up the mirror to the odd and sometimes frightening actualities of the American social processes and its effect on housing demand. The changing formation of households, for example, is also a statistical fact, but in human terms the increase in household numbers reflects a social and emotional revolution, with the breakup of the nuclear family and the young and the old living separate lives.

Only the pursuit of happiness and the American dream is seemingly unchanged. The out-migration continues from city to suburb to coun-try, unchecked in spite of rumors to the contrary, and as the suburbs develop urban ills the movement is to exurbia, where the pattern is being repeated over again.

Because it is not just the city that is being abandoned, but the older suburbs as well, for the more spacious house on its own lot for the working class, the two-car garage and rec room for the middle class, Arcadia for the upper class, and an extra bathroom for everyone. All the same defects are being created in all the same ways; nothing suc-ceeds like failure. The only thing that will slow down the process is costs, and possibly the energy crisis.

Although the report offers no recommendations, conclusions are implicit. We must understand that housing deprivation in this country is much greater and more complex than we had believed. We must see that the stock of low cost housing is declining, and as cost hardships rise we must accept the idea of subsidies other than those for construction. Housing production alone is not the answer; it is neither a complete nor successful response. Neighborhood rehabilitation, about which we still know so little, must be high on our list of priorities.

Most important, there is no national norm for housing, as formerly believed or sought; areas vary in problems and potential solutions and programs must be devised and administered locally, with a mix of answers. A large-scale and generous response is necessary, but it must be more sensitively conceived than ever before.

"For men expect more than the safe and sanitary box," the Douglas report concluded. "Men seek a new quality in urban life and its setting and they ask for this on a scale no society has ever provided." As for the city, it "has become the place where the poor and the discouraged cling together in neglected houses along dreary streets." There are places where they don't even have the American dream.

December 23, 1973

SOME HANDSOME HOUSING MYTHOLOGY

Since Habitat made its stunning appearance on the scene at Expo 67 in Montreal, its architect, Moshe Safdie, has been demonstrating both the theoretical potential and the frequent dead end of one of today's most intriguing, seductive, frustrating, and self-defeating approaches to housing construction.

Habitat was the handsome, custom-made, almost hand-crafted prototype (including, anachronistically, a fine prefab bathroom) meant to demonstrate the beauty and practicality of systems building. It also demonstrated everything that could go wrong with the process of developing new techniques against impossible deadlines, and how attractive housing could be created by an architect who cared. Safdie has an unshakable faith in two things: the human, intimate, personal scale of the optimum housing environment, and the ability to produce

A garden for everyone out of the factory—
Safdie's industrialized building.
Model for Coldspring New Town (Baltimore)
courtesy The Jewish Museum

it industrially. His professional life is dedicated to the realization of this idée fixe.

The Jewish Museum exhibition of 1974 traced his work from Habitat forward. It consisted of photographic enlargements, films and models over a six-year period. There have been Habitat proposals for Rochester, Puerto Rico, Israel, and New York City. Other projects include the San Francisco State College Union, resorts for Saranac Lake and the Virgin Islands, a rabbinical college and housing, and a Western Wall Square for Jerusalem, and a new-town-in-town for Baltimore.

It is all fascinating work, and it has remained quite consistently unbuilt except for the schemes for Puerto Rico and Israel.

The projects themselves are so well done that one does not dispute the ability of their designer. It is a quite amazing production, even in schematic terms. It forces one to examine their basic premise, and the society into which these schemes seem to fit so well only on paper.

What one disputes, reluctantly, is their logic. That is an odd thing to say, because they are founded on a bedrock of logic that is, in the abstract, indisputable. The argument is as follows. We need housing. The twentieth century has developed industrial expertise. The mass-production system that turns automobiles off the assembly line should be able to do the same thing with houses. Standardization could move housing into factories for prefab units to be site-assembled to save money, labor, and time. Industrialization should be the sane and rational answer to the housing problem.

There is absolutely nothing wrong with this logic, which is why most of us have bought it, promoted it, and prayed for it. It has worked in some parts of Europe, and there have even been token imports of European systems here, but the process has never succeeded in getting off the ground in this country. For some reason, the logic does not work. For a lot of reasons, in fact, but they tend to be swept aside by those to whom the arguments are intellectually irresistible.

For one thing, we have a building system already, which is admittedly full of faults, but it is quite capable, with the right confluence of the moon and interest rates, of turning out a lot of houses. The industry has also quietly incorporated a lot of modest and unspectacular prefab techniques, aimed at conventional taste and markets rather than at the avant garde.

The gospel of industrialized housing demands revolution. It cannot work within the established system. It takes on existing practice, labor unions, custom, and even life style, with missionary zeal. It would require the total reorganization of the building industry into a coordinated, vertical, production-shipping-assembly format.

There was a time when such assembly line production might have been set up as a reasonable investment, but it is now an outrageously costly procedure. Add to the huge capital investment the expense of special carriers and long and short range transportation, and the first costs approach the stratospheric. Purely economically, the time has apparently passed when the logic worked. Even with on-site factories, as tried with London's Thamesmead, the diminished costs expected through increased production became an idle fantasy as prices continued to rise. Inflation deflates the dream. The arguments of speed and quantity tend to become academic.

A further fallacy is the premise that we are dealing with the main cost of housing by industrializing the product. The house itself— materials and labor—represents only half of the total costs; the on-site cost is less than 1 percent. Big chunks of housing costs are in land (23 percent) and money (25 percent), problems no one is solving.

HOUSING THE AMERICAN DREAM

Another fallacy has been indicated in the report on America's housing needs by the Joint Center for Urban Studies of the Massachusetts Institute of Technology and Harvard University. Standardized solutions, the argument of proponents of industrialization goes, can still be flexible enough for regional or other variations. But the Joint Center study concludes that there is such a wide variety of need and taste, in different places, for different people, that any generalized or centralized solution will not work. The recommendation is for specialized, local solutions of many kinds, on many levels.

That was the unreality of HUD's Operation Breakthrough, which not only struggled against established procedures and union practices with token systems building, but addressed itself to the academic equation of shortages, rather than to the actuality of human expectations. In this sense, industrialization is self-defeating. It either solves through standardization or it cancels out its advantages trying to specialize adequately. It is hard to have it both ways.

But perhaps the ultimate demonstration of failure of the logic involved is in Safdie's Habitat proposal for Lower Manhattan. This is truly spectacular visionary architecture. Sail-like configurations of prefab units are suspended from masts 50-stories high. Adjusting the prefab concept to the New York City "givens" of high land costs and densities inevitably created this extraordinary, unbuildable result.

If, in addition, one looks carefully at these "systems," their simple logic is found to be extremely complex in terms of what must be done to construct them. This is actually custom design. Because these houses are both more complex, in this sense, and more unconventional than ordinary houses, and in the case of Safdie's work, markedly better, their concept is simple only when figured in terms of a mass production fait accompli. Clustered and sometimes cantilevered, their totality is an elaborate and costly undertaking. It is just plain cheaper, if not nearly as exciting, to build conventionally.

On the one hand, one would like to see these elegant, brilliant, sensitive schemes built; on the other, one doubts if it is remotely possible except under conditions of climate and labor and cost that do not hold for much of the industrialized world. Architecture's love affair with the factory and the megastructure is running into serious trouble. Housing remains architecture's and society's chief unsolved problem.

January 13, 1974

Art and Theory

A BIZARRE MONUMENT
TO NON-ARCHITECTURE

To the long list of ancient and historical ruins that figure in the annals of architecture, the United States has added a stunning example of instant twentieth-century archaeology: the abandoned ABM site near Grand Forks, North Dakota. The announcement that this $5.7 billion investment in the miscalculations of the cold war is to become a dead installation virtually on completion could keep social commentators busy and bitter indefinitely. But as architectural commentary it is even more intriguing. The implicit message of this group of structures as design and symbolism could occupy a generation of polemicists.

First, the stark engineering composition of severely abstract forms, grimly silhouetted against open sky and flat land, upstages architecture totally. It is without doubt one of the most peculiarly impressive built groups of our time. Architects trying consciously for impact and meaning might just as well call it quits in the face of this kind of brute esthetic force. Non-architecture wins over architecture, hands down.

The newspaper description of the installation's deactivation delivered the message succinctly. "The huge missile-tracking radar structure that is Safeguard's major landmark—a majestic concrete pyramid with the point sliced off, visible for miles—will become as much a relic as the pyramid of Cheops, and its air intake vents as abandoned as the Stonehenge ruins they resemble." One thinks also of those giant geometric instruments that the Indians erected to the heavens, or some sinister Necropolis. The effect is singularly, appallingly dramatic, as much by pure esthetic imagery as by chilling evocation.

The modern movement, of course, puts a great deal of faith in pure esthetic imagery. And as every student of modern architectural history knows, engineering was praised and promoted over architecture, with particular emphasis on American examples of the early twentieth century such as factories and grain elevators. They were invoked as the models of the new architecture, their rational forms equated with truth and beauty. The engineer's esthetic, Le Corbusier told us in *Vers Une Architecture,* was "at its full height," while architecture was in "an unhappy state of retrogression." A new kind of world was to follow the lead of the engineers and of industrialized technology; its artifacts were to be light, airy, mass produced, and somehow morally superior to anything that went before.

"Styles" were to be supplanted by the sphere, the triangle, and the cube; Le Corbusier's description of building as "the masterly, correct and magnificent play of masses brought together in light" was basic to the modernist revolution. When these abstract forms have the power to evoke emotional response, the reasoning went, then true architecture has been achieved. "The sight of these forms affects us immediately by their delicacy or brutality," Le Corbusier explained; "elementary or subtle, tractable or brutal, they work physiologically on our senses. . . ." We are, in a word, moved.

In the case of the ABM structures, we are assaulted; our senses are shattered. The architectural power, the imagery and the symbolism, are overwhelming. "Passion" said Le Corbusier in the same seminal treatise, "can create drama out of inert stone." So can fear and loathing—a more popular set of emotions 50 years later—create drama out of concrete.

The ABM installation seems to offer a satanic twist to history—prophecy perverted rather than prophecy fulfilled. The abstract forms are all there and we are moved by them, but the values represented seem poles away from those intended. What has happened is simple enough; time has provided one of those unexpected twists that turn theory into irony, that reveal truth and destiny to be considerably grimmer than expected. We are dealing with the death of optimism rather than with the death of art. All of that engineering elegance and efficiency born of rational, industrialized solutions that was to make a better world—led by the architect—did not bring a new dawn. It brought an era of more gigantic problems in the nature of life and survival than history has ever known.

THE PRESENT—BUILDINGS

Next to the reality that produces an ABM, the monuments of architects often seem like arbitrary toys. They know this, which accounts for a lot of desperate posturing; they are increasingly uncomfortable with their unresolved relationships to the social and symbolic realities of the age. This has as much to do with a current professional malaise as the fact that so much building, in speculative or specialized technological hands, can get done quite efficiently without them. There has been a tremendous upsurge of non-architecture.

Whether the architect is being one-upped by the engineer or by-passed by the investment builder, he is being pushed increasingly from the stage by non-architecture of every kind. He is less central to the scheme of things than when architecture was an academic art and his place as social and esthetic arbiter was secure. On the pragmatic level, almost every professional meeting in recent years has dealt with the threat of non-architecture in terms of jobs. To compete, the architect has tried to turn himself into a deliverer of computerized commercial services—a role and a set of values more easily understood and more highly prized by society today than a good building. Most recently, he is trying to get it all together by acting as developer.

On the intellectual level, paradoxically, non-architecture has had a noticeable vogue. First there was the anonymous, ethnic, geographic building recognized and promoted by people and publications like Bernard Rudofsky and *The Architectural Review* for so many years—really another aspect of the modern movement's rejection of academic

Our senses are shattered. *The New York Times/ David Wallis*

style—from Italian *trulli* and Dogan huts to the blinding whitewashed shapes of Greek island towns. The "natural," or peasant production, as well as the engineer's contribution, was enshrined by the Museum of Modern Art show "Architecture Without Architects."

Later came the definition of the spontaneous, American pop landscape and the non-architecture of the highway, the strip and the tract house and motel by Robert and Denise Scott Brown Venturi and Herbert Gans. This is the architectural counterculture in which the dumb-and-ordinary is celebrated and the monument is taboo. It is not accepted by the modernist establishment. But both establishment and anti-establishment non-architecture have an elite cachet.

On still another level, those who see architecture primarily as a social act have espoused a kind of non-architecture that deals more with qualities of amenity and environment than with art. The way a building serves the processes of life takes precedence over sophisticated esthetic skills.

Non-architecture has come a long way since it was raised as the antithesis of academic style and the banner of revolution more than a half century ago. It would no longer be possible, in the name of non-architecture, for Bruno Taut seriously to redesign the Alps, a perfectly acceptable exercise at a time when improving nature was as legitimate an aim as improving life, and all you needed was a manifesto to make it so. Who now would have the innocent architectural arrogance to recrown a peak or remake a valley with "walls erected on hillsides out of colored glass in rigid frames, light shining through a variety of changing effects, as much for those in the valley as for the pilots of aircraft overhead?" Christo wraps mountains today, but it's not the same thing. And a less-than-earth-shaking avant garde issues manifestos denouncing any form of architectural practice at all.

In 1919 Bruno Taut could say, "My torch dazzles me, but I am determined to carry it." In 1975 the austere and awful geometry of the abandoned ABM is an architecture of nightmare, not of dreams.

December 14, 1975

BUILDING BY THE SYSTEM

Cities are built and unbuilt by the forces of law and economics, supply and demand, cash flow and the bottom line, far more than by the ideals, intentions, talents, and visions of architects and planners. Buildings are designed by competitive economics and cheap energy. They are fiscal and mechanical marvels. Yes, they have been designed by architects too, but forget any Fountainhead idea of genius fighting business and the mobocracy for art.

The art of construction is a very pragmatic thing. It is usually the art of cash flow and code compliance and hitting the market right. It is not artistic inspiration transferred to paper to be executed by compliant craftsmen-builders. It is a conditioning and sometimes crippling set of limitations through which the architect may guide a concept, if he has one, with considerable struggle.

What comes out of the process may eventually be art, depending on the quality of the mind and the idea and the talent engaged in the struggle. But the process of design, and the art of architecture, are a lot of things most people never think about.

Abundant, cheap energy harnessed to twentieth-century techno-logical innovation created today's big buildings. It has also made them extremely profitable, by bringing into existence huge volumes and floor areas artificially ventilated and lit and totally climate-controlled, which society and its builders measure by the rentable square foot.

Historical restrictions on building size—the practical height of a bearing masonry wall or the weight an arch could carry—have been swept away by modern technology. The architect sees this technology as a challenging design and building tool; he is fascinated by new materials and structural systems and radical engineering techniques, and he has done a fine job of utilizing all of this functionally and programmatically.

But he has invented nothing, or very little, except for using the new engineering innovatively. This, however, is no small accomplishment. In fact, this is where art comes in: The architect has devised a system of esthetics to deal with and express this structure. As mechanical advances have helped, he has pushed these functional and expressive design systems—the skin wall, the glass box, the concrete form, the superskyscraper—to adventurous esthetic limits.

Normally, which means almost always, this has to be done within

The art and act of building are shaped by the rules
and regulations of the system. *Garth Huxtable*

allowable costs. That can vary from tight speculative lids to regal corporate indulgence, but with today's extraordinary inflation of land, money, and materials, the demands get harder to meet all the time. The architect's job is always to translate an engineering-economic formula into a building.

That building is further liable to all of the restrictive regulations with which the modern community has surrounded the act and art of construction. The structure and its surroundings are shaped, quite literally, by zoning codes that may demand setbacks, towers, or open space and determine height and bulk. There are construction and fire codes that require certain materials or dictate performance standards that rigidly affect specifications and design. Materials vary in supply and cost; there can be a switch from steel to concrete or vice versa at a time of market shortage; manufacturers tempt with newly developed kinds of metal, glass, and plastic.

And then there are the further restrictions of custom and practice. The wheels of production, from manufacturing and distribution to union operations, are set in certain inexorable grooves, and to change course would be derailment—expensive, time-consuming, and destructive to the system. It would, in fact, be revolution. There is a stunning rigidity and inertia involved in all such established processes that is equally destructive of creativity and architecture. It is also frequently destructive of simple logic and efficiency. Find a better way to do something, and you can't do it. As society becomes more complex, the system becomes more elaborately intractable.

All of which means that the architect who designs today's buildings within this system, faced with an energy crisis, isn't going to make a revolution tomorrow. He can't, and no professional vows or manifestos will make it possible. Quite aside from the serious economic dislocations that would result, the system won't adapt that quickly, if at all.

In fact, a look at some of the energy crisis recommendations in connection with building, from suggested code revisions to structures that would seal themselves even tighter into life-support boxes with minimum glass and less contact with the outside world, reveals proposals that are both frightening and depressing. Their advantage and their inevitability is that they are achievable within present practice.

There will be some sensitive exceptions, of course. But this further dehumanization may be the only immediately viable way of combating waste within current production methods, without radical industrial dislocation. It is certainly the course of least resistance. And the rigidities of the much-vaunted efficiencies of the investment and building system created by the economics created by the system will only be intensified, for the still greater loss of art and humanity.

There are several villains in this picture. One is known as low first cost. If the initial cost is cheaper for certain kinds of wall systems and sealed windows, even though different kinds would lead to long-term savings in money and energy, the ones with cheap first cost will be chosen. The higher subsequent costs of maintenance and operation will be passed on to the user. If customized climate design and environmentally responsive details add to first costs, they will not be considered. If uniformly controlled air and light throughout the building make not only standardized sterility but a lower initial bill, that is the choiceless choice. First costs are everything to the investor and the banker, and proven first costs are preferable. This is no road to innovation or amenity.

Another factor is society's slow awakening to the deleterious effect of this kind of inhuman, standardized building on people and the environment. And it is only being recognized now because this effect, too, is being read in dollars and cents, in the decaying or lifelessly renewed city core, the uncertain tax base, and the inability to attract business or residential activity. Many of those who are able have fled the dehumanized city; those who cannot, riot or rot in the dehumanized slum.

The knife against the architect's throat, if he wants change, is always economic. Both his ambition and his results answer ultimately to this factor. Today a lot of building is simply a set of standardized minimums, from dull to shoddy. If the architect's good ideas are costly, although they may be good for art, humanity, and building, they get axed.

Society is beginning to pay a fearful price for all this, and concern is increasingly apparent where none existed before. You don't measure social or urban health in kilowatts and foot candles. You don't predicate livable cities on first costs. It is not only costs and dwindling resources that must be dealt with, but people and life and urban amenity and environmental quality and the pursuit of happiness that the founding fathers thought essential, but the builders of cities consistently subvert.

It is all part of the art of architecture. Where there is enough talent, concern, and persistence, combined with a hard grasp of these depressing realities, the architect and urban designer can make a conspicuous difference. Does anyone really question the importance of the building art?

December 16, 1973

ARCHITECTURE IN THE 1970s

I wish people would stop asking me what my favorite buildings are. I have favorites, because I believe quite passionately in the elegance and beauty of an appropriate solution to a problem. Quality, while almost a lost art, is never obsolete. The new false gods of cheapness and expendability bring more problems than they solve. Excellence always has, and always will, ennoble man and his surroundings if it is properly combined with a sympathetic involvement with the human condition.

But I am not that wildly attached to my favorite buildings, even though I will champion the new ones or fight for the old ones—to the death, naturally. I do not think it really matters very much what my personal favorites are, except as they illuminate principles of design and execution useful and essential to the collective spirit that we call society. For irreplaceable examples of that spirit I will do real battle. It has been too long ignored, with increasingly disastrous human consequences.

The reason the question turns me off is because it demonstrates such a profound misunderstanding of what architecture in the 1970s is all about. There is a tragic lag from the historical definition of architecture to the definition and comprehension of the art of building today.

The problem is as basic as the definition of the word architecture. The history of architecture has been taught as a progression of monuments. Thank God for them. Without them, we would have a hard time claiming a civilization. As a consequence, however, most of us think of architecture as a series of isolated great structures, related only by style, country or sequence in time, which are the historian's tools for order and classification. They have little to do with the building of the real world, of which masterpieces are such a small part and "non-architecture" is such a large part, for very tangible better or worse. I find myself talking about that world to people who are thinking about monuments, with a disturbing communications gap.

Architecture is the art and science of building the entire man-made environment, in terms of the way it works as much as the way it looks, and like everything else it is in a state of metamorphosis and revolution. I am not suggesting that works of architectural art are obsolete. That would be ludicrous. The point is that we are in the midst of an extremely important shift in the perception and consideration of the critical relationships between a building and its surroundings and the people who use it or are affected by it, with emphasis on effect.

The effect can be salutary or catastrophic; it can even have a chain reaction over a large area. It can help shape or destroy anything from a neighborhood to a society. That makes architecture, correctly understood and practiced, almost frighteningly important. And it is.

The architecture critic is dealing only tangentially with the production of beautiful buildings. What counts overwhelmingly today are the multiple ways any building serves a very complex and sophisticated set of environmental needs. What is it part of? How does it work? How does it relate to what is around it? How does it satisfy the needs of men and society as well as the needs of the client? How does it fit into the larger organism, the community? What does it add to, or subtract from, the quality of life?

In these terms, even a very beautiful building can be very bad architecture. And what Robert Venturi has indelibly dubbed the "dumb and ordinary" building may serve cheerfully and well. It is a matter of measuring by the priorities and values that a critically changing world not only requires, but demands. We have not, until recently, subjected architecture to this yardstick, and that is in some part responsible for our environmental debacle.

The new architecture is a humanistic equation for which creative and qualitative standards are absolutely essential. I part company with those who find it intellectually fashionable to jettison these standards for a kind of cosmic sociology. The results of the lack of qualitative standards are all too clear in the junk around us. Creative poverty has a lot to do with poverty of the spirit, which is a direct byproduct of poverty of the environment. The architect has a lot to answer for.

So has the client, the administrator, the banker, the lawmaker, and a host of others. But appalling results are not justified by fingering the faulty machinery that cranks them out. Every one of these sources is being questioned today, along with a lot of other institutions as well.

Our cities are polarized. Architecturally, they consist of formless masses or tremendous statements. We build the impressive, overtly costly behemoths of the affluent commercial society while abandoned housing, without replacement, turns into architectural and sociological disaster by the mile. Building is for the rich. Think about that. In New York, the towers of the mammoth World Trade Center rise aggressively over everything else, gleaming like new-minted money—the architecture of power. Housing is unaffordable. What is built for ordinary people and ordinary purposes, like a place to live or the pursuit of happiness?

Plastic flowers are almost all right—Guild House in Philadelphia
by Venturi and Rauch. *William Watkins*

Like every profession, architecture is indulging in considerable soul
searching and self flagellation with social issues. It is groping toward
a redetermination of purpose and practice in a revolutionary period
that has left conventional practice behind because it provides no
answers—or the wrong answers—to environmental questions.

Today we expect the architect to deal with these environmental
matters. However, we err if we do not still expect him to be an artist.
If, in our own time, he has created an inordinate number of "ducks,"
as the Venturis put it, buildings straining after symbolism when there
is nothing to symbolize, it is because he has misjudged or dead-ended
his artistic role. This role is, and always has been, to solve a problem—
symbolic or functional or both—with brilliance and beauty. And this
work has produced the peaks of civilization and subjective experience.

April 11, 1971

BUILDINGS YOU LOVE TO HATE

The fuss that greeted Robert Venturi's *Complexity and Contradiction in Architecture* (Museum of Modern Art and Graham Foundation, 1966), and the article "Learning from Las Vegas" with Denise Scott Brown, his wife (*Architectural Forum*, March, 1968), came to a slow boil for the Venturi and Rauch exhibition at the Whitney Museum (1971).

This is in large part because almost everything that the Venturis have to say is heresy, if you have been brought up as a true believer in modern architectural doctrine as formulated in the early part of this century. Everything Venturi and Rauch designs is a slap in the face of the true believers. And to use irony or wit in the pursuit of either theory or design—as a tool to shock awareness or as a comment on the cultural condition—is the original sin.

Architects will tell you this is not so—that they are just appalled by the Venturi brand of design. But then why go into such a rage? There is a lot of work around that people don't like. The answer is that architects do not build the way accountants add up figures; through education and inclination they design from a set of strong philosophical and esthetic convictions, a polemical position, that has the highest place in their scheme of essential beliefs. Attack that, and you've got a religious war.

As a historian, I don't believe in religious wars. What is despised today was enshrined yesterday or will be tomorrow. I believe not only in complexity and contradiction but also in continuity and change. I do not share a good part of the modernist dogma of the modern architects whose work I admire most, at the same time that I recognize and respect its place in the development of modern architectural history. And I think the dogma of the recent past, in the light of the problems of the present, is doing the others in.

The modern architect is a hero figure who sets his buildings in shining isolation. He sees his job as showing a benighted populace, by terribly limited example, how "rational" and "tasteful" things should be. In this anti-environmental, anti-historical stance taught by the modern movement, the architect has become the man clients often cannot get a direct answer from because he is too busy being heroic and original, or the man contractors double their estimates for to take care of the problems of unconventional construction to serve those heroic and original designs.

Now that the "environment" has been rediscovered, it seems that the architect has never been there. Its mixed bag is not his bag at all. And because its mix is exactly what society is made of, the architect is looking more and more like a mastodon than a savior.

Which brings us back to the Venturis. The Venturis tell us that "the world can't wait for the architect to build his utopia, and the architect's concern ought not to be with what it ought to be but with what it is—and with how to help improve it now. This is a humbler role for architects than the modern movement has wanted to accept."

To play this role the Venturis suggest that the architect meet the environment on its own terms, because it is there. And because it is there we might study it, including the despised highway strip and the subdivision, to see what works and why. Their two eyebrow-raising studies in this vein, done as studio exercises with Yale architecture students, are called *Learning from Las Vegas* and *Learning from Levittown*.

I will go clearly on the record by saying that I think these studies are brilliant. There are the inevitable blind spots of the totally committed; the fast buck has shaped the scene as much as real need. The big sign often means the big deal. There are false values behind the false fronts. But complexity and paradox are the stuff of which the Venturis are made.

Their insight and analysis, reasoned back through the history of style and symbolism and forward to the recognition of a new kind of building that responds directly to speed, mobility, the superhighway, and changing life styles, is the kind of art history and theory that is rarely produced. The rapid evolution of modern architecture from Le Corbusier to Brazil to Miami to the roadside motel in a brief 40-year span, with all of the behavioral esthetics involved, is something neither architect nor historian has deigned to notice. All that has been offered by either are diatribes against the end product.

The Venturis see much of Pop Art in this Pop Scene, and they admire both. This admiration extends to the full range of expediency and mediocrity with which America has housed and serviced itself while the architect looked the other way or for "enlightened" clients. The Venturis vie with each other in the acceptance of the commonplace. And because these are cheap and practical answers, they suggest we use them.

They use them. But with such an educated filtering to suit their own subtle and ironic "pop" tastes that perversity and paradox is the name of the game. When one outraged architect called their work "dumb and ordinary" they said that in a way he had exactly gotten the point and adopted the phrase themselves.

They have a gift for that kind of outrage. Not content to score the "personalized essay in civic monumentality" they add the ultimate insult, "It's a bore." With more-than-candor they point out that the renunciation of decoration has led the modern architect to so manipulate his "structural" forms that the entire building becomes a decoration. Then, with less-than-innocence, they draw an analogy between the building as decoration and symbol and the building in the shape of a duck on the highway. Furious, architects reply that the Parthenon is a duck, too.

The Venturis design "ducks" and "decorated sheds." To them, Main Street "is almost all right." So is history, and it is not surprising that mannerism suits them best. They accord the dumb and ordinary the full seventeenth-century treatment. Piling paradox on paradox, they combine the obvious and the arcane. You can peel off the layers of meaning. Call it Pop Mannerism.

Guild House, a perfectly dumb and ordinary, and incidentally very satisfactory, apartment house for the elderly in Philadelphia, is a mannerist exercise that uses blatant facadism and a perverse assortment of details that sets other architects' teeth on edge. Like all Venturi and Rauch buildings, it is intensely personal, idiosyncratic, and arbitrary, done in an intelligent but totally unsettling way. It is meant to make the educated viewer look twice, to see why the ordinary is extraordinary. Because, never doubt it for a moment, the Venturis are determined to make it so.

The results are undeniably extraordinary, and many qualified judges think they are perfectly awful. I have a kind of love-hate relationship with Venturi designs, more for their ideological input, their profound comments on our culture, their intense and often angry wit, their consummate oneupsmanship, than for their architectural results. But there is no doubt of the Venturi talent; the ultimate perversity is that these buildings are so much better than their avowed models.

I suspect that the conscious application of theory always produces noble experiments and abysmal failures. If theory is valid, it usually leads to something else. The ultimate irony is that the cost of building today is making the dumb and ordinary inevitable. The prophecy is self-fulfilling. But this work is eye-opening and catalytic and if my response is complex and contradictory, so are the Venturis, and life, and art.

October 10, 1971

A LOSS OF FAITH

The British tend to plant bombs, intellectually, in scholarly publications. The fallout can be deadly. Have you heard about "the breakdown of the architectural belief system?" You have if you've read a book by Martin Pawley called *Architecture Versus Housing*, published by Studio Vista, London. Or a June, 1969, article in the British *Journal of Sociology* called "The Architectural Belief System and Social Behavior" by Alan Lipman of the University of Wales Institute of Science and Technology. In the blunt, dull, "objective" documentary prose affected by scholarly investigators, of which the British are deadpan masters, the article draws real blood.

It says that the architect must have an "architectural belief system" to respect himself as a professional and to have the respect of others. Such a system, made up of tenets and myths, is a tool for survival; it helps to define his role in contemporary Western society, creating it with status and value.

The architect used to believe that he was an artist. But in the twentieth century he has moved from artist to technician. The pressures of technology and economics and the overwhelming shift in emphasis to a non-art, pragmatic kind of building in enormous volume pulled the comfortable esthetic rug out from under him. So has the rising pressure of social problems on an environmental scale.

The hard truth is that the architect's role has changed from arbiter to servitor. He is not able to build much more, or much better, than the strictures of cost, techniques, and multiple restraints permit, which makes him the victim of a set of circumstances that generally produce adequacy at best and undistinguished or even bad building as the rule. He is neither the master of an art, nor of the environment. It's a shabby comedown from previous centuries, and he can't face it without some kind of soul- and face-saving rationalization.

Rationalization came, thanks to the masters of the modern movement. "Functionalism," the declared new doctrine of the twentieth century, announced that by building practically one could also build beautifully. Form was to follow function in the new art of architecture.

In the light of reality, this was compellingly convenient. It also made considerable sense in terms of direct and logical building. But it didn't make a lot of good buildings, because form following function becomes art automatically in theory only. Still, the thesis saved a lot of architectural souls.

But not enough. The architectural belief system of functionalism proved to be full of holes. It imposed rigid doctrinaire restraints, willfully limited choices and frequently made the environment an adversary. It may have been the beginning of alienation. Never has the architect so totally divorced himself from public preference in the name of "living solutions" for the masses. Never has there been a more arrogant, detached disregard of all that went before and all that people desired. Housing was built on the revered, abstract models of the Deutsche Werkbund, even when the economics of land and construction and the social patterns of the users failed to justify it. And the architectural beliefs were stated with tyrannical paternalism.

It became noticeable that some "functional" buildings seemed to be serving people rather badly. And so the architectural belief system was revised. "Retreating from the uncompromising moral pronouncements of their peers," says Martin Pawley in a chapter on "The Breakdown of a Theory" in *Architecture Versus Housing*, "a later group of theorists seized upon the demonstrable truth that a relationship exists between context and behavior and developed a kind of superfunctionalism based on scientific evidence . . ." The new thesis: "The built environment must influence or even control the actions that take place within it."

This gave the architect a handle on the age of science and the future. And it gave him a new role—savior-technician. But his claim that design directly affects or can change human behavior is pseudoscience, and in its attempts to humanize earlier modernist theories, it introduced new fallacies.

Mr. Pawley may be the Jane Jacobs of architectural theory. In addition to exposing these scientistic fallacies he indicts "the blindness and deafness of the architectural belief system to the mass client." He points out how the unpopularity of the current housing models based on this belief system needed only the collapse of one unit—The Ronan Point housing explosion in London that destroyed a single industrialized model of the architectural belief system—for the collapse of reluctant public acceptance. Resentment was not restricted to safety; it included style.

The irony is that the architect has come to his new humanitarianism at a time when the profession is farther away from the people than ever before. Today the architect rarely serves a client directly or has first-hand knowledge of his life style. He usually works for government, for corporations, for boards or committees. There is an insuperable gap between him and the "masses" he builds for; they are unknown to him, through lack of direct contact, and across unbridgeable social, educational and behavioral barriers.

The naive faith that a certain kind of design will result in a certain kind of human response is simplistic nonsense. For confirmation we have only to look at the vision of America's "safe and sanitary housing" (now there was a belief system) that has turned into some of our most vicious slums.

Still, it is equally true that the kind of design that builds high-rise housing for unsophisticated families with small children, without ground floor toilets, is asking for behavioral trouble. It invites antisocial actions including fouled elevators, and through the inability of mothers to supervise their children from hundreds of yards in the air aggravates still other social problems.

There is obviously a connection, a kind of chicken-egg relationship, between design and the environment and human response, and even between design and such abstractions as self-esteem and social hostility. The small matter of no showers and no closet doors is cited constantly by public housing tenants as "demeaning."

I believe, with the new theorists, that the architect is on dangerous ground when he claims that he can remold society. There is no such thing as simple environmental determinism. The architect cannot determine human patterns any more than he can control the society that produces the multi-problem family. He has no real answers.

At the same time, I believe that he must work constantly and conscientiously within a sociological framework. And I do not believe, as the theorists do, that the character of the man-made environment in no way affects the kind of man we make.

A great deal of irreparable damage can be done to the complex human psyche, and even to patterns of human behavior, by bad building. Non-neighborhoods that are the amenity-less residue of speculative greed reinforce the sense of worthlessness of those who cannot escape. You can create desolate wastelands of the spirit as well as of the environment. You can scar people as well as land.

But these are value judgments that social scientists shun. Fortunately, environmentalists go where scientists fear to tread.

July 4, 1971

VISIONARY ARCHITECTURE

In a sense, the essay that follows is a personal confession. For years, I have dealt with the urban environment—a grim, demanding world of constant crisis and catastrophe. The search for an impossible balance between society (imperfect) and art (equally imperfect) has been my steady theme. The visionary architectural project, the intellectual or esthetic exercise, held little allure, since fantasy is not much use in the desperate battles with reality. The critic involved with the facts of disaster doesn't wait around for brilliant ideas to prove themselves with the hindsight of history.

And so by any measure at all, an informal exhibition of "Architectural Studies and Projects" held in the penthouse of The Museum of Modern Art could claim absolutely no relevance to the serious business of building anything. The 50 drawings by American and European architects were selected by the architects themselves as most representative of their work or as examples that they particularly cherished. Directed by Emilio Ambasz, Curator of Design, and sponsored by the Museum's Art Lending Service, the show contained drawings for sale at prices ranging from $200 to $2,000.

Provocative and frequently baffling, these drawings are often quite beautiful. But all are profoundly suggestive of philosophical and esthetic values that go beyond the obvious talents revealed. All, in Mr. Ambasz's words, are of "imaginary creations never intended to be built . . . an expression of an idea, or an attitude toward architecture." There is the usual ritual bow to the belief that such paper projects can influence the course of architectural history. You may take that as Calvinist truth (nothing should be useless or without redemptive value) or pious claptrap. Sometimes it may even be correct. Abstract exercises invariably reflect the convictions and directions of a historical moment with a singular purity that looks like prescience.

But that is not really the point. Released from the restraints of programs and clients, from engineering and economics—in fact, from any kind of reality at all—these architects have expressed, or groped toward, their inner convictions about the nature of late twentieth-century art and life. What we get is not a picture of a buildable building, or anything remotely resembling it except in the most lyrically perverse way. The architectural forms that appear are used as icons or symbols. This work has nothing to do with the basic design mandate of problem-solving. It is a kind of poetry.

And my confession, after years of struggling conscientiously with the social and practical aspects of the art of architecture, is that I now find poetry essential. Something is required to pull one out of the quagmire of the political-bureaucratic, economic pragmatism of the built environment. Cities decay and regenerate, buildings are replaced, history heals or destroys; only the spirit is eternal. Poetry is the gossamer absolute that transcends the vicissitudes of a flawed and impermanent world; it endures, while almost everything else disappears. Perhaps it is the only reality.

Obviously, architects need it too. Some of these drawings are sheer poetry. What else does Raimund Abraham's "House with Flower Walls" say to us except that walls, freed from the humdrum business of holding up buildings, become simple, unattached planes with a cutting-edge beauty and extended, independent esthetic of their own? The drawing is refined, sensitive, and very elegant: a trompe l'oeil three-dimensional, mock-architectural composition evoking a delicately ironic, insubstantial world.

Friedrich St. Florian, in "Himmelbett, Penthouse Version (with Holographic Heaven)," gives us an ethereal open pavilion of dematerialized arches containing a crisply levitated square of sky plane touched by floating clouds. The base and floor of strict, single-point Renaissance perspective provide the kind of formal reality that makes the whole even more unreal. In Rodolfo Machado's "Fountain House," the architectural elevation is liberated into pure fantasy. It is a carefully constructed "found object" composed of the scraps of architectural practice and history. Or the fantasy may be more illustrative and obvious, as in Ettore Sottsass's "Temple for Erotic Dances" and "Rafts for Listening to Chamber Music."

Sometimes the vision becomes darker. Gaetano Pesce's haunting "Project for the Remodeling of a Villa" leaves a nineteenth-century classical villa as a hollowed-out, dead shell, the floor replaced by a colossal flight of steps spanning the entire structure, angled deeply downward to a crypt-like underground addition. There is Surrealism here, and necrophilia, and a Ledoux-esque love of the crushingly inhuman.

The most magical of all the drawings, for me, at least, create their fantasies in terms of pure architectural geometry. Peter Eisenman's handsome "house transformations" play complex three-dimensional games with aloof isometrics suggestive of the 1920s. (One of these is a house design that is actually being built.) With the same sophisticated architectural nostalgia, John Hejduk transforms Corbusian motifs into a very special kind of lyricism. He calls his pastel-hued rendering of an impossible house "Villa of No Consequence." It is designed to delight the senses with loving use of the forms of near-history. And for controlled, aristocratic, consummate end-of-the-line intellectual passion, I would buy, if I had the $1,700, Richard Meier's superbly intricate "house" studies that translate the vocabulary of the International Style into a pure system of linear and spatial esthetics—particularly the red one that isn't for sale.

At the other extreme of expression are the fantasies of the avant-garde groups with names like Eventstructures, Inc., from Holland ("Sea Ruins," a watercolor photo-collage of inflated columns anchored in the sea with ruined ancient columns pictured on them) and Super-studio, from Italy (mankind photographed naked on a ruled grid representing a world-wide network of energy and interrelations). This section includes work by the now venerable British Archigram and an Austrian contingent.

The sources of all this are fairly clear. There are echoes of Sur-realism and Pop Art and waves from the prophetic (or dead-end?) radical "anti-architecture" school, which believes that the system—from architectural practice to the cities themselves—must go. Their weapons are visual ironies and glorious generalities and the refusal to perpetuate the system by producing any architecture at all. They seem to have a very good time. (An American group, SITE, actually erects some of its inspired environmental commentary.)

Historically, there has always been "visionary" architecture. Among the most striking and enduring examples is the innovative, megalo-maniacal version of late eighteenth- and early nineteenth-century ro-mantic classicism by Boullée and Ledoux—paper projects that genu-inely prefigured the modernist esthetic. They dealt in strictly structural fantasies; today's visions are clearly post-Freudian. But they were men, according to the historian J. C. Lemagny, who "began to sense that there was poetry in a smooth surface, in two lines meeting at a right angle."

Poetry and protest are a twentieth-century architectural alliance. There is protest against the restraints of mediocrity and necessity. Poetry is a synonym for another suspect value in today's culture: beauty. Architectural fantasies can be a lot better than building in a bankrupt society.

April 27, 1975

WHAT'S IN A WALL?

To think about walls at all—and the point is that one doesn't—is to conceptualize, with difficulty, something blank, neutral, and finite that dead-ends space. A totally negative thing, a wall—or is it?

Think again. The wall is the sleeper of the environment. There is nothing more infinitely expressive than its receptive expanse: It establishes style and setting, creates mood as well as enclosure, defines time and place. The wall is an environmental event.

The architect, for one, has always known this. The walls of Borromini are brilliant, playful refractions of surface, light, and form, manipulated with a passionate intensity and skill. In front of these stage-set facades modeled by sun and moonlight, pedestrians become actors in a Baroque drama. The classical walls of Sir John Soane are cool and clever; Ledoux's are suavely sinister; Gaudí's whiplash curves are exercises in the Freudian and the surreal. Today's walls come out of catalogs. The blank exteriors of the modern shopping center state the visual poverty of consumer affluence. Urban walls tell the city's history from grandeur to despair.

Walls communicate. They deliver signals, images, and messages. In the modern city, the messages are minimal, beyond the state of technology and real estate, and they are delivered as often by the graffiti artist as by the architectural designer. But the wall is increasingly recognized as one of the few resources of popular expression with substantial public impact. It is utilized for everything from self-advertisement to environmental improvement. It can be decorative, witty, sardonic, or sad. But it is never without implicit comment on its surroundings.

The most obvious and traditional wallwork is the mural. The affinity of the blank wall for political comment is a condition of history, whether it is used for protest or propaganda. Robert Sommer, a professor of psychology and environmental studies at the University of California at Davis, who has written a book called *Street Art*, deals with this kind of outdoor painting in a deeper sense, both as community statement and action. He sees it as a therapeutic, unifying group effort that is an instrument of pride and place for the poor and underprivileged. Far more complex than folk art or propaganda, it is a socioesthetic act often tied to the frustrations and dislocations of today's urban condition.

At the other end of the scale, many cities now have a mural or wall-painting program devoted to purely environmental-esthetic ends. Artists, dealing mainly in large, colorful abstractions, camouflage the wounds of the city. At their best, they are miraculous city brighteners.

Some examples of this genre go beyond abstractions of eye-pleasing color and pattern. Artist Richard Haas, working for City Walls, has turned the bleak, dingy brick side of a cast-iron-fronted landmark building on Prince Street in Manhattan into a *trompe l'oeil* triumph. His design simply continues the ornate iron front around the side of the building. It is an exercise in art and wit and instant architecture.

Every elaborate detail of the windows (the wall incorporates two random real ones), columns, and piers has been reproduced from measured drawings, and then the artist has added shadows and a basking cat. This solution is both a tribute to the building's architectural quality and a visual punch line for the original, unintended joke of its one-sided excellence.

Both political and decorative wall painting are highly organized in cities across the country. In New York, City Walls has commissioned artists to embellish more than 35 of those raw building surfaces that disfigure so many streets and vistas. They provide bold, professional designs. The City-arts Workshop supplies paint and guidance to community groups for more polemical efforts, and while the results are messier, they make up in sincerity and *Zeitgeist* what they lack in graphic expertise.

There are walls that deny the environment, that willfully turn it into something that it is not by simply painting out the existing condition and substituting something else. And because what is suggested is clearly more desirable than what is there, and no one is really fooled for a minute, there is a sad or bitter edge to the decorative act.

In Yellow Springs, Ohio, a blank wall carries a picture of a bucolic railroad station that once stood on the spot where its presence is nostalgically invoked. In Stamford, Connecticut, a Bicentennial project conceived by Renée Kahn and carried out by Melanie Melia has covered the walls of a warehouse (the only thing blanker than warehouse walls are shopping-center walls) with an eye-fooling row of houses in perspective on a pleasant street. This dematerializes an ugly reality into the neat propriety of a cozy scene, or another kind of street entirely.

But some kind of record for dematerialization of the real environment has been carried out in Vernon, California, with the transformation of the Clougherty Packing Company's Farmer Jones Sausage factory into "Hog Heaven," a porcine panorama believed to be the longest mural in the world. This is a bucolic spectacular of serene, full-scale farmland and frolicking pigs, with grassy fields, outbuildings, fences, roads, and distant hills under a blue sky and cotton clouds. It is continued on every side and surface of the building. The work was begun in 1957 by Les Grimes, who died in a fall from a scaffold, and was continued from 1961 to the present by Arno Jordan.

This is an environmental fantasy that not only denies the existence of its unattractive setting but also denies the nature of modern industrial development. The scale and insistence and specificity of this denial create both a definitive environmental comment and a Pop Art masterpiece.

There are simpler, more cosmetic messages: an architect's office in New York—Doman & Associates—has turned an unprepossessing brick facade into an overscaled architect's blueprint as a lively form of improvement and identification. The Schmidt Music Center in Minneapolis has covered one of those omnipresent parking-lot walls on the side of its building with the tidily painted score of Ravel's "Gaspard de la Nuit." Detroit's Eastern Market added painted pigs, chickens, and produce to old sheds for instant revitalization, as one of many graphics projects under the direction of Alexander Pollack and the Mayor's Merchants Assistance Program.

And then there are the walls that nobody designs, that appear spontaneously to add color, communication, and gaiety to grim streets and demolition sites. These are the graphic accidents of posted advertisements that turn walls into billboards overnight. Unpremeditated murals, they are walls with Warhol impact, from rows of movie posters to Sun Myung Moon faces stretching to infinity.

But the most provocative walls have more complex aims. They make both visual and philosophical points about the state of the city and society. These are not decorative or informational in the traditional sense; they deal in more esoteric environmental observation. Their imagery is sophisticated, obscure, and controversial.

One artists' group, called SITE, specializes in a kind of constructivist-nihilist treatment of the elements of the environment. Their projects are set forth as "the conversion, or recycling, of architectural banalities," in the words of James Wines, the group's spokesman. They are the ultimate in facade communications.

An early design envisioned an irreverent red stripe up the side of the General Motors Building's vertical marble facade to parody its pretentious pseudoelegance. A recent project was an "iconographic proposal" for an abandoned grain building on the Island of the Giudecca, prepared for the 1975 Venice Biennale.

This design simply reverses the building wall and the canal. A replica of the structure's nineteenth-century "German Gothic" front would be laid down horizontally over the water, and a glass wall erected in front of the building, washed by a built-in sprinkler to represent the canal. A deliberately unsettled visual device, this proposal does more than suggest the ephemeral quality of substantial architectural undertakings. It is meant to call attention to the area's need for revitalization.

SITE's artists refer to their work as an "inversion of situation or of public expectation," an "imagery of uncertainty," or "de-architecturization." It could also be called a superb example of the architectural pratfall or put-down.

Nor does it all end as an intellectual exercise. The group has designed and executed two showrooms for the Best Products Corporation, a national mail-order firm. (For whatever it is worth environmentally and esthetically, Best Products was one of the three top performers in last year's stock market.) These buildings are, ordinarily, the archetype of the dull, omnipresent, commercial roadside box. But SITE does not dress them up. Instead of applying "style," it apotheosizes the implications of the standard crumminess of their accepted false-front vocabulary.

One building, in Richmond, Virginia, has an applied brick wall, shaped, sculpturally, to look as if the facade is peeling off. Another,

Not a ruin, but a succinct commentary on the environment.
A Site Project, photo by Michelle Stone

in Houston, has a facade of concrete block laid up to appear to be crumbling, with jagged outlines and a small avalanche of blocks spilling over the entrance marquee. (A local story suggests that a building inspector, given the choice of deliberate design or hurricane damage to enter on his forms, chose the latter as the more believable.) Still another, projected, design sets up a stylish box with a smart logo, of which one corner is casually rotting away.

The approach owes something to Pop Art in its celebration of the ordinary and the vulgar and something to Environmental Art, with its accent on natural phenomena in outrageous packaging, and something to the fantasy of the avant-garde. What it adds of its own is a succinct critique of the built environment which reaches independent levels of esthetic expression.

Beyond that, a wall cannot go. It was a much simpler matter when the Diego Rivera mural on a wall of the newly built Rockefeller Center of the 1930s scandalized the world with harsh portraits of American capitalists, including the sponsors. They were removed on Rockefeller orders, inspiring the E. B. White poem with the memorable refrain, " 'And after all,/It's *my* wall. . . .' "

Today the wall has gone public. It has become one of the most universal art objects of our time. Beautiful or ugly, barrier or invitation, it is the arbiter of city environment and life.

February 29, 1976

REDISCOVERING THE BEAUX ARTS

The Museum of Modern Art's major fall exhibition, "The Architecture of the Ecole des Beaux-Arts," is clearly meant as an object lesson to architects (particularly to young ones) and a question raiser for everyone. These questions are serious and heretical ones about the doctrine and dogma of modern architecture—the movement that the museum was sublimely instrumental in establishing. They are part of a broader questioning of the whole modern movement reflected in a rising interest in the work of the rejected Academy, the establishment mainstream in all of the arts against which the modernists rebelled.

The Modern's show is, therefore, an extremely significant polemical and art historical event. It follows the Metropolitan's eye-opening and ground-breaking display of nineteenth-century academic French painting last spring, which proclaimed the Academy's return to respectability in powerful, tastemaking art circles, and its assumption of the position of a kind of reverse avant-garde. That show was also a brilliant act of scholarship.

All this is equally true of the Beaux-Arts show. As everyone who follows events of the art world probably knows by now, this is a whopping, more-than-200-item presentation of architectural drawings produced by the students of the Ecole des Beaux-Arts in Paris from the late eighteenth to the early twentieth century, representing the kind of building (and training) that was specifically rejected (and despised) by the leaders of the modernist revolution.

The concept of the exhibition, the painstaking selection of material from forgotten and neglected archives, the application of rigorous research and a knowing eye, must be credited to Arthur Drexler, the director of the museum's Department of Architecture and Design; his achievement is an impressive one. His collaborators in organizing the exhibition and preparing its catalogue, which will be augmented by an important, profusely illustrated book of detailed and murky scholarship later this year, are David Van Zanten, Neil Levine, and Richard Chafee.

There is considerable shock effect for the viewer entering these galleries, so long sacrosanct to the modernists' cause, now filled with huge, precisely and exquisitely rendered classical and eclectic facades of monumental, palatial, and arguably unnecessary casinos, cathedrals, conservatories, water circuses, royal residences, and reconstructions of Greek and Roman antiquities. It is even more of a shock to realize that these frequently superb, if occasionally wildly overreaching, exercises in grandeur were largely the work of students in their late teens and early twenties, responding to a discipline of the hand and mind absolutely unknown today.

While each student progressed individually, his development was rigidly controlled by the *concours* given at every stage of advancement, and by the expertise with which he executed his competition entries. (The Beaux-Arts system, with its indentured ateliers copied from France, dominated architectural education in the United States from the 1860s to the 1930s, until the advent of Gropius and the Bauhaus. It led to the establishment, in emulation of the Prix de Rome and the French Academy, of the American Academy in Rome—a gentlemen's club for creative and scholarly research that is only now facing extinction.) The basic solution to an architectural problem had to be set down in a twelve-hour *esquisse* and then adhered to in the *projet rendu*, which took three to six months to execute. The architects were relentlessly separated from the boys right at the start by the ability to devise a solution immediately, and then to execute it with the highest degree of skill—a painstaking, perfectionist rendering of plan, section, and elevation in a style and technique formularized over two centuries.

The drawings, just as drawings, in ink and colored wash, are magnificent. They are at once grand and delicate, detailed and abstract. In their finished precision, they parallel the Academy in painting, but the similarity stops with the care of execution. The detail was there not to satisfy a nineteenth-century taste and sentiment for verisimilitude but because these were professional architectural renderings upon which the next step, the production of measured working drawings for construction, would be based—if they had not been student projects. Literal, perspective renderings were disdained as less-than-accurate, unprofessional illustrations of the architect's intent, and although they were pushed by Viollet-le-Duc during his aborted Ecole reforms, they never caught on. This careful drawing, therefore, does not approach the polished or licked surface (*"le fini"*) of Academy painting,* in part because the work was never meant for the public, which judged by realism and finish, but for the professional architectural juries that evaluated them in the endless Ecole competitions. In fact, this is probably the first time that the public has seen these drawings at all, at least in a coordinated display.

A point that Drexler doesn't mind making with the show is that few architecture students can draw today, any more than they can spell or write; there is no requirement for this level of skill. Model-making has become a substitute for draftsmanship. It also frequently substitutes for thinking, and even for design, because it so drastically cuts down the range of conceptualization that can be achieved with the far more flexible pencil in hand. Drexler frankly hopes that this fact will not go unnoticed.

What he hopes most of all is that people will be startled and even seriously upset by the show, which does not—in the museum's customary fashion—present its historicism as proto-modern, but as countermodern. Because Drexler is hellbent on counterrevolution. "History," he says, "is written by the victors, and what they leave out

---

* See the interesting discussion of *le fini* in nineteenth-century French Academy painting by Charles Rosen and Henri Zerner in their essay *"L'antichambre du Louvre ou l'idéologie du fini"* in the French journal *Critique*, November 1974.

is the losers." In fact, what the architectural modernists attempted to do was to bring history to a halt. Not only was the past rejected out of hand, but the present was to have nothing to do with it. Unlike modern painting, in which a sense of continuity with the past can be traced, however tortuously, from, say, Courbet and the impressionists to cubism, architecture attempted to make the break absolute. The Bauhaus and its successors succeeded in jettisoning history—the Futurists had only hoped to destroy museums and their contents. They were aided by the fact that the industrial and technological revolution made the materials of their art, unlike paint and canvas, totally new; so by abandoning masonry for steel and concrete and a new structural-aesthetic potential, a new vocabulary of forms was made legitimately possible. In one very real sense, this made history and its lessons irrelevant, although they were lessons that the early, Beaux-Arts-trained modernists were never able to forget.

A new absolute was invented—timelessness—and its justifications were ruthlessly edited. For the orderly progression of civilization a false kind of scientistic myth of art-as-technology was substituted, married to the quasi-religious morality of the machine aesthetic. And to make that aesthetic more complex, a new kind of relationship was established with painting. In spite of vows of structural functionalism, both new and old materials were used in building to create a romanti-cized resemblance to the flat, painterly, geometric abstractions of cubism. Although modernist painting and architecture shared the rejection of the Academy and both contributed to the distortion of the past, only architecture abolished it. But history did not pack up and go away; it stayed, all too solidly, in the cities, and the new buildings violated their historic context with an unprecedented vengeance.

And so the exhibition is first of all a revisionist reconsideration of history. But Drexler brusquely rejects any idea of it as an incentive to revivalism. He does not, however, reject the idea of eclecticism as a next step in architecture, although he claims no clairvoyance about the forms it will take.

It is therefore possible to enjoy the display just as a treasury of nineteenth-century styles and standards—revelations of a now unreal world. The drawings are all competition-winners, from the lesser *concours* to the coveted Prix de Rome. The consistent theme is the now discarded classical tradition, the underpinning of the French Academy. But the examples cover everything from late-eighteenth- and early-nineteenth-century romantic classicism to the exotic revivals of the later nineteenth century and the final, consummated, official Beaux-Arts style.

Official meant more than establishment. This is all official architecture in a sense we no longer comprehend—it was not just that it was concerned with public buildings, which was how the Beaux-Arts defined architecture, but that it was state architecture, taught, commissioned, and controlled by a central government authority. The Ecole was a state school, an outgrowth and affiliate of the Academy established by the monarchy in the seventeenth century. The Academy dominated teaching and practice. Its graduates went on to do all official, state-sponsored construction and private construction simply followed along. Ecole graduates automatically received the prominent or prestigious commissions, and were eventually elected to the Academy, a position from which they continued to dictate style and practice to the Ecole.

The exhibition selection begins with the eighteenth-century work of Peyre and Vaudoyer, who influenced so much of the Ecole's teachings, and goes through a galaxy of nineteenth-century ornate and eclectic modes. The arcades of Louis-Ambroise Dubut's Granary of 1797, stretching to near-infinity, recall the almost surreal serenity of Boullée and Ledoux (Dubut was a pupil of Ledoux), and they prefigure Durand's prototypical classical solutions for France's civil engineers. Charles Percier, later one of the chief architects for Napoleon and the Empire, is present with a student project for a colonnaded Menagerie of a Sovereign in 1783. Louis Duc's Colosseum studies (1829), Marie-Antoine Delannoy's Restoration of Tiber Island (1832), and Edouard Loviot's Parthenon Restoration (1881) contributed significantly to the nineteenth-century's lust for classical (not to say imperial) antiquities. François-Louis Boulanger's Library of 1834 could be the work of an

Exquisitely rendered and arguably necessary . . . Victor Baltard's
Prix de Rome project of 1830.

ancestor of Louis Kahn (and is, in a sense, since Kahn and other early modernists were Beaux-Arts products) in its "served and servant spaces" and love of courts and walls.

By the end of the nineteenth century, as projects grew ever larger and more elaborate, Louis-Hippolyte Boileau's Casino of 1897 offered a pastry-fantasy in a facile, painterly rendering of a world *perdu*. An 1891 railroad station by Henri-Thomas-Edouard Eustache is so super-colossal in scale that it had to be framed on the museum wall, or it could not have been brought into the building. Tony Garnier's Central State Bank of 1899 symbolizes and synthesizes what had by then become known, internationally, as the Beaux Arts way of building: the axiomatic French classical manner for the imposing free-standing public monument composed in a calculated, progressive hierarchy of functions, movement, and spaces—composition, *marche*, and *parti*.

A single gallery is devoted to two of the most important, realized structures of leading Beaux-Arts architects—Henri Labrouste's Bibliothèque Sainte-Geneviève of 1845–1850 and Charles Garnier's Paris Opera of 1861–1874, each a textbook study of successful nineteenth-century design. Modernists have been able to admire the library for its handsome and progressive metal framing; the Opera, in spite of the brilliant social and ceremonial planning that it displays, has baffled them with its sensuous decorative excess. Two other galleries contain photographs of executed Beaux-Arts buildings in France and the United States. And as a complement to the exhibition, the Architectural League has prepared a guide to Beaux-Arts buildings in New York, available at the museum.

In the final analysis, however, the chief purpose of this show is to serve as the big gun of the re-examination of the modern movement that is currently under way in episodic fits and starts. The aim obviously goes far beyond historical or esthetic exposition. Its calculated objective is to provoke a far-reaching critique of all contemporary architecture. There has already been much criticism and debate about this subject of course, but most of it tends to be either smugly academic or chicly exotic and arcane in its cultural and historical references. The architect-debaters themselves are given to such gestures as adding naughty paste-on moldings to their safely modernist facades. Most of this has been a tempest in an eyedropper, based on self-indulgent *épater la bourgeoisie* esthetics. The one real contribution has been the heretically perceptive work of Robert and Denise Scott Brown Venturi, with its emphasis on the aspects of complexity and contradiction in architecture, and of inclusivity rather than exclusivity in the environment.

But as important as such a contribution may be, it is still a fragmentary response to a large philosophical problem. In addition to polemical discussion, there is a burgeoning interest in the phenomena of the near past and the modern movement's near-misses. Books are proliferating on Art Moderne and Deco and the Skyscraper Style and such early figures as George Howe, who, with William Lescaze, designed the seminal Philadelphia Savings Fund Society Building. There is bound to be a resurgence of critical analysis of work by almost forgotten or downgraded names, among them Ely Jacques Kahn, Barry Byrne, and Irving Pond. The transitional buildings of Bertram Goodhue and James Gamble Rogers, who have always made the modernists profoundly uneasy, are in for inevitable re-evaluation.

The focus will shift, not always clearly. It is also likely that this esthetic revival will further obscure the essential contributions of men like Clarence Stein to social planning. The cardinal virtues of the modern movement—clarity, simplicity, and logic, qualities extremely rare in art and life—are going to be compromised and downgraded. They are fragile, easily compromised values at best, the first casualties of confusion, pretension, and perverted creativity. These rational responses are the essence of good and great architecture of all periods and styles, as necessary to the Beaux-Arts as to the Bauhaus. Bad architecture is by nature unclear and irrational (not to be confused with the delights of complexity and contradiction). But elaborate bad architecture, the worst kind of all, is what the wrong kind of theory can produce.

Not the least of the probing will be institutional—the role of the Museum of Modern Art then and now. Indeed the relation of the Beaux-Arts administration in Paris to state and economic power could usefully be examined and compared to the situation in architectural patronage today. There will be a lot of belated bandwagon-jumping. But we have reached a point in history where a kind of flawed perspective is beginning to emerge. And the mirror of hindsight combines revelation and narcissism to a seductive degree.

One lesson always looming implicitly in the Beaux-Arts exhibition is that less has indeed become less. Its primary protest is against the relentless stripping down that has characterized the modernist esthetic. By demonstrating what the modern movement denied, it forces the thinking viewer to reconsider what Drexler calls the "platitudes of functionalism," or the modern doctrine of functionalism as a "euphemism for utility." It is also a euphemism for economy and a rationalization for cheapness when building costs are rising relentlessly—a factor Drexler might consider more seriously. (The non-thinking viewer, as always, will like being told what to think by the Museum of Modern Art. But that brings up another subject—whether trends are found or made by our powerful institutions.)

Drexler's point is that utility, or the narrow adherence to use and functional structure as the primary source of the building art, has had an unexpected and undesired result: the impoverishment of architectural design. So many of the expressive and stylistic possibilities of art have been rejected by the modernist practitioner either as superfluous hedonism or as a dangerous kind of playfulness that is not essential to survival—a rationale and rejection that are the routine, predictable, joyless accompaniment of all revolutionary doctrine. Not just decoration but sensuosity and symbolism are casualties. In architecture the suppressed (and unsuppressable) instinct for pleasure and experiment has reemerged as a distorted kind of "play" with form—the stretching and torturing of structure into perverse works of object-sculpture with equally perverse structural and functional rationales—the Venturis' "ducks." Today's architect has built himself into a corner.

At the same time that the Museum is pointing out these failures, it is perpetuating one of the most serious fallacies of the modern movement—the exclusive ideal of the isolated monumental building carried over from the Beaux-Arts by the modernists, a concept that proved impervious to revolution or modification. This institution, dedicated to the life and art of our time, is insisting that nothing of importance has changed except style—that only the monument is still architecture. And it is saying this in the face of a radical change in environmental perceptions that has profoundly altered the art of architecture in our day.

Still, the examination of the Beaux-Arts has an almost eerie relevance right now. By the end of the nineteenth century the work of the Academy reached the point where it was increasingly dedicated to forced and fantastic formal invention, while fundamentally adhering to the monumental conventions of the Beaux-Arts style. Modern architecture has reached that same point (it is also today's Academy) of strained invention within what appear increasingly to be the crippling restrictions of functionalism. The problem here is not with functionalism per se, but the doctrinaire and almost mindless paralysis to which it has been reduced. Today there is also the jarring effect of such architecture on the receiving environment to be considered as well as its place in the history of cities, which are the remarkable survivors of continuing, temporal catastrophes. The barriers to dealing understandingly with the academic past are still great, however; in painting there is the overload of unacceptable sentiment and emphasis on surface, and in architecture the hurdle of a puritan ethic of structure and design.

These questions of art and function, meaning and invention, of creativity and sterility, of commission and omission, are being asked in all of the arts today. But the situation is perhaps unique in architecture. If what is being debated, to a large extent, are the limitations of reduction, or the validity of minimalism, it is above all architecture that has made the philosophy and practice of reduction into a moral imperative rather than an esthetic exploration. Modern architecture since the Bauhaus has based its claims not just on purity of form but on purity of art and soul and societal mission. Only now are we seeing the death of the architect as a self-conceived superman, or kind of god, in a world that scarcely wants him.

Perhaps he was more of a god when he built palaces and pantheons, but both princely and social roles have turned out to be exercises in futility. The end came to the Beaux-Arts in small things: the design of an elevator, an electric chandelier, a utility pole. They had to be conceived of as a sedan chair, an electrified candelabrum, a torchère or baldachino with wires. The intrinsic failure was the inability to visualize the needs of a newly industrialized society, to come to terms with the kind of construction it would require. This the Beaux-Arts never even grasped. It could not recognize the real substance and challenges of the twentieth century. Modernism is clearly entering another age of problematic transition. Are the answers eluding us now?

The New York Review
November 27, 1975

Art and Building

PENNZOIL: HOUSTON'S
TOWERING ACHIEVEMENT

New York architects Philip Johnson and John Burgee have completed one of the best big buildings in the country—not in New York, but in Houston. That is not surprising. Houston is the place where money, power, and patronage are coming together in a city of singular excitement and significance for the 1970s.

The $45 million Pennzoil Place, in Houston's downtown, the work of Johnson/Burgee with the Houston firm of S. I. Morris Associates, is that rarity among large commercial structures—a notable work of architecture. It is, by any measure, a dramatic and beautiful and important building. It is also a highly profitable investment. It successfully marries the art of architecture and the business of investment construction—a union essential to the American economy and the urban environment.

Pennzoil is the product of Houston developer Gerald Hines, who is also responsible for another of the city's standard-setting buildings that happens to be its tallest, One Shell Plaza. Shell is a handsome tower with a strong structural rationale; Pennzoil goes farther as a work of art. It engenders a special kind of visual and conceptual excitement.

The building is hard to describe, and no picture can fully represent it. That is because it is a complex and unconventional three-dimensional form—actually two forms—that meets the eye differently from every viewing point, changing as that perspective changes, in a brilliant, shifting geometry.

The richness of its esthetic impact suggests sculpture. The architects speak of it as sculpture, but that is a dangerous reference because of its implications of arbitrary and superficial novelty, something that has already infected too many architects lusting after style and symbolism, and produced too many dreadful results. Like all of the best architecture, however, this is a formal statement at the same time that it is a working building and part of the environment—a synthesis passionately to be desired and rarely achieved.

The building consists of two 36-story towers that are trapezoidal in shape, in the form of a square plus a right triangle, set down on a square city block as mirror images of each other. In plan, each tower has a sharp, 45-degree angle at one corner. The towers are separated by a 10-foot space, or "slot," a division visible from some viewpoints and not from others. The tops of the buildings slope, sliced off at a 45-degree angle. The two towers are joined at the base by a glass court 117 feet high at its apex, with a roof that also slopes at 45 degrees, to make a covered pedestrian space eight stories high.

It sounds complex, and it is, visually, because all of those angles add up to a very sophisticated series of stunning geometric images. "All is a play of simple, angular volumes," Mr. Johnson says. That narrow open slot, or sliver of air and space between the towers, determines the relationships and effects of the two volumes as one moves around them. And those effects are best seen—characteristically for Houston—from the freeway, where the elements come together and apart, compose and recompose, with the kinetic advantage of the moving car.

The taut skin of the building is a grayed-bronze, modified mirror glass, in a bronze-colored aluminum grid of flat spandrel strips and delicately raised and slotted mullions. The ground-level galleria enclosure is clear glass in an aluminum space frame. The building is a sharp, dark presence on the skyline; it gives weight and focus to the glaring, almost levitating whiteness of the neighboring cultural center. The dark color seems to make that 10-foot separating slot a mysterious opening, and the pleasure of suddenly catching and losing the creamy *tempieto* of the 1927 Niels Esperson Building in this narrow slit is a bit of architectural lagniappe.

But there is no mystery to the building's economics. Mr. Hines has calculated the actual costs and cost advantages with a finesse that equals the architecture. One tower is called the Pennzoil Building, and the other is the Zapata Building, after the two principal tenants. The taste of an interesting corporate client, Hugh Liedtke, chairman and chief executive officer of Pennzoil, for something different and dis-

A union of the art of architecture and the business of investment
construction. *Steven Anderson*

tinguished, figures as prominently in the results as the willingness of an astute investment builder to capitalize on the financial assets of an exceptional design. In fact, this building proves once and for all that architectural excellence pays.

"The point of difference," as Mr. Hines puts it, is a building of such recognizable quality that it achieves both immediate status value and long-term investment value. By his own figures, these values translate directly into money. The tallest building in a city may have a temporary advantage. But a notable building has a permanent advantage.

Nor does achieving this end mean artistic or financial license for the architect, or extraordinary costs for the builder. Item by item, the elements of the design—steel weight, curtain wall, mechanical systems—were worked down to the developer's acceptable figure by the architects, with the developer's staff. Final costs were a reasonable $28 a square foot for the building, exclusive of interior partitions, and $7.50 for the curtain wall. This includes special lobby details and the striking 45-degree corner that is cantilevered, rather than having an exterior column, for maximum elegance and drama. Because the developer wanted distinctive features as much as the architects, the cost compromises arrived at were mutually agreeable.

Again, by Mr. Hines's figuring, the construction cost of this kind of architecture is 10 percent above that of a basic, bottom-quality box. But that 10 percent difference is immediately reduced to 5 percent by the advantage of lower interest rates and fewer delays. A better building, provided ownership and management are equally good, gets faster and more favorable financing. When money is tight, it goes first to the better product. And quality construction with long-term value offers the kind of security that insurance companies and pension funds like for their investment dollars.

The other 5 percent is made up in the higher rentals that the prestige building commands. Pennzoil Place rent rose from $7.50 to $9.50 and $10 a square foot during the leasing period alone, and the lower floors, ordinarily the lowest-priced, commanded a premium because of the galleria base.

Beyond that, the financial advantages accrue. Space rents faster and the quality of the income stream is not only greater, but it will increase—or at least stay level with inflation—while it drops in other buildings. And the building tends to stay full, even in bad times. A prime structure in a prime location with prime tenants has greater liquidity; it also has the "hidden" asset on the corporate books of potentially profitable sale or lease if the corporate position changes.

70

Pennzoil is already subleasing its expansion space at a profit. Liquidity and lower capitalization are important future protective advantages. In fact, it is this kind of stockholder protection, in addition to the immediate, favorable financial features, that is the conclusive answer to those who protest higher initial costs.

These are all powerfully persuasive arguments for superior architecture—beyond the usual ones of quality of life and environment. If Houston has found the formula for turning prosperity and growth into beauty and elegance, it is indeed the city of the future.

February 22, 1976

AMERICAN CAN:
IT'S SO PEACEFUL IN THE COUNTRY

One of New York's worst-kept secrets and best-manipulated statistics is the exodus of major corporations. City Hall shivers for its tax base with every new company count.

Where do the corporations go? To the country, even as you and I. What do they get? That can best be illustrated by one of the most architecturally distinguished corporate additions to the country scene, the American Can Company.

American Can has moved its headquarters to 175 acres of spectacularly beautiful wooded and rocky land in Greenwich, Conn., not far from another corporate exurbanite, IBM. While the building was in construction, the company transferred 2,200 employes from the office building at 100 Park Avenue in Manhattan. This represents its central, administrative operation. American Can is a giant with 54,500 employees in areas from the United States and Canada to American Samoa, with subsidiaries, affiliates, and licensees in 23 countries. That's not corporate peanuts.

The new plant has a setting of idyllic splendor. It was designed by Gordon Bunshaft of the firm of Skidmore, Owings and Merrill, the country's notable purveyors of good architecture to corporate clients whether their taste runs to sylvan campuses or city skyscrapers. It

71

offers comfort, efficiency, and structural grand luxe, tastefully controlled. And it is a triumph of environmental consideration.

The impact of such a plant on its surroundings is considerable. Communities that previously welcomed tax benefits on this corporate scale have been taking a hard look recently at some of the problems raised. Studies have been made of how much new revenue is offset by new demands for increased facilities and services and an enlarged administrative burden. There is a rising concern with ecology and conservation.

In Greenwich, apparently, if local officials and corporate executives shadow-boxed at all, it ended in a marriage dance. For benefits received—zoning was changed from residential to commercial—American Can worked to make its host community happy.

All of American Can's traffic is taken off local roads as quickly as possible by a sweeping four-lane highway that enters and serves its own property. The corporation has built its own sewage disposal plant. Water comes from its own wells. Neighborhood views are unspoiled. Since Greenwich land is expensive and zoning is restrictive, it is unlikely that new housing on a mass scale can adjoin the new plant to bring expansionary problems. You may read whatever sociological message you want into this and it will not be irrelevant. But these are the current facts.

The building is a beauty. It costs a lot of money to be environmentally considerate, and the real American Can construction figure isn't even available. First, there is the least possible coverage and destruction of the site. What the architect has done is to bridge a ravine and a stream with his building, in effect, creating a dam. Most of the structure has been dropped into this ravine and the building itself is the dam. With one level partly below ground, five beneath that, and three above ground, nine floors look like a three-story building. Nothing has been leveled, almost every tree has been spared, and a lake has been created at the end of the ravine.

Second, with between one and two thousand people commuting by car daily, there are no visible automobiles. Repeat, no asphalt parking seas. Five of those underground levels are a 1600-car parking garage. No one need put foot on the site. One enters and leaves on wheels.

One large and one small building are constructed in this fashion, connected below ground. The large structure, 525 by 255 feet, with three administrative floors above its parking podium, is the general headquarters operation. The smaller structure, 165 feet square, is a one-story executive building, also on a parking podium inserted into the slope of the land.

ART AND BUILDING

Both buildings are stunning structural bravado. Structural bravado does not mean whizz-bang visual effects such as fins, curves, and other eye-stopping gimmicks. That kind of flash is a cheap substitute for the real thing and you can see its corporate fall guys in nearby Stamford.

What it means is the use of unprecedented modern structural techniques for a rational combination of functional purpose and dramatic architectonic effect. But effect does not come first. And it is not faked. It derives from appropriateness. The use of structure at American Can is to bridge that ravine and provide large, clear-span floors with a practical working module.

This is done with poured-in-place concrete walls, columns and girders, and precast double-tee beams on office floors of the main building to make 30 by 60-foot bays. Two vertical spines contain elevators and services, and between them at ground level is an open, landscaped central court 95 by 195 feet, making the building into Mr. Bunshaft's favorite shape—the squared, or rectangular, doughnut. The span and strength of the construction are impressively, handsomely evident.

The concrete finish is a grayish granite aggregate exposed by sand-

The corporate addition to the country scene.
Ezra Stoller © ESTO

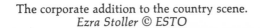

blasting: the precast tees are white. Recessed windows are of gray glass, with muted incandescent lighting at the perimeter to keep the building from being a beacon at night. On a recent winter day, the gently mounded white curves of snow swept against the strong gray concrete planes next to jagged out-croppings of gray and black rock and the black tracery of bare trees. There was the combined power and delicacy of a Japanese wash drawing.

The supremely elegant executive tempieto is framed by huge, 165-foot-long, post-tensioned beams that provide 60-foot spans. After erection, when the steel inside the beams was tightened (in a very elementary sense, that is what post-tensioned means) to make the beams enormously strong, the exposed ends of the steel were covered with a jeweler's touch—polished stainless steel caps. This may be understated overreaching, but it is pretty breathtaking stuff, structurally and visually.

On to the main office building interiors, alas. Structurally they are excellent, with exposed beams permitting an integrated lighting and air-conditioning system that allows higher than normal ceilings in most of the work areas. These work areas are serenely and efficiently organized around the central court. Higher echelon offices ring the edge of the building, with views of the site. If the gentlemen in these outer offices are kind enough to leave their doors open, everyone else can see part of the carefully conserved view. But the court is pretty, too.

There is high intensity red carpet throughout. If you like insistent red carpet, fine. If it gives you a headache, stay away. It must be said here that S.O.M. furnishings sink deeper and deeper into a familiar, formalistic rut. At American Can, it is no less deadly because it is red, white, and blue. I suppose you could stand up and salute.

Back in New York, there is slush and crime in the streets. Disturbing questions enter one's head. What part of a work force does a commuter's country-club plant set in Greenwich's restrictive zoning serve? What does it do for larger considerations of regional planning? After how much captive pastoral beauty does one crave the lively, bad vibes in town? Defectors are few, according to American Can's low turnover figure. After all, you can get out of your car or leave the cafeteria with its lovely lake views and humdrum food for a scenic walk to the carefully preserved swamp or the sewage plant. And you can breathe the air, which is fully conditioned and artificially controlled in a sealed building all year round.

January 17, 1971

AKRON ARTS CENTER:
AT LAST THEY'VE GOT IT RIGHT

The Edwin J. Thomas Performing Arts Hall is located on the campus of the University of Akron, a stone's throw across the railroad tracks (which the university hopes to bridge) to the city's downtown. Its superior design is the result of 13 years of collaborative effort on similar projects by theater designer George Izenour and acoustician Vern Knudsen, and the lessons learned from the ambitious Jesse Jones Hall in Houston by the architects, Caudill, Rowlett, Scott.

Everybody's learned a lot. "The theater of experience," a distinguished drama critic colleague of ours calls it, with not a little irony, and adds, "At last they've got it right."

Architecturally, this is a strong and sophisticated work, conceived with unusual care. It is a structure of essentials, in which nothing is there without a reason, and all the elements are utilized rationally and creatively, for a powerful effect. Dalton, van Dijk, Johnson and Partners of Cleveland worked with Charles Lawrence of Caudill, Rowlett, Scott, and Ian MacGregor was the university client as vice president for planning.

Acoustically, we cannot pretend to judge, but the hall contains, and in fact consists of, one of the most flexible acoustical systems yet devised, and there were happy faces among the experts at the opening performances of the Akron Symphony. And whether inevitable compromises have had to be made for a multi-use structure meant to accommodate music, dance, drama, and a full grab-bag of cultural events remains to be seen in practice.

Programmatically, the building raises all the questions that these centers habitually pose, of how to match the facilities with arts resources, although as part of the university it will also be used for educational purposes, which eases the strain. Financially, it will surely be no stranger to the economic problems that haunt the performing arts and their physical plants and are the cultural cross of the communities that have taken on these extravagant centers. But Akron's resources are considerable; this is a $13.9-million hall and its sponsors are feeling no pain. Akron desperately wanted this building.

It is a big, as well as an expensive, building, providing a 3,000-seat auditorium. Like other big performance halls in smaller cities—Greater

Akron numbers about 250,000—it is designed as a multi-use, multi-form facility.

A striking hung ceiling of steel sections that move in mitered catenary curves can cut off parts of the house to make it serve smaller audiences of 2,400 or 900 people. It takes an incredibly short 15 minutes to make one of these changes; we know, we watched. The cables from which the ceiling is hung are counterweighted to lighten it, so that the 44-ton ceiling is balanced by 47 tons of weights, which hang, as 27 massive chrome-plated steel cylinders, in the soaring lobby. Their polished geometric forms, suspended in 90 feet of space, surpass any sculpture.

The building is poured concrete, its weighty mass lightened by entrance walls of glass on two sides, butted and joined without metal, in the European fashion. This crystalline delicacy juxtaposed to solid walls makes a facade of great visual elegance, in which boldness and delicacy strike a breathtaking balance.

From the outside, the angled structure—the result of an asymmetrical plan—appears to be folded into terraced steps and plantings which lift people from a fountain below to entrances on several levels above, with parking tucked underneath. Nothing is static. The upper and lower plazas, banked tiers of flowers and patterns of movement, turn this architecture into a multidimensional solution through extremely skillful site planning and the treatment of the act of entrance as a complex and ceremonial sequence of spatial experiences.

Inside, the lobbies are also a spatial experience. This is just about the handsomest public area to be seen anywhere, barring some not-quite-appropriate furniture. Three continuous lobbies flank the auditorium and stage house, and they can accommodate all 3,000 occupants of the hall at one time.

The focus of this splendid space is the clerestory lit-main lobby that rises to the full height of the 90-foot wall which contains and insulates the whole complex against the bordering railroad. Bridges, balconies and stairs lead to this great room from orchestra, grand tier and balcony levels, and the movement of people is like an architectural fugue. Dominating the space are the shining giant cylinders of the counterweights with their intricate pattern of wires and pulleys. A lower lobby continues down steps, under the grand tier, and up again to open full height on the other side.

It is space—functional and formal space sensitively controlled—that is the chief ingredient here; beyond that there is the restrained effect of white plaster, discreetly used pale gumwood facing, and vermilion red (not "theater" red) carpeting that sends a warm reflective glow to all surfaces, including the splendid steel "sculpture." See this play of scale, movement and color and sense the public and esthetic presence here, and then think of the big, banal box that stretches across the Kennedy Center's halls as a public foyer for depressing contrast. And if you haven't had enough, think of the kitsch of New York's Metropolitan Opera House.

Inside, the auditorium breaks many rules. It is fan-shaped, rather than the more conventional rectangle, a 30-degree hall in which no seat is more than 132 feet from the stage. How the far side seats will work in terms of vision and intimacy for drama is still to be tested. There is a noticeable lack of traditional acoustic treatment of broken surfaces, wood, and fabric.

What one sees is a three-level sweep of vermilion seats in so-called "continental" arrangement, topped by a floating abstraction of a ceiling consisting of 3,700 steel sections hung invisibly on 20 miles of wire and cable in natural catenary curves, looking like an undulating black-veined white mosaic. Computers control the movement that cuts off the hall's back sections. Lighting, indirect except over the stage, shines up from balcony and tier edges, reflecting softly from the irregular ceiling.

Below the patterned white ceiling, and surrounding the vermilion seats, are plain, straight, undecorated walls of a soft brownish tone, and what one does not see is everything that goes on behind them. They are made of heavy bronze mesh screen, through which sound travels. In back of this screen are the curves, baffles, absorptive surfaces and adjustable felt curtains that respond to computerized directions for "tuning." The stage walls, of the same composition, are moveable.

It must be noted that there is not one "glamour" cliché, and this is a genuinely glamorous house. There are none of the expected touches of "theater" nostalgia; no one has fruited it up with mock-modern chandeliers or giftshop crystal and colored it conventional red. This technique never works anyway; the result always has a cheesiness that looks second-rate even when the stuff has been turned out by royal factories and supplied by government gift. Elegance is not a handful of beads or gold trim. It is drama and sensuosity, as practiced here.

One hopes that, unlike Houston, it will not be found necessary to sell the full 3,000 seats for every performance, suitable or not, to balance the books, so that expensive flexibility becomes a bad joke. Or like still other halls that started with gala performances, it will not be reduced to an amateur-night formula after its initial schedules run down.

Elegance is not a handful of beads.
Bob Wilkey

Sir Rudolf Bing, at an opening luncheon, served notice that the Metropolitan Opera's costs were too great to abandon the 7,000-seat Cleveland Auditorium, no matter how badly performances suffered there, and no matter how tempting Akron might be. He painted a dismal picture of unused houses and arts without subsidy.

There is only one thing that can be said with certainty on the uncertain cultural scene today: Thomas Hall is a splendid performing arts center, synthesizing all that has gone before it. But unless there is content to match, architecture becomes an empty art.

October 21, 1973

THE NEW SENATE OFFICE BUILDING: HOW TO SLIPCOVER A BLOCKBUSTER

There will be a new Senate Office Building on Capitol Hill, and for the first time a major building for the Hill is not being planned behind closed doors. Even for Washington, it is to be a very expensive and important structure. It will also be very big.

In a virtually unprecedented step, the Senate Public Works Committee held an open hearing on the design by John Carl Warnecke and Associates. Traditionally, the Architect of the Capitol, under whose auspices this and any other structures for Congress are designed and built, is the King of the Hill who answers to no one—review board or planning commission—except the Congress and God.

The Senators were probably as interested in protecting themselves from an architectural disaster of the magnitude of the Rayburn Building (the New House Office Building of 1968) as in soliciting design review and informing the rest of the Senate and the world of the project's details. The approved political end run in such touchy situations is to be sure that everyone else shares the knowledge and, if necessary, the blame.

Considering the fact that the Rayburn Building was, and is, an esthetic and economic scandal of monster magnitude, the hearing was a good move. It has not escaped observation that in the way of such edifices, the image of Mr. Sam has become fused with a solid gold turkey rather than with his sterling virtues.

The proposed building is the new, New Senate Office Building, because the last New Senate Office Building was completed in 1958 and named the Dirksen Building in 1972, and that was also a solid gold turkey.

It followed the original Senate Office Building now called the Russell Building, begun in 1904 and completed in 1933, which was an impressive classical exercise with appropriate columns and porticos when money still could buy them.

The two buildings are disposed on a massive line along Constitution Avenue from Delaware to First Street, and halfway from First to Second. The second half of that block will house the latest and most overpowering addition to the group, at an estimated cost of $60 million, which is already being pushed up by a 16 percent construction inflation rate, when only 4 percent had been predicted.

The history of recent large-scale building on both sides of Capitol Hill, for both House and Senate, and also of the ill-advised monkeying with the Capitol itself, is one of extraordinary expense and consistent esthetic catastrophe. Each building was characterized as the most costly of its day, and each was replete with ludicrous functional failure and laughable details. (If you can laugh at the Rayburn Building's $120-million with record overruns and the mutilating extension of the Capitol's East Front.)

Most of these earlier Congressional building misadventures took place during the tenure of the late non-architect Architect of the Capitol, George Stewart, who was notably consistent in producing bombs. There is now a new real-architect Architect of the Capitol, George M. White, approved by the American Institute of Architects, and it is under his aegis that Warnecke has developed the present design.

This is a turkey of a different feather. Within limits, it is a distinctly better bird. It is so far beyond the recent buildings in quality of planning and design that one is tempted to leave it there. But where it is weakest, in its facade treatment—which wraps around an extremely well thought-out office and circulation plan—is where most Washington architecture falls on its face, or its rear, hamstrung by a set of inexorable rules that the capital imposes on its official buildings. And there are 450 feet of this facade on both C Street and Constitution Avenue, and even more on Second Street where it will seem to stretch to infinity.

In sum, what is required is an extremely large, but low building, to accord with a zoned, low skyline, in a non-style tortured to conform to something viewed as a "classical" tradition. This tradition has gone through assorted stages and standards of real and spurious historicism from commendable to meretricious, from the nineteenth to the twentieth centuries, with degrees of distortion and dilution that make it increasingly clear that the battle for both contemporary expression and classical recall have been lost.

The problem might be called how to slipcover a building, according to the Washington cut. Sometimes the outside relates to the inside, and sometimes not. What is wanted is not a really classical cover, of course, because inflationary dollars can no longer pay for that kind of detail in any legitimate form. The accepted rationalized version is one in which the architect says, look, boys, no hands (columns), but we are using proportions and forms that with a little double-talk and double-take create the illusionist trick of classical order. At the same time, we are being true-to-ourselves modern.

The answer is—no way. The result is an esthetic bastard, by any measure. But the fact is that in official Washington there is hardly a choice. Capital design rules say make it white, make it marble and make it reminiscent of something older and vaguely Greco-Roman, no matter how farfetched or tenuous the connection may become. Architects who do well in other places flunk out in Washington with predictable regularity.

These restrictions will never produce great architecture because great architecture, like all great art, rarely, if ever, comes out of this kind of compromise. The best architecture not only reveals structure

Make it big, white, marble, and vaguely classical. . . .
Louis Checkman

and function with direct, creative clarity, it is also a powerful, unadulterated expression of its time. It cannot be less.

Washington architecture is all soporific accommodation, done with varying degrees of skill. On the other hand, what could be more suitable for the capital than compromise? There are symbols and symbols. Even if it is at the expense of art, this has the virtue of retaining the city's lulling, sunlit serenity, a character so worth keeping that we continue to build stupefying non-monuments to it.

The Warnecke design is more skillful than many. It makes the most of the handsome, tall windows of duplex Senatorial offices and adds a marble brise soleil with measurements comparable to the modules of columns and column-to-wall interstices of the Capitol dome—a truly monumental rationalization. The addition looms higher and bulkier than its predecessors, a skyline encroachment that could cause real pain if, on a direct lateral axis, the far more offensive bulk of another gilded turkey, the Madison Memorial (Congressional) Library, were not taking awful shape.

In the end, these slipcovers don't wrap up much more symbolism than a monumental amount of work space, and this building is a little more honest in that respect than most. One look at the flaccid, overblown phoniness of the Rayburn Building's pompous facade with its intellectual and esthetic insult to the classical tradition, and it is easy to love the new Senate Office Building. Everything is relative. By comparison, it is an eagle.

Accepting the crippling reality that genuine twentieth-century creativity is outlawed in the capital, this is a far more competent job of design than Congress has received in 40 years. Gentlemen, you are getting about the best possible example of Washington's curious Pratfall School of Architecture and you might as well go ahead and build it. The interiors promise considerable senatorial comfort, some dignity, and a measure of celebration of symbolic space. We've got to keep those birds flying. Even on one wing.

June 23, 1974

THE NATIONAL GALLERY:
BREAKING THE ROLE OF MEDIOCRITY

Washington is finally going to have a good twentieth-century building. I will go further: Washington is finally going to have a *great*
twentieth-century building. The rigid rule of mediocrity through uneasy compromise with an uncertain past that has characterized the
best and worst of Washington construction in our day will be broken
by the new East Building of the National Gallery of Art. Let's go even
further: it can be a great building for all time.

I am, of course, judging from architects' plans by I. M. Pei and
Partners, and that is risky business. But the promise of these plans is
enough to make one go dancing down Pennsylvania Avenue.

Washington is a wide-skied, seriously troubled, lovely city in which
the whole is greater than the parts. It doesn't have many great buildings. (London, for example, is studded with them like raisins in a
pudding.) But it has a style, due to its plan and its period—a genuine,
spacious, formal, classicism of the nineteenth century that was historically and esthetically true to its time, and a failed classicism of the
twentieth century when changing times made it a futile gesture—and
it is embellished, softened, and embraced by all those trees.

No matter what an architect may be at home, he becomes a monu-
mentalist when he comes to Washington. Even iron-willed modernists
succumb to marble double-think. They are soon mouthing rationalizations of how to make a contemporary building "go" with a tradition
now so confused and weakened that trees are a necessity. This is the
Washington play-it-safe syndrome. It is also the fall-on-your-face syndrome.

Ieoh Ming Pei, the designer of the new East Building, is a gifted
man in his ebullient, productive maturity who may very likely be
America's best architect. Each building he does attests to growing taste
and power. For the National Gallery he is not playing it safe; he is
playing it right.

This is fortunate, because the site of the new building is one of the
most important and conspicuous in Washington. It is the curiously
awkward trapezoidal plot where two of L'Enfant's radial avenues,
Pennsylvania and Constitution converge on the Capitol.

It is made even more sensitive by the fact that the Constitution
Avenue side is on the Mall, and that it adjoins and must relate to John

84

Russell Pope's last magnificent fling of frozen mega-classicism that houses the National Gallery. The new building will be one of Washington's most focal structures, functioning like an arrow pointing directly at the Capitol, while it forms the capstone of the superscaled row of monuments ranged along the Mall. That is practically a script for falling on your face.

In addition, the plot is awful. What do you do with a lopsided triangle? Pei's answer is perhaps the golden rule of design—or should be. You don't fight it; you join it. You don't torture it, or try to make it something it's not. You accept the "givens" and make the most of them. You design rationally and creatively with what you have. Not surprisingly, this leads to rational and creative solutions.

One critical "given" is the National Gallery itself, and the fact that the odd-shaped plot and anything on it must tie into this overpoweringly formal, axial, and symmetrical structure. Another "given" is the program.

It consists of two parts: gallery space of a kind to deal with the art experience of today—architecture is a legitimate part of that experience—and provision for a Center for Advanced Study in the Visual Arts. Visual, rather than fine arts, denotes another step into the twentieth century. And then there are all those complex museum problems, some peculiar to the capital, such as feeding hordes of national cultural sightseers in an enlarged cafeteria and dealing with busloads of children, and the juggling of curatorial functions now spread unsystematically through miles of misused marble halls.

In the Pei plan, it all seems to come out just fine. New and old buildings will be linked by a plaza across Fourth Street, with a glass-sided fountain providing a skylight for a cafeteria-concourse below ground, between the two structures. The Fourth Street entrance, closed now—a gigantic bronze door behind which one expects at least the Delphic oracle—will be opened. Escalators and stairs will ease and redirect circulation.

This is all logical, efficient, and except for the numbing scale that one must adjust to in our national institutions, inviting. But the new building is more. It is brilliant.

The trapezoidal shape is divided diagonally into two parts, making two nested triangles. The larger triangle is the new exhibition gallery, with its blunt end facing the present building to provide an on-axis entrance facade. The smaller triangle becomes the Study Center, entered at its point, well to the side of the main entrance.

Every natural peculiarity of this scheme, dictated by the nature of the "given" space, becomes an asset—both as rational design and as

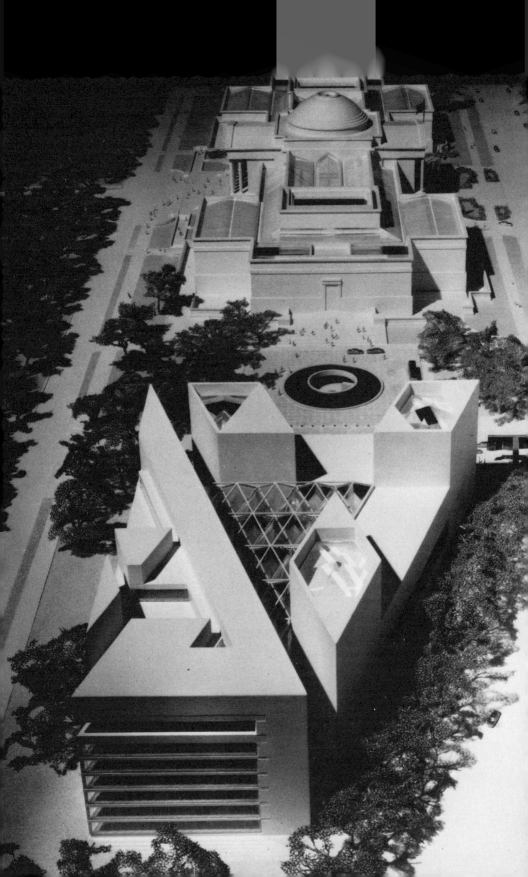

esthetic effect. The two building triangles are joined by a triangular skylit court, a feature that gives essential orientation to the visitor. (This function of the central court is one of the great lessons of the National Gallery.)

Instead of surrounding the court with bulk gallery space, the concept devised by Pei and the National Gallery's director, J. Carter Brown, divides the space into "houses," scaled like "house museums" —the happiest way to view art. These "houses" form four-story units at the three corners of the triangle, and are connected by stairs and bridges.

The design is intricately vertical; one floor opens to another visually, in a variety of ways, with a layering of spaces that reveals gardens or galleries above or below, and that always takes one from the full enclosure of a gallery to the full openness of the skylit orientation court. Unlike the serene, static, horizontal classicism of the present building, the new one will be a dynamic, sense-awakening, multi-level experience.

The Study Center focuses on a six-story library core. This part of the building will contain offices for staff and scholars, and there will be a terrace cafe with a view of the Mall for visitors. The long Mall facade, unlike other long, Mall facades, will not look like the wall of a tomb.

A sense of scale can be suggested by the length of the avenue facades, which will be 405 and 382 feet; a New York avenue blockfront is 200 feet. The walls will be faced in the same Tennessee marble as the original structure. Modern technology will replace Pope's marble-over-masonry construction, however, because it cannot be duplicated today even for the Mellon family's generous $20-million gift. Structural members, such as horizontal trusses, will be exposed concrete.

Anyone who has seen Pei's small Everson Museum in Syracuse knows how superbly he marries the sensuousness of space and art in a seamless contemporary blend. That is art, and Washington deserves it.

July 11, 1971

PRINCETON INSTITUTE:
AT THE HEAD OF ITS CLASS

The air is a bit more rarefied at the Institute for Advanced Study than in the rest of Princeton, and the new architecture, generally, is better. The institute, the prestigious center of advanced research in the fields of mathematics, historical studies and natural and social sciences, is the country's sacrosanct temple of pure learning at ionosphere levels. From those wonderful people who gave you Einstein and relativity, now comes a distinguished complex of new buildings. And for once, there is a tie between standards of scholarly endeavor and the setting where it takes place.

The new, \$4-million Academic Office Building and Dining Hall Commons by Geddes, Brecher, Qualls, Cunningham is the institute's major expansion, completed over the last year and in full use now for its first semester.

The level of the building's design suggests immediately the level of the work being done, and the appropriateness of an environment that matches intellectual and artistic excellence. If that is élitism—and it is —the most should be made of it.

The addition is no monument and does not strive for Parnassus— and what a temptation, considering the client, that could have been. At a time when arrogance is often synonymous with architecture, these buildings teach humane and artful lessons in the built environment.

The result is an extremely thoughtful exercise in solving functional needs with a maximum of taste and sensibility, a modicum of homage to some great architectural innovators of our time, and a thorough understanding of all those relationships of space, scale, and personal response that make a structure work.

It all seems a great deal farther away than New Jersey. A grassy courtyard with birch trees seen through glass walls, smooth white surfaces and the warmth of teak and fir evoke Alvar Aalto's Finland and the master's low-keyed sensuosity.

Round concrete columns and framing, formwork patterns, sunshades and the indulgence of half-sphere "viewing" balconies bow to Le Corbusier. A glass-enclosed geometric stair is a genial gesture to Gropius.

But there is not the rigor of the originals, because these details are no longer absolute, revolutionary statements; they have become absorbed by another generation that bows to its sources without didacticism and makes them part of an evolutionary whole.

As another master, Mies van der Rohe, wisely said, "You don't invent a new architecture every Monday morning," although a lot of architects keep trying. Current campus construction is full of acrobatic novelties and vacuous vulgarities, such as Princeton's own Woodrow Wilson School of Public Affairs by Minoru Yamasaki.

The Institute for Advanced Study is an autonomous school, with its own land, tied to Princeton through academic courtesy. It is part research institute, part university and part home away from home.

Working on subjects from astrophysics to the recruitment of political leadership in Mexico and other non-nitty-gritty matters, members tend to be solitary and inner directed. They need privacy, quiet, and the opportunity for shared seminars and optional socializing.

This is the mandate the new buildings meet. There are two structures—a three-story academic office building and a two-story dining facility, with a garden court between. They are parallel, linear buildings on a sloping site of approximately 80,000 square feet, connected by the court and bridges.

Construction is poured-in-place concrete, with column and beam framing and concrete slabs. The system is modular, forming a flexible grid.

The handsome dining hall, two stories high and glass-walled, allows intricate views of the academic building beyond. Within it there is a

An environment for more than equations. *Tom Christie*

"coffee balcony" partially walled for intimacy, without destroying the space, and a lounge below. The areas range from open to closed with many subtle variations between, on a graded scale of activity and psychological need.

The two buildings are joined on a single axis that leads to the original Fuld Hall and outbuildings, neo-Georgian nonentities that can never be viewed dispassionately because they have been transfigured by association with great men.

All this is implicitly respected by the new construction, which is so much better in every way than the old. The cornices of the latest buildings are level with the eaves of the old ones, and scale is consciously related.

New and old are further married through freshly landscaped courts and quadrangles, the work of Zion and Breen Associates. The new landscape provides a forecourt for the 1964 library by Wallace Harrison—one of Mr. Harrison's more felicitous buildings that is also well integrated into the complex—as well as a setting for the additions. It does this at the same time that it respects a singularly lovely existing landscape: beautiful lawns and woods of an English-country quality that stretch beyond the buildings. The institute is producing environment as well as cosmic equations.

September 22, 1972

THE WORK OF MARCEL BREUER

It is some of the most photogenic architecture in the world. It occasionally promises more than it delivers, and sometimes lives up to its promises. It is building as art—strong, stylish and preoccupied with form, rich in dramatic contrasts, proudly insistent on structure as sculpture—concepts treated with extreme suspicion by those who prefer a Salvation Army esthetic.

This is the life work of Marcel Breuer, covering a half century, celebrated in a retrospective on view at the Metropolitan Museum of Art showing models, photographs, furniture, and structural mockups.

ART AND BUILDING

Partly by timing and partly by talent, Marcel Breuer is one of the leading figures of the modern movement. Born in Hungary, in 1902, he was a young man at the Bauhaus, that legendary incubator of "modernism" in Germany from 1919 to 1928. He carried the "revolution" with him to England in the 1930s and then to the United States in 1937, where he joined Walter Gropius at the Harvard Graduate School of Design.

In the New England of the thirties and forties, a small, elite group knew his houses—shelter as simple, expressive geometry in fieldstone, glass and taut white surfaces, cantilevered over the countryside or precisely placed in fields and on hills, eloquent windows cut into walls with surgico-esthetic skill.

But in recent years, Breuer has had a lion's share of the big, prestigious commissions: UNESCO in Paris, I.B.M. in the south of France, H.U.D. headquarters in Washington, a new resort town in France, corporate headquarters in the United States.

The now-familiar Breuer trademarks are the powerful, repetitive patterns of precast facades, artfully sculptured columns, Y-shaped buildings, folded and fanned concrete and elevated, sculptural shapes. They push reinforced concrete technology into the realm of abstract art.

Like so much innovation, these forms have inevitably been imitated and debased by others into contemporary clichés. But their thoughtful genesis as early as the 1920s and '30s is clear in the model of the Civic Center of the Future, a London project of 1937 done with F. R. S. Yorke, a kind of mother lode of future forms.

No one has ever surpassed Breuer's furniture. Now approaching the age that is some people's definition of antiques, these superb chairs of tubular steel, wood, canvas and cane are still in production, increasingly popular and timelessly elegant. They will continue to be "classics" when the punching-bag novelties of current camp chic are gone.

As for the buildings, it is hard to judge them by photographs, particularly when they lend themselves so brainwashingly to a kind of theatrical, abstract imagery. There are wide variations of quality and success.

New York's Whitney Museum, for example, which photographs less well than other buildings, continues to be—in spite of museological criticisms—an extremely rewarding structure celebrating a small, awkward site and turning it into a rich variety of spatial, visual, and tactile experiences. Details such as the stairs, with benches and outside views, warm wood and somber stone, are infinitely revealing of the architect's sensibilities.

In contrast, the I.B.M. Building in the south of France looks like a modern Parthenon. But once past its stunning exterior with its sweep of sculptured columns the interiors are ambivalent, patchy and ill-related to the spectacular show. The Y-plan is so disorienting that finding one's way is like being given three blindfolded spins and told to pin the tail on the donkey.

It is unpopular to say so, but the philosophy of much of this work is a kind of structural and sculptural overreaching. One suspects that this is dead-end theory dangerously close to a perverse point of no return.

Certainly in lesser hands this is true—form can become a kind of ornament that is questionable and vulgar stuff. In at least one Breuer building not shown, it has led to dubious and off-putting gymnastics.

But the Metropolitan's show provides an illuminating perspective that is achieved only by the act of definition of a man's work and times. It is an act that illuminates the twentieth century as well.

November 30, 1972

ALVAR AALTO: MT. ANGEL LIBRARY

Importing the work of a famous Finnish architect known for his beautiful use of wood to the Pacific Northwest may seem like bringing coals to Newcastle. The woods are as full of architects as they are of Douglas fir.

But imported architecture, unlike some imported wines, can travel well. The new library of the Mount Angel Abbey, a Benedictine monastery 40 miles south of Portland, brings a small and perfect work of a master of the modern movement, Alvar Aalto, to the United States.

As surprising as its presence here on an Oregon hilltop is the fact that this is only the second building, and third work, of this internationally celebrated architect in this country. The Baker House dormitory at the Massachusetts Institute of Technology was built in 1947, and the Kaufmann Conference Room was designed for the Institute of International Education in New York in 1964.

Aalto's elegant humanity, full of sophisticated skills. *David Falconer*

Mr. Aalto takes only those commissions that please him. When a letter came to Helsinki in 1963, quite out of the blue, from Father Barnabas Reasoner, postmarked St. Benedict, Oregon, asking him "to give us a building that will fill our needs in a beautiful and intelligent way," Mr. Aalto agreed to do the job. It was an act of faith on both sides.

The result is a three-story, fan-shaped structure that cost $1,272,000 and was paid for by an anonymous industrialist. It fits snugly into the side of a hill that overlooks a vast, quilted panorama of rolling farm country.

There are fields of red clover and bursts of orange poppies. But it could just as easily be a monastic hilltop in Bavaria or the south of France, with the cultivated land spread below, except for a backdrop of Mounts Hood, Adams, St. Helens, and Rainier. This is green north country, as hospitable to Alvar Aalto's architecture as his native Finland.

The whole building is from the master's hand, down to the smallest fitting. Furnishings, lamps, and movable objects were brought from Finland. All structural and trim details are on-site work. The classic Aalto-designed chairs and stools in vanilla-pale birch have a "B" brand mark on the bottom to identify them for export from Finland. The

Benedictine brothers at Mount Angel raise their own beef and sent their cattle brand to the factory.

Only the library's top level shows above the hill at the entrance side. It is flanked by other abbey structures built in a bland mid-1920s medieval manner that might be called Lapsed Lombard. With no compromise of its own style beyond a blending buff brick, the new addition displays a kind of good environmental manners rare among name-architect "star" structures on institutional or educational campuses.

The design was begun in Mr. Aalto's Helsinki studio from photographs and plans of the site. In 1967, before construction, he visited the abbey. He moved the location of the building 10 feet to save two handsome Douglas firs and to insure an opening between buildings for the view.

The library itself does not maximize the view; it does not focus attention on the outdoors. It is a place to work, flooded with controlled daylight, with equally controlled glimpses of the countryside.

The fan-shaped plan, with a two-story central, curving skylight, reveals the entire interior to the eye from the entrance. There is no rigid, straight-line, geometrical progression of shelves or stacks; they enclose the space and the user in a gentle arc. The two floors of light-bathed stack and working areas can be seen at once, in a functionally and esthetically inviting relationship. The whole operation can be controlled by a single librarian.

The Aalto palette of white walls, black seating and pale, warm woods, a beauty intensified by natural light from high windows and skylights and warmed by a carefully supplementary incandescent glow, proves again that no color can be the richest color. The characteristic, lovingly used Aalto woods are birch, oak, and fir crafted here, with insistently natural finishes that make American wood products look like cheap wood imitations.

A slatted, sunburst ceiling of fir strips is repeated in slats finishing the ends of the book stacks. The free form, an Aalto innovation that suffered near-total degradation by the 1940s, is here in curving walls that define a small lecture hall, also fan-shaped, that seats 100 in Aalto black-and-birch chairs facing an oak "shell." The building is superbly finished and detailed.

The structure contains about 43,000 square feet of space, with room for 250,000 volumes on theology, philosophy, and related educational subjects, to serve the abbey and its seminary and wider ecumenical scholarship. There are microfilm, periodical, and map rooms, a bindery, and staff offices. The associated local architects were DeMars & Wells of Berkeley, Calif., and Eric Vartiainen represented the Aalto office on the site.

Beyond the facts, there is a kind of architecture that is elegant, humane and full of sophisticated skills. These skills never date. Vintage Aalto and 1970 Aalto are the same—subtle, sensuous, full of wisdom about the environment and man.

Aalto architecture continues to teach basic truths about space, light, and function. Two generations brought up on pictures of his landmark library at Viipuri, destroyed during the war when the Russians took over the Finnish province of Karelia, can find the essential lessons here. They are lessons of humanitarian sensibility and a quality of design that must be applied to whatever new sociological role the architect defines for himself in a troubled world.

May 30, 1970

LOUIS KAHN: EXETER LIBRARY

A serene, distinguished structure of considerable beauty by Louis I. Kahn, the new library at Phillips Exeter Academy, exemplifies much that made Kahn the dean of American architects.

The building was a year and a half in design and two years in construction, and cost $3.8-million. Its handmade, wood-fired bricks (the last production of a local company going out of business) and its teak, slate, and solid white oak (milled in Maine) are quietly sumptuous and keyed to tradition. Tradition is strong at Exeter.

But the building is anything but traditional. The paradox and fascination of Kahn's work is that it seems to embody the whole history of architecture, as it proclaims how contemporary his work and thought really are.

That proclamation is strong and subtle. His buildings evoke the primal simplicity of materials used with an almost religious respect for their basic structural qualities. They also convey a keen awareness of the most sophisticated achievements of historical styles.

But none of his designs ape the mannerisms of the past. The sense of the past is just there, through the architect's remarkable, extremely personal, and very passionate love of all that is logical and beautiful in building, at all times.

Kahn's designs frequently carry this love to the point of great achievement by stretching existing concepts and techniques to new frontiers. The result is the impression of a stunning symbolic synthesis of all that has gone before, and all that is still to come. Sometimes that symbiosis is imperfect, but his buildings are full of that special kind of vital inquiry called art.

The process works at Exeter. The library makes its creative statement without jarring the school's ambience, a felicitous blend of New England campus and ivied neo-colonial. "Totally nice," Kahn calls it, "not really vintage, or early, but warm. I have a sympathetic response to brick, and I am taken with American history."

The library is a 108-foot square. It has traditional, exterior bearing walls of brick, with piers thickening toward the bottom. There are no "quickie" brick veneers. Solid brick arches carry this construction 17 feet into the building's interior, forming a kind of square outer ring. This ring contains the reading areas.

The brick arches (old technology) join concrete structure (new technology) to form an inner ring. In this inner square, the concrete provides wide-span, heavy load-bearing floors for book stacks, something brick cannot do. The two separate but equal structural systems meet consciously and interact.

Kahn explains the structural interaction in the anthropomorphic terms he favors. For him, buildings feel, think, and act. "The brick was always talking to me, saying you're missing an opportunity," he recalls. "The weight of the brick makes it dance like a fairy above and groan below. Arcades crouch. But where brick is stingy, concrete is tremendously generous. The brick is held by the concrete restraining members. Brick likes this so much, because it becomes modern."

The two nested square doughnuts, Kahn points out, create a leftover, central interior space. This space, soaring the equivalent of eight stories, is daylighted from above and walled by massive natural concrete with huge circular openings revealing the tiered bookstacks. Unsuspected from the outside, the space breaks on the viewer with breath-taking drama.

"I just put a roof over it," says Kahn, with the ultimate understatement. But he calls the great room an "event," and, he adds, "A room is the beginning of architecture."

Light is used as skillfully as structure. The outer glass walls are

rimmed by daylit, built-in carrels with views. Bookstacks are away from the windows, at right angles. All have vistas out to the reading areas and into the giant room. Light seems to flow from edge to center, and from the roof above.

After describing these exceptionally sensitive and complex structural-esthetic relationships, Kahn says, tongue gently in cheek, "It's just a box, isn't it?"

The superior results are due in no small part to the sympathetic working relationship of the architect and client, the Exeter Librarian, Rodney Armstrong, and his building committee, Elliot G. Fish and Albert C. Ganley.

"Book," says Mr. Armstrong, obviously not believing it, "has become a dirty four-letter word."

"No one ever really paid the price of a book," Kahn says, "only the price of printing it."

His beautiful box celebrates books, and art.

October 23, 1972

LOUIS KAHN: THE MEANING OF A WALL

For Louis Kahn, there were ten years of great buildings, and a lifetime of preparation. Which made his sudden death in 1974 harder to take, because it was not a promising talent that was cut off, but one that flowered late, and magnificently, to create works of architecture of such enormous fullness and richness that they stand not only as masterworks of this age, but with the agelessness of great art, for all time.

Some of the best of his work, in Bangladesh and India, was still coming out of the ground; even more of it, for New Haven and Baltimore and other American cities, was still on the drawing board in his Philadelphia office. The Salk Institute at La Jolla, of the 1960s, and the Exeter Library in New Hampshire and Kimbell Art Museum in Fort Worth, of the 1970s, are established landmarks. He had reached this point of achievement slowly and painstakingly, and without much fanfare; it was just quietly accepted that he stood alone in creative stature at this critical phase of twentieth-century art.

The poignancy of his death was made even more tragic by the circumstances. Alone in Pennsylvania Station on a Sunday night, returning from a working trip to India and on his way back to Philadelphia for a Monday morning class, he apparently died quickly. His passport provided identification and the New York police attempted to reach his office, which was closed for the weekend. Inexplicably, they did not call his home, but gave the information to the Philadelphia police, who never notified his family at all. It was Tuesday before inquiries found his body in New York. Such is sudden death in the age of alienation and anonymity; anguish aggravated by an uncaring bureaucracy.

Lou Kahn was in his prime at 73; no other architect approached him. And all other architects, including some very good ones indeed, knew that the work he was doing was the catalytic kind that changes cities and culture, and the way man thinks about himself and his world.

Kahn was not a pioneer, breaking the frontiers of architecture, leading the modern movement into radical territory. He was not one of the initial formgivers, offering revolutionary definitions of twentieth-century esthetics. He was a fundamentalist, seeking beginnings, and meanings, fond of saying that he consulted not volume one of civilization, but volume zero.

During the early years of his career he built little, and taught and thought much, developing a personal language that combined poetry and philosophy in tantalizing and elusive intimations of deeply felt universal truths. They were truths that he sought persistently in architecture—the meaning of a wall, or a roof, or a door, the way light brought spirit to a structure, what the building "wanted to be." He pursued basic answers, in the deepest terms of art and humanism.

He tried, in a process of sophisticated purification, to "reinvent" architecture. He looked for something he called, interchangeably, Order, or Form, which he saw as a kind of self-revelatory information about building—if one looked hard enough—that forged functional and social needs and the "will" of materials and structure into a humanistic whole. He probed constantly for this "reality."

It involved intense analysis of what he called "served and servant spaces," both of which he felt deserved equal design consideration and expression. He "asked" materials what they "wished" to do. At

THE PRESENT—BUILDINGS

Ahmedabad the brick answered, in Kahn's words, "I like an arch." At Exeter, the brick arches "requested" the greater support of concrete. Everywhere, he pursued the "thoughtful making of spaces."

The style he developed with much painstaking searching—if one can use a superficial word like style for something that now seems so elemental—is a fusion of past and present. It represents the rare and indescribably important moment when modernism came to terms with history. In the struggle for this stylistic resolution, his early buildings were a combination of startling strengths and unsettling failures. Sometimes they were seriously flawed. "It is better to do the right thing badly," he taught his students, "than to do a bad thing well."

He worked this way, out of the mainstream, all his life. For much of it, he was poor. He had been brought to Philadelphia from Russia as a child, in 1905. He learned art, religion, and music at home; later he learned Beaux Arts classicism at the University of Pennsylvania School of Fine Arts, where he earned a Bachelor of Architecture degree. Paul Cret was his professor, and briefly, his employer. He never lost his sympathy for Beaux Arts style and substance.

Still later, convinced intellectually by the modernist revolution, he worked with George Howe and Oscar Stonorov. But his attempts to jettison the Beaux Arts tradition in favor of radical structural lightness and thin planes were never totally successful. Visits to Europe reinforced his love of antiquity and medievalism.

It is not surprising that for many years Kahn was a puzzle to his peers. He had no definable place on the bandwagon of modernism. He seemed out of step with his times. It was this personal phenomenon, perhaps, that slowed both his own development and general understanding and acceptance of what he tried to do.

The profession watched his "ugly" buildings grow with fascination; their probing experimentation and deliberate roughness caused continuing interest and debate. Clients were less sure. The Yale Art Gallery of 1951–53 broke the deadlock; the building was a successful, much-praised step toward his later manner. The Richards Medical Research Building of 1957–61 at the University of Pennsylvania earned a small, significant show at New York's Museum of Modern Art.

But whatever his natural bent, Kahn's fully developed work would not have been possible without the crucible of the modern movement. When he went back to the brick wall and the arch, he joined them to reinforced concrete, and he did so with the new esthetic vision and functionalist philosophy of the International Style. He was, at once, the interpreter of Le Corbusier and the Parthenon.

His buildings, full of strength and grace, have persuasive presence.

They belong to their own age, and to all ages, with equal ease. Their almost primitive beauty, deceptively simple and yet extraordinarily sophisticated, is already an unassailable part of the progress of civilization and its arts. Louis Kahn was more than an architect; he was an elemental force.

April 7, 1974

The Present—Cities

New York

SENZA RISPETTO

There is a New York lady who had a Tuscan father and an English mother and has been married to an American and watching New York architecture for most of 50 years. She has seen the old buildings go down and the new buildings go up. Observing a typical apartment house rising on York Avenue recently she asked a workman, in Italian, "How do you build them so fast?"

"Senza rispetto," he replied, "without respect."

AN URBAN SPECTACULAR

Lower Manhattan is an urban spectacular. The area is packed with the twentieth century's most characteristic, cosmopolitan architectural drama; it is tough and beautiful and bold and rich. There is quality and a sense of time and place. Its form is the result of accident and plan, of vision and greed; it is an urban design laboratory and a demonstration of laissez faire. It is to be experienced and explored in

The Chase Manhattan Building and Dubuffet's "Trees"
reward the explorer of Lower Manhattan. *Garth Huxtable*

the same way one visits Florence and Rome. This is the quintessential New York. Even New Yorkers don't knock it.

Try the South Street Seaport at night—that burgeoning historical enclave that represents a triumph of obstinacy and cunning by New Yorkers, both official and unofficial, who care about their past. Enjoy the unabashed romantic beauty of the jeweled and filigreed Brooklyn Bridge with its massive Gothic stone towers, the old ships in the river, the lights and sounds of passing craft, and the music or drama of special Seaport events on the piers.

Or join the daytime rhythms of the financial district, an epicenter of commercial vitality that is also a living museum of early twentieth-century skyscrapers of incomparable art and style, from palatial lobbies to stepped and gilded spires. Go into those lobbies—Cunard, Woolworth, 60 Wall Tower—for a dazzling display of the arts of decoration and design.

Try shadowed, small streets, for the contrast of nineteenth-century brick and cast iron; there's not too much left, but it is a revealing record of New York's art and history. And take a moment to mourn something you can no longer see—the Georgian and Greek Revival streetscapes that existed here for well over a century, until they were ruthlessly "renewed" about 10 years ago. The new Water Street, which lost its brick and granite warehouse rows to street widening, now offers I. M. Pei's chaste, white, number 88, one of its better features, and a sanitized Jeanette Park. You can still find the old buildings functioning on South Street, at least until the Fulton Fish Market moves.

Summer is the season to see it all, with breezes from the river gentling the austere new plazas and sun glinting from glass walls. There used to be dark old bars on Front Street (there used to be a Front Street) in small 1830s houses that were perfect refuges from the heat; today's retreats are less historical.

For sheer delight, do not miss the ongoing "reconstruction" of Manhattan, a studio project being carried out by Red Grooms and his Ruckus group in visible ground floor quarters at 88 Water Street. For most of this year (1976) you can watch Lower Manhattan's landmarks being built in cardboard, fabric, and wood, all slightly askew—colorful, cockeyed Wall Street towers wear their spires at a gently drunken angle like fancy crowns, the World Trade Center is weighed down crookedly but ingratiatingly by its own banal pretensions, and there is an insouciant, dressmaker confection of a City Hall. When this fantasy-mockery Lower Manhattan is completed the public will be invited to enter it over a rocking recreation of the Staten Island ferry.

Perhaps the unforgivable sin of this troubled city, to outsiders, is its refusal to take itself too seriously. New York, thy name is irreverence and hyperbole. And grandeur.

July 20, 1975

HOW TO BUILD A CIVIC CENTER

You've got to be around New York for about ten years and watch the progress of a major project or two to develop a proper sense of the ludicrous, or the miraculous, or both. That the two are not mutually exclusive gives this city its special flavor. It is also a New York truism that if you wait long enough for something to happen, it will happen, but not remotely in the way you expected. It can be an epic disaster or a cockeyed miracle, as in the case of the new Police Headquarters downtown.

The Police Headquarters comes in the miracle class. Designed by Gruzen and Partners, the $58-million building is a solid, sober, brick and concrete structure carried out with skill, sense, and taste—rare enough commodities today. It is, as Brooks Brothers says of its sportswear, good-looking, meaning it has quality without flash. And it provides a headquarters of computerized twentieth-century efficiency for a police department that has been begging to be let into the twentieth-century for some time. Curious place, New York.

The cockeyed miracle part comes in with the realization that this structure has been 15 years in the making, through two mayors, six police commissioners, and nine public works commissioners or municipal services administrators (the last have a very high mortality rate in New York). The project has had to be expedited by a special mayoral assistant through interdepartmental jurisdictions. The result still came out, wonder of wonders, an esthetic whole. It managed to escape such maudlin bureaucratic fates as having its handsome glassed-in lobby, with its essential view, chopped up for a computer room. It was very, very close.

But the real cockeyed miracle, and the greatest homage due to the architects, is for the public space that the building creates around it. Here, suddenly, is a civic center, or the spirit of a civic center, where only chaos existed before. You've got to know how much talk there has been about a civic center for New York for the last ten years to appreciate that statement.

In the city's civic center plan—of which more later—the new Police Headquarters ended up in a hole in the ground at the back side of McKim, Mead, and White's Municipal Building, smack against the approach spaghetti to the Brooklyn Bridge. Just to get to it over the tangle would have required an overpass rising 15 feet and then dropping down again. Without the guidance and goading and departmental coordination of the Office of Lower Manhattan Development—one of the Lindsay-sponsored innovative city planning offices—the story would have had a different and too-familiar ending: more piecemeal design and incremental chaos.

Not only have Gruzen and Partners, with the collaborating landscape architect, M. Paul Friedberg and Associates, redeemed the irredeemable, they have also created the city's finest public plaza and given a kind of coherence by extension to the entire fragmented area of City Hall and Foley Square. This is much more, and much more important, than architecture alone. An esthetic masterpiece isolated on that grotesque, cut-off site would have been meaningless. But the level of planning that turned the site into connective tissue, increasing the pleasure and efficiency quotient of all the space around it, is significant urban design.

In fact, the city's and the firm's architects thought first about the environmental aspects of the building, before any architectural design was done. They started with the surroundings and worked from the outside in. The solution was to depress Park Row, at the western boundary of the site, and to create a 75-foot-wide bridge-overpass across it to the Municipal Building, leading directly to, and through, its wide central arch. In the other direction, to the east, the open site's lower level affords pedestrian access to the Al Smith Houses. To do all this, Brooklyn Bridge approaches were modified and Park Row utilities were moved.

The bridge-overpass is the spacious new three-acre Police Plaza, brick-paved, planted with mature honey locust trees, with a fountain wall and raised green buffer strip against Brooklyn Bridge to the south. Part of Duane Street, closed to traffic and also brick paved, continues the plaza as a pedestrian way into Foley Square. The plaza is connector and catalyst for everything around it; all the spaces and structures it touches take on totally new meanings and relationships, where before there were no relationships at all.

It also connects with the Federal courthouse annex to the north, another Gruzen and Partners job. The corner of this structure has been chamfered to follow the line of the street, the first three floors have been hollowed out for visual penetration, and the building's detailing is related to the height of the capitals of the church columns next to it. At the particular urging of Richard Weinstein, head of the Office of Lower Manhattan Development, the colonnade and frieze lines of the Municipal Building and adjacent court buildings, which make a surprisingly unified, monumental urban order in the area, have been picked up in the proportions of the lower floors. This, too, is significant urban design.

And so, miraculously, it all—sort of—comes together. The irony is that what has been built is a kind of beautiful back door to the city's official civic center plan, a study produced and adopted in 1963 with great fanfare that proposed a $168-million reordering of the area to the west centered on City Hall Park and Foley Square. It was called the ABC plan for the architects who drew it up, Max Abramovitz, Simon Breines, and Robert Cutler.

After eons of putting the wrong buildings in the wrong places at the wrong time, it looked like vision. It at least dealt with a whole, rather than with disjointed parts. Hindsight reveals it as a simplistic bit of Beaux Arts pedantry, with lots of axial symmetry and greenery

A Civic Center where only chaos existed before.
David Hirsch

used like glue, but at the time there was public rejoicing, with this voice in the chorus. Everything is relative.

There ensued a passionate donnybrook with the federal government, which was engaged in its own architectural misadventures on Foley Square. The city wanted the site of the new Federal Building moved west to Broadway to allow those pointless axial vistas to go on and on. The Feds, in the role of bully boys, refused, and then something even sillier happened—weakened by the excavation for the new building, the small structures on the Broadway side fell down. The Feds still wouldn't budge their blockbuster, which has subsequently become known as the Great Checkerboard and is so horribly visible from anywhere at all that its placement is academic.

The job of designing a mall and new municipal office tower was given to Edward Durell Stone and Eggers and Higgins. The saccharine scheme that resulted died a natural death. All this went on to an obbligato of public protest by Nathan Ginsberg, the civic center gadfly. But in New York, silliness can lead to success. With the establishment of the Office of Lower Manhattan Development, under Richard Buford at that time, the first commendable scheme was produced, by consultant architects Conklin and Rossant. It sensibly emphasized circulation patterns. An elevated "ring" was to be the magic device to make the Brooklyn Bridge mess disappear and tie everything together.

The new Police Plaza actually builds one eighth of that ring, debouching near the Municipal Building. Today you can stand in the Police Headquarters lobby and look out through the glass wall to the handsome new public space, through the Municipal arch and along Chambers Street toward the Hudson River. That splendid view, which never existed before, is a 100 percent architectural achievement. It is also a fine demonstration of how to practice the art of civic center building and environmental design.

November 18, 1973

BAD NEWS ABOUT TIMES SQUARE

It is not the best of times, and it is not the worst of times, just somewhere discouragingly in between. With the commercial market overbuilt, New York no longer has the look of a city in construction, which means that at least fewer good old buildings are being torn down for bad new ones. The developers are crying all the way to the Caribbean. And the city's planners, theoretically, have time to sit and think.

They have plenty to think about. The change in the economy and the change in the municipal administration have left the city's planning offices in a kind of paralysis, or limbo. After establishing a remarkable record for tangible achievements in the guidance of private development through progressive urban design, they have virtually no construction to guide. This means that there must be a radical reordering of programs and priorities if the planners are to continue as an effective force in the city's life. And unless this reassessment is made with vision, speed, and skill, there is no place to go but down. As the planning offices go, so goes New York.

Most of the news about Times Square, that symbolic heart of New York and crossroads of the world, is bad. On the plus side, it has what every city needs—tremendous vitality. On the minus side, much of that energy is channeled into high-visibility pornography and other fast-buck operations. The area is encrusted with the dark and gritty sediment of endless seasons of concentrated use and abuse that no rain or garbage removal ever touches. But the crime statistics are down. And the theaters are virtually full.

So much for the surface. Underneath, the district is particularly hard hit by both recession and inflation, in terms of rentals, building health, and the future of certain key projects. Because the area is tenuous anyway, these factors are critical. Within months, Times Square and its environs lost a Liggett's, a Woolworth's, at least two restaurants, and the Royal Manhattan Hotel. The Franklin National Bank demolished one of the area's few fine buildings to save taxes and maintenance. The real estate base is in serious trouble.

The hotel, stores, and restaurants represented the kind of sound, diversified services that the district desperately needs. But when rent and expenses went up, the tenants went out. Whenever rents rise and legitimate commercial activities leave a fringe area, peep shows and massage parlors come in. After the demise of Deli City on 42d Street, only the withholding of a state liquor license staved off a topless bar at this focal point of Times Square. It was an empty gesture; it became a porn supermarket. The trend in such an economy is inevitably down. And the farther down the ambience slips, the greater the pathologies of the public it attracts, and the more difficult it is for any stabilizing, legitimate activities to remain and compete. (No one is looking to make Times Square genteel or the playground of the effete rich, only reasonably secure and appetizing.)

In fact, the future of Times Square seems to depend on one large, tide-turning project: the $160-million hotel planned by the Atlanta architect-entrepreneur, John Portman, for the west side of Broadway between 45th and 46th Streets. In size and scale, in design bravura, in its ability to attract the middle class tourist and to be an environmental catalyst, it would provide an essential stability for Times Square, in character with its traditional functions and style. But this hotel, in turn, depends on a $200-million convention center proposed for a riverfront site a few blocks west, and this project is hung up on the city's financial crisis and the present state of the economy.

That is the situation, and the future is clearly in the balance. In the Lindsay era, the city's planners would have been in there with a strategy compounded of Machiavelli and Sixtus V. When Fifth Avenue began to change in character and style a few years ago, the Office of Midtown Planning and Development (OMPD) devised the mixed-use Fifth Avenue zoning district to control and upgrade the street's activities. The special theater district was taken over by OMPD from the Urban Design Group that had devised the zoning, and the planners worked with the builders to bring new playhouses to the Times Square area. It initiated plans and negotiations for the convention center and the Portman hotel. Farther east—OMPD's authority extends to both rivers—there was the defeated, but imaginative Madison Avenue Mall.

OMPD, one of about a dozen special planning offices located throughout the city according to districts, is in uneasy transition. A new director, Dick G. Lam, has replaced the first director of the office, Jaquelin T. Robertson and acting director William Bardel, after months of delay due to changes at City Hall. (Mr. Robertson has embarked on the redevelopment of Teheran for the Shah of Iran, with the planning firm of Llewelyn-Davies International—a far cry from Times Square.)

None of the planning offices have the high priority status in the Beame administration that they enjoyed under Lindsay; at that time the top-line authority of the Mayor's office was actively behind them.

The power of his concentrated interest and backing was no small advantage in getting things done. In the uncertain transition from Lindsay to Beame, some of the best urban planners and directors left. In the midtown office, five of the top planners were lost as a result of insecurity and conflict, and the Robertson team has been reshuffled.

Now that the period of high publicity and dazzling innovation is past, New York has ceased to attract the brightest young professionals in the field. Loss of talent is matched by loss of leadership; the charismatic directors, such as Robertson and Richard Weinstein of the Office of Lower Manhattan Development, who put the public and the private sector together with a blend of political magic and pragmatic idealism are gone. The days of working with large-scale development are also gone, at least temporarily, and so are the charismatic, large-scale projects. There are limited funds for anything at all in the current budgetary crisis.

If there is neither money nor development, what are OMPD's planners doing? There are some commendable undertakings: a continuing study of zoning controls for signs and street access that could reduce the impact of porn joints around Times Square, coupled with an ongoing collaborative effort with law-enforcement agencies to monitor and clean up illegal and dangerous activities. There is a study of proliferating single-room occupancy hotels with the aim of controlling their conversion. Block by block, surveys are being made for computer digestion and other forms of analysis. There also seems to be an increasing amount of planning busywork, such as "exchange and comparison" of information from other cities from Caracas to Miami, for which grants are usually available. These have, at best, risky and limited input into the New York planning process.

No longer are developers being pulled in by their jacquard silk ties to take a strong dose of higher design standards, often for mutual benefit and stimulation. The Villard Houses-Palace Hotel project in east midtown is not being guided into appropriate as well as profitable design solutions by the midtown office. Nor is the planning being done during this building hiatus that would prepare the city for development when construction resumes. (A "public entertainment district" could be mapped out for Times Square where peddlers and tourist activity could be coordinated. A comprehensive midtown traffic study needs to be pushed while pressures are low.)

What is actually coming out of the office is less than encouraging. A Broadway Mall, a holdover from the Lindsay years, has been shorn of its most important element in its most recent public appearance. Part of its purpose as a pedestrian precinct was to have a tourist information billboard, or building, at one end that would centralize visitor activities attractively and informatively. That is gone, and the Mall is reduced to street dressing, rather than something that deals inclusively with the needs and functions of the area. But what is most disturbing is the planning climate: not apathy, but slowdown; not lack of interest so much as lack of vision; a lowering of standards and a lessened conceptualization of the job. What has noticeably slacked off is the passionate pursuit of a better city through the imaginative, far-reaching application of the creative processes of urban design. It was a kind of passion that pulled bureaucrats and businessmen along with it to very real planning achievements. It is not just Times Square that hangs in the balance; it is all of New York.

February 9, 1974

THE BLOOMING OF DOWNTOWN BROOKLYN

Generally, it is easier to get New Yorkers to cross the Atlantic than to cross the East River. Still, the blooming of downtown Brooklyn should not really take them so very much by surprise. It wouldn't if they didn't keep looking the other way. A walk across the Brooklyn Bridge on a magical early spring day or evening reveals more than its accustomed romantic beauty. (How spoiled we New Yorkers are; but this is part of our dubious charm.) Downtown Brooklyn is still fraught with real and continuing problems, but there is enough visible accomplishment in terms of design, development, and the creation and reinforcement of community and amenity for a dozen other cities.

Brooklyn's lessons in architecture and urbanism—which largely involve informed efforts to turn around an area decimated by a residential and commercial flight to the suburbs of the 1950s and 1960s—are heartening. And so are the role and achievements of the city agency in charge, the Office of Downtown Brooklyn Development, under the direction of Richard M. Rosan, working in collaboration with exceptionally strong and dedicated local groups. This is one of those on-the-spot Mayor's planning offices that have done more for New York in terms of positive development policy than any single idea or action initiated by city government in the last decade.

You don't have to be a closet Brooklynite to know about Brooklyn's brownstone revival, but the first thing that strikes the visitor is the startling dimensions of the residential renaissance. These neighborhoods go on literally for miles, ringing downtown Brooklyn. They have an incredible population of 275,000—at least as big as three medium-size cities. Beginning with Brooklyn Heights, the revival moved to Cobble Hill, Boerum Hill, and Park Slope—four areas that have been declared historic districts. Still another, Fort Greene, is in the process of designation.

Almost all of these seemingly endless, superb streets of nineteenth-century row houses were once slated for the bulldozer brand of urban renewal. That figured, of course, since the easiest thing to demolish is a treasury of intimately scaled, rich architectural styles of exceptional craftsmanship and quality. The revival that took place instead was a spontaneous, snowballing, bootstrap operation of individual and collective gut faith, born of a dedication to the principle that New York is livable, made by a young, committed, urban middle class.

If you want to know the extent of such faith, it is worth noting that with the exception of a few local Brooklyn institutions, New York banks would give no loans or mortgages on any of these houses in any of these areas. Has anyone ever estimated the disastrous impact of such "sound banking policy" on cities, even when street wisdom was in the act of proving the bankers wrong? They have a lot to answer for. (They'll handle the buildings now, at quintuple markups in sound, marketable neighborhoods.)

This charm, comfort, and beauty, from tree-lined streets and blooming back yards to Eastlake parlors and sun-filled kitchens, is within a stone's, or a subway's, throw of the big apple. Transportation facilities are excellent, although they need upgrading like the rest of New York's mass transit. Everything converges on downtown Brooklyn. And if the natives don't want to cross the river, they have an overwhelming concentration of their own cultural and educational institutions.

Again, if one stops to think about it, the score is stupefying. There are at least a dozen educational institutions, with 45,000 enrolled in them, as compared to 26,288 students in Cambridge, Mass. Baruch College is now moving toward realization on 13 acres of the Atlantic Terminal renewal site after ten years of backing and filling. There is a small, steady, loyal stream to the dance programs (outstanding) and exhibitions (ditto) of the topflight Academy of Music and Brooklyn Museum. (One draw, even with Manhattan's easy riches, is dinner at Gage and Tollner's landmark restaurant, an island of authentic food and atmosphere in the expensive *ersatzschmier* of New York dining.)

And that's not all, as they say in boostersville. Just beyond the bridge is Brooklyn's civic and commercial center. About 67,000 people, divided between the public and private sectors, work in its businesses, courts, government agencies, law and insurance offices, and retail enterprises. And these are not just buildings—we are also talking about architecture. From the solid granite Romanesque Revival Post Office and the neo-classical Borough Hall to the nifty Art Deco of Corbett, Harrison and McMurray's 185 Montague Street (headquarters of the Office of Downtown Brooklyn Development), there is more substantial, stylish, top-quality building in downtown Brooklyn than one can shake an architectural historian at. Block for block, it is some of the best, most underpublicized landmark territory in New York.

Most of the pivotal change and the concentrated redevelopment effort have taken place in this central business district, around Fulton Street. There has been commercial spillover beyond, from the brownstone neighborhoods, revitalizing Atlantic Avenue as well, with its older ethnic strengths and burgeoning antique and specialty shops. Atlantic Avenue is now surprisingly reminiscent of New Orleans's Magazine Street in both character and renewal. The development office has devised a special Atlantic Avenue zoning district to protect just those urban and architectural features that would be lost, without controls, in the regenerative process.

With the Downtown Brooklyn Development Association, the planners have made steady progress in the Fulton Street area. Abraham and Straus and May's have held on, while the famous movie houses died and traditional shopping turned into a redundancy of fancy shoes and wigs. But even with suburban defection and social change, this section still has the sixth largest sales volume of all U.S. central business districts, and one of the planners' proposals is a Fulton Street pedestrian mall. This seems about to go ahead. (Not the least problem is the repeated political, social, and commercial mobilization needed, year after year, as every project inches forward one hearing at a time.)

A good deal less visible remedial action has also been under way. The Livingston-Bond garage that opened recently does more than provide parking space; it is a coordinating facility for off-street unloading, goods handling, and new shops. Two handsome new, key buildings have been completed by the firm of Skidmore, Owings and Merrill— for Con Ed and the New York Telephone Company. Under careful planning persuasion, they feature such mandated urban assets as arcades and new subway entrances as well as far-above-speculative-quality design.

There have been disappointments. Dreams of large amounts of new office space have died with the real estate market. Housing plans have collapsed, brought on by the failure of UDC. But nothing is too big or too small for the Brooklyn planning office. A clear indication of its eye and attitude is a series of tidy, tiny, "traffic island" parklets throughout the area—carefully repaved, with trees and benches. The strength of a local planning office is that, unlike a centralized agency, its attention is focused on every street corner. This is the only kind of planning that really works.

We have saved the best till last. Downtown Brooklyn not only has the unparalleled view of Manhattan, it has a wonderful waterfront. The development office's Fulton Ferry waterfront plan ranges from the building of a small park and ferry slip, almost complete, to a pair of imaginative schemes to use a fine "modernistic" factory for the Brooklyn Museum Art School and the city-owned Fire Boat House for a Brooklyn Bridge Museum. (One of New York's secret treasures is the set of Roebling's inch-by-inch watercolor renderings of the bridge in the original wooden file cabinets.)

Long-range plans would link the area with the South Street Seaport on the Manhattan side. But it isn't necessary to wait for that to happen to explore the architectural marvels of the dramatic brick Empire Stores with their griffins and eagles and arched gates at the water's edge. Last one over the bridge is a loser.

March 30, 1975

BATTERY PARK CITY: DREAM OR DISASTER?

It is doubtful if any city has had so many incarnations before it was even born as Battery Park City, the new community being built in the Hudson River at the edge of Lower Manhattan. There have been three official plans and numerous city reviews to get the project moving. However, observers note that the moves are more like a slow gavotte than a headlong rush to acceptance by the city, with its planners known to be clearly unhappy with what they have been given.

Three versions make up a lot of planning since 1966, when the project was announced, and, except for one brief creative spurt in 1968, it seems to have been downhill all the way. The questions being asked in professional circles are whether New York is getting a dream city or a disaster area, and why.

These are not small questions. Battery Park City will cover 100 acres of landfill in the Hudson River extending from the Battery to Duane Street, for a community of 90,000 people. This is a full-size city by any standard.

There has been continuous, concerned debate about density transportation and services in relation to the already overburdened streets and systems of Lower Manhattan, exacerbated by the arrival of the World Trade Center. The resolution of the "great divide"—the West Side Highway—is still being studied as state and city agencies argue the method of its mandated rebuilding. At present, it is a barrier between the landfill and Lower Manhattan.

A large part of the basic financing for the project has had to be switched from office building with private capital, when the office boom collapsed, to housing with state funds. With the troubles of the State Urban Development Corporation and the shaky status of the State Housing Authority bonds, even that has become tenuous. Although the New York builder Harry Helmsley has signed on as office developer, commercial construction will now be last instead of first, when the market permits. Commercial financing can no longer carry housing, schools, and services, as planned.

Bonds already issued by the Battery Park City Authority, which was set up by Governor Rockefeller and the State Legislature with power to plan, finance, and construct the land and buildings, are troublesomely remote from yielding a return. All moral obligation bonds are in trouble.

If these were not problems enough, the question of design authority, in this totally new piece of Manhattan, is confused and chaotic. Design quality is under attack. And costs mount daily.

The Battery Park City Authority, headed by Charles J. Urstadt, sits high over the Hudson on Rector Street watching the landfill take shape. A bit farther east, on Lafayette Street, the Office of Lower Manhattan Development is watching the Battery Park City Authority. City and state have been involved in a continuous hassle over what the project will be since the Rockefeller-Lindsay battles at its initiation.

The very first proposal, announced with great fanfare by the Governor in 1966, was a slick, brochure-type presentation of sterile high-rise towers in vacuous open space that caught the city completely off guard. It was pure "box-top architecture"—something that can be torn off at the dotted line, because it has no relation to anything around it.

Almost simultaneously, the city released a master Lower Manhattan Plan that had been in preparation for some time. This was a thoughtful proposal for land use, residential and commercial development, and waterfront reclamation that set a new standard for urban-design sensitivity. It also proposed landfill development. But it had nothing to do with Battery Park City, and Battery Park City had nothing to do with Lower Manhattan.

Some fast political footwork brought reconciliation and, in time, a new Battery Park City plan. In 1968, both the Mayor and the Governor unveiled a scheme developed by a team of designers that could only have been put together by a clubhouse deal or a marriage broker, or both.

The coalition included the Governor's original architects, Harrison and Abramovitz, in addition to Conklin and Rossant, the New York architects of the Lower Manhattan Plan, which had also been prepared by Wallace, McHarg, Roberts and Todd of Philadelphia and Alan M. Voorhees and Associates of Washington. Architectural diplomacy was provided by the firm of Johnson and Burgee.

The result was a brilliant, schematic compromise to which all had contributed, containing urban-design ideas from the waterfront parks, inlets, and marinas of the Lower Manhattan Plan to a multilevel "service spine" along the length of the development.

It was conceived as a "linear city" with a platform 28 feet above the river, and most of its features were predicated on the profitable, first-stage erection of three huge office towers at the southern tip.

The city and the state then signed a lease that virtually built in the plan's basic elements. The coalition architects dropped from sight. The plan's virtues were its imaginativeness and its comprehensiveness—until that point, New York had been built as a series of disconnected, block-size speculative adventures. It was received enthusiastically, and then its troubles began.

The Manhattan office market went soft. That blew the three office towers and the scheme's essential financial base.

The city's urban designers at the Office of Lower Manhattan Development grew increasingly disturbed at the plan's lack of relationship to existing configurations of Lower Manhattan. They were developing large plans of their own for contiguous areas, stressing waterfront promenades, views through to the water, and an attempt to create human scale at the street level of massive new construction. They feared a "Chinese wall" effect offshore and wanted connections and continuity with the new development.

Battery Park City now found its heralded scheme elaborately expensive, in conflict with the city's objectives, and financially inoperative. To keep it alive, the Authority switched from commercial construction to 5,800 units of housing as its base and first phase, using $4.5-million of Mitchell-Lama funds from the state. It began to redesign.

The Authority acquired Samuel Lefrak and the Fisher Brothers as potential housing developers. It also acquired an architectural consultant, Max Abramovitz of Harrison and Abramovitz, and a director of architecture, William Halsey. The developers brought their "in-house" architects and preset formulas. A design deadlock set in.

It is an open secret that bruising battles went on between consulting and city architects and the developers. Mr. Urstadt sits in a Solomon-like position, adjudicating the developers' demands and the architects' objections. The result is a disastrous draw.

The plan is a curious one. It started out looking a lot like Lefrak City. The "service spine" with its separate levels of cars and people and skylit gallery of stores and restaurants became a "future shopping center," and waterfront coves and inlets were reduced to tokens. With pressure from the Office of Lower Manhattan Development and the consultant architect, some modifications have been made. But it still looks like outer borough limbo.

Those modifications include a slight staggering of the towers to form some relationship with existing Manhattan streets and the city's demand for water sightlines, a park backing on the World Trade Center, and some circulatory connections. The city-state lease has had to be totally rewritten.

The consultant architect fought for underground parking by adding unpromising platform bases to the buildings. He also fought for low-rise units to temper the inhumanity of the towers. Still later, the firm of Lawrence Halprin and Associates was brought in to humanize the open spaces.

Since the developers' mortgage money will come from the Battery Park City Authority, higher standards and tighter controls have been possible from the start. The problem is whether those standards are really understood, and how a hopelessly fragmented and emasculated architectural setup can possibly achieve them.

"We are losing $50,000 a day while we sit and wait," Mr. Urstadt has said nervously. The real question is whether the city is losing a $1.1-billion planning opportunity for the future.

July 14, 1973

BIG BUT NOT SO BOLD: THE WORLD TRADE CENTER

The towers are pure technology, the lobbies are pure schmaltz, and the impact on New York of two 110-story buildings and auxiliary structures with a projected population of 130,000 workers and visitors using a city-size amount of services is pure speculation. These are the three areas in which an undertaking of the size and scale of the World Trade Center must be evaluated: engineering, design, and planning.

As engineering, the buildings' roots are in Chicago in the 1880s, where technology and esthetics combined for that uniquely American contribution to art and urban life, the skyscraper. By the 1930s it had shaped the Manhattan skyline and the twentieth century. However, even as the World Trade Center is dedicated, the palm is going back to Chicago, where the Sears Tower will be still higher and even more advanced in its tall building technology.

In the sixties, new developments in framing techniques that increased strength and rigidity and decreased bulk and cost made megalomania compatible with economics. Don't knock the twentieth century, when art finally equalled man's aspirations. Big buildings are beautiful by accident—through sheer size and drama—and by design.

As design, the World Trade Center is a conundrum. It is a contradiction in terms: the daintiest big buildings in the world. In spite of their size, the towers emphasize an almost miniature module—3 feet 4 inches—and the close grid of their decorative facades has a delicacy that its architect, Minoru Yamasaki, chose deliberately. The associated New York architects are Emery Roth and Sons.

The module is so small, and the 22-inch-wide windows so narrow, that one of the miraculous benefits of the tall building, the panoramic

122

view out, is destroyed. No amount of head-dodging from column to column can put that fragmented view together. It is pure visual frustration.

Mr. Yamasaki is a modest size, and he talks insistently of "human scale." He believes that this miniaturization "humanizes" the huge buildings and relates them to the man in the street. Because the delicate aluminum grid covers the closely spaced columns of a load-bearing exterior wall, he claims structural justification.

But the most beautiful skyscrapers are not only big, they are bold; that is the essence and logic of their structural and visual reality. They are bone-beautiful, and the best wear skins that express that fact with the strength and subtlety of great art. These are big buildings but they are not great architecture. The grill-like metal facade stripes are curiously without scale. They taper into the more widely-spaced columns of "Gothic trees" at the lower stories, a detail that does not express structure so much as tart it up. The Port Authority has built the ultimate Disneyland fairytale blockbuster. It is General Motors Gothic.

Still, there are things to be grateful for. Whether one likes the style or not, the Port Authority tried for something special. And those lobbies are high and spacious, if cheesily pretentious. Everything else, however, is monumentally average.

The third factor, planning, is bringing the big building increasingly under attack in cities today. It is being looked on more as monster than as marvel. The tall building is recognized not as an isolated object, but as an element of the environment. These buildings cannot be considered yet as a total complex or measured in the all-important terms of how they work in their surroundings, because they must function as part of a vastly replanned and rebuilt Lower Manhattan.

But belatedly, questions are being raised about energy use and pollution, and all those city troubles that a city-size structure complicates. The World Trade Center will take 80,000 kilowatts of electricity a year, for example, or 20 percent of Con Edison's growth. With hindsight, it seems obvious that the Port Authority has no business being in the real estate game, and that the huge structures, combined with their unfairly advantageous position as to taxes and subsidies, have dealt the Manhattan office market a lethal blow.

The skyscraper has become a sophisticated problem in environment. And that is how the World Trade Center will ultimately have to be judged, rather than for its esthetic effect on the skyline, or its status value, or even its economics. Survival is the issue now.

April 5, 1973

The World Trade Center, the daintiest big buildings in the world.
The New York Times/Jack Manning

SMALL BUT SIGNIFICANT:
HENRY STREET SETTLEMENT

The Arts for Living Center—the new building of the Henry Street Settlement on Grand Street on the lower East Side—sums up in its name everything that urban architecture should be. It is a building meant to serve and expand the life of a community, and no better definition of architecture exists than that.

The fact that it is a good building, not only in the fulfillment of this basic objective but also in terms of the more esthetic qualitative criteria in which architecture deals, makes it doubly satisfying. The successful integration of the two requirements—one very much tied to the life of society and the other a timeless requirement of the art of architecture—is a complex and rewarding achievement.

Henry Street is a name both familiar and revered in the annals of social reform. The Settlement has served its neighborhood since 1893, and its activities, from assisting the adjustment of immigrant families to the dramatic successes of the Playhouse, are legendary. As a pioneer in the use of the arts for socially oriented services, Henry Street has become a part of New York and national history.

Like almost everything else, this institution has been in troubled transition in recent years. The once predominantly Jewish area has become largely black and Puerto Rican with a mix of Jewish, Italian, and Chinese; the neighborhood has exchanged stability for a state of flux symptomatic of the times; the urge for upward mobility within accepted middle-class standards has been replaced by rebellion against those standards. Only poverty and underprivilege remain the same.

There has been a matching upheaval at Henry Street as to how its programs, within the framework of its aims and values, could best serve this new kind of disadvantaged, multi-cultural community. The objective remains the same as it has for the last 80-odd years—a kind of triumph of its own when it is fashionable to turn all values upside down—to improve the quality of life in an area of urban poverty. The resolution of the dilemma has led to significant changes in approach and style. Under the leadership of the Settlement's executive director, Bertram M. Beck, all this is reflected in the form and use of this exemplary building.

The Arts for Living Center has been designed by Lo-Yi Chan of the architectural firm of Prentice, Chan, Ohlhausen to house an extensive performing and visual arts program of highly professional standards that serves all elements of the community from children to the elderly. There are facilities for painting, sculpture, silkscreen printing, pottery and crafts, dance, drama, and music from chamber to rock, and such refinements as individual piano rooms for practice.

Nurturing talent is as much a part of the agenda as the primary purpose of helping people. A new emphasis is placed on the cultural heritage of minorities, and on film and television. A recent Playhouse success was Ed Bullins's *The Taking of Miss Janie*. But you don't have to know anything of this to see and respond to the building's obvious role in the community, for this is a design that states its pur-

Henry Street Settlement, an architecture meant to serve and expand the life of the community. *Elliot Fine*

pose immediately, in visual, three-dimensional, urban terms. The structure opens to the street in a very special way to ask people in, to say that it is part of the neighborhood, to invite everyone to use it.

Instead of hugging the building line, it takes the shape of an open arc, with shallow, curving steps creating an informal entrance space that is used actively for sitting and socializing. Doors and studios, wrapped around the plaza, are visible and welcoming. This public area carved out of the building site and flowing in from the street, yet part of the building itself, demonstrates architecture as a social and urban art in the very best sense.

The aim is equally clear in the plan. The Center is actually a basic shell for people and their products. The shell holds many multipurpose rooms adaptable to changing needs. Arranged in five levels around the entrance arc, all of these performance, meeting, and instructional areas are related constantly to it, either through large areas of glass on the ground floor, or smaller, sometimes eccentrically positioned windows above.

This gives immediate orientation and visibility. To state a basic fact simply, nothing in a building like this can be closed or hidden. Part of its function is to turn energies commonly directed to vandalism to other interests and pursuits. Trashing and attack are today's societal norms, with complex motivational roots. A too-high concealing wall outdoors, next to the adjoining Bialystoker Synagogue, for example, meant merely as a back to benches, has become a place to hide and jump emerging elderly worshipers. The wall will be lowered. Design becomes a kind of behavioral or architectural fencing to the end of making the building something more than an adversary environment.

Even with a budget of close to $2.5-million, there are no frills. The creative work—exuberant banners, stained glass, surprisingly skilled prints—is the building's only adornment. Construction is the most reasonable kind of cast-in-place concrete; facing is brick to blend with the connecting Playhouse. The costs include renovation of the Playhouse, built in the 1920s in a tentative Federal style, which is now a designated landmark. Its stylistic naucheries, colored by its creative and community roles, are endearing and non-expendable after 50 years, and it is a further credit to the architects that the new and old buildings sit together with comfort and style. Both use red brick, but it is more a delicate adjustment of planes and proportions that does the job. The Bialystoker Synagogue flanking the center on the other side is another designated landmark, with a required 30-foot separation well handled as a supplementary outdoor space.

After visiting the new Center, it is a good idea to go back to the original Henry Street buildings, a few blocks away, for a fine demonstration of cultural continuity. These are also landmarks—small, brick row houses of the early nineteenth century with delicate columns and carved entrances and a Georgian street scale that are a precious link to New York's past. Their museum-quality interiors, used actively and sympathetically for administration and living, are beautifully proportioned, flooded with daylight from large double-hung windows, rich in moldings and mantels, linked in the manner of old houses by steps at changing levels. Informal staff lunch is in one of the handsomest dining rooms in the city. These buildings are full of architectural grace. The past and the future are in good hands.

August 10, 1975

PERSPECTIVE ON THE CITY:
THREE BUILDINGS

Sometimes the best exhibitions are in the most unlikely places. On second thought, sometimes the most unlikely places are the best places for exhibitions. I don't know when I've seen a better architecture show in a more appropriate setting than the one called "Three Buildings," in the City University Graduate Center Mall at 33 West 42nd Street, prepared in collaboration with the New York City Landmarks Preservation Commission.

The show's unique virtue is that its subject matter is only steps, or blocks, away. One leaves the mall—a covered passageway forming the ground floor of the Graduate Center's handsomely recycled building that is a fine urban achievement in its own right—to encounter the buildings themselves. This gives the display an extraordinary dimension.

The "Three Buildings" of the title are the Fifth Avenue Library, just across 42nd Street, and Grand Central Terminal and the Times Tower, due east and west. The first two are designated landmarks; the third is not. The Library is safe, the Terminal is threatened, and the Times Tower has been changed almost beyond recognition.

All three buildings straddle the nineteenth and twentieth centuries. They are all examples of progressive planning and formal, academic style. And all profoundly affected the character and development of their surroundings. Together, they are responsible to a large degree for the form and content of midtown Manhattan. And they have continued to serve practical and symbolic purposes well into our own time. They are, in fact, much more than buildings; these three are New York icons, touchstones of its identity, generators of function and legend, a part of the city's soul.

The Library, started in the 1890s and completed in 1911, soon turned a quiet residential area into a cosmopolitan avenue of commerce and culture. Because the new building incorporated the earlier Astor and Lenox Libraries for a larger, central facility—it was a time of consolidation, growth, and the grand civic gesture—the Library's new president, John Shaw Billings, devised an innovative and functional plan. This grand plan received a grand French classical form when a competition for the building's design was won by two young Beaux Arts-trained architects, John M. Carrère and Thomas Hastings. The murmurous sea of the huge reading room is still sanctuary for scholars and life's gentler failures; its collections are available in great rooms of marble, carved wood, and bronze.

Today, the building's mellowed classicism, seen from the east, is one of the city's finer vistas. The superbly planned complex of the Library and Bryant Park and the set back, green front—now designated as exterior, interior, and landscape landmarks in full and wise application of the law—creates an urban space beyond price. (Try to imagine New York without it.)

There are those, however, who can imagine such things very well. For example, the bankrupt owners of the Grand Central Terminal, the Penn Central Railroad. They have succeeded in having the Terminal's landmarks designation overturned, and the city's appeal is now in the courts.*

When the Terminal was built, between 1898 and 1913, it too was the result of consolidated growth and a grand civic gesture. The brilliantly functional, intricately related, multi-level plan, with the Terminal built over the tracks, was connected by pedestrian routes and "circumferential drives" to the circulation of the area and the large-

---

* The city won the appeal and the decision was reversed.

scale development around the station. It is one of the most stunning achievements in the history of urban design.

Ramps, passageways, subways, shops, services, and offices all converge on one of the greatest interior spaces of this or any other city, the Grand Concourse—125 feet high to its star-studded, once blue, vaulted ceiling. The planning concept, based on electrification of trains, came from a railroad engineer, William J. Wilgus; the design was the result of a competition won by Reed and Stem of Minneapolis; the stylistic grandeur was the contribution of Whitney Warren of the Beaux Arts firm of Warren and Wetmore.

The elegant facade is now black with soot and the huge arched windows are blind with grime. Ugly leaks in the concourse quietly threaten the structure. But the worst threat is from the Penn Central and the developer. After the show's photographs of the Terminal's early splendor, a picture of the proposed commercial tower for the Terminal's air rights, designed by Marcel Breuer in the 1960s, is like a slap in the eye. The design shows a waffle-faced slab, obliterating the Terminal's facade, supported by giant canted legs from the elevated roadway. The new tower would form one side of a huge sandwich board (the Pan Am Building would be the other side) and together they would squeeze the old building in a brutally arrogant embrace. The grand civic gesture has been replaced by the grim economic gesture.

In fact, this picture and the view of the Times Tower after it was sold to Allied Chemical in the 1960s, and its facade stripped and refaced, are the shockers of the show. The Times Tower was another turn-of-the-century hybrid—nineteenth-century picturesque in its Gothic detailing by the architectural firm of Eidlitz and MacKenzie, and twentieth-century modern in its remarkable, early steel skeleton and underground links to mass transportation. Both the area and the brand new subway station were named Times Square shortly after the building's completion in 1904. (Can you think of it as Longacre?) Through its special site and eccentric shape and style, the building became part of the city's cultural folklore.

The distinctive character of the old building was replaced by the lowest common denominator of nondesign; if the remodeling had set out to be artless, banal, and ordinary, it could not have done a better job. There is a proposal now (the building has been sold again) to reface it with mirror glass, and anything would be an improvement. It cries to be turned into a badly needed center of tourist information and services, as part of a coordinated city plan to revitalize Times Square.

The Times Tower trivialized, or remodeling to the lowest common
denominator of design. *The New York Times*

Curiously, even in its mutilated state, the structure's symbolism survives. The illuminated news banner courses around its sides in a gesture to tradition: the ball still drops at midnight on New Year's Eve. In the end, buildings are the survivors, and the barometers, of our world.

November 6, 1975

PERSPECTIVE ON THE CITY: THE PHOTOGRAPHER'S EYE, I

Photography as art has had a lot to do with the way we perceive the world and react to it, and to some extent the accepted image of our environment is one that the art of photography has given us.

The concept of the "landscape/cityscape" show at the Metropolitan Museum (1973) stressed the characteristic way in which the photographer chooses to record these surroundings. The question is whether that process actually involves environmental as well as esthetic responses.

On the evidence of this one show, it frequently does not. As a survey of photographers' images of the twentieth-century land and city, the exhibition documents what might be called a significant trend of philosophical vision—a vision primarily poetic and abstract.

For the city, in particular, and for an urbanist, this vision seems disastrously deficient. Even at its most elegant and effective, it is seriously disappointing. To anyone who sees the city, quite apart from its role as a human heaven or hell, as one of the richest and most complex art forms of history, the selectively narrow preoccupation with formal pictorial elements that dominates these works leaves a sense of something terribly important missing. Life, substance, structure, the city itself—call it what you will. As lovely as these pictures are, and they are consummately skilled, to one who has spent a lifetime trying to grasp the life and art of the city, they are sometimes very thin art, indeed.

Photographers as image-makers of the city—
Andreas Feininger's "Midtown Manhattan from Weehawken, N.J."

THE PRESENT—CITIES

The early observers of the American scene in this century tended to be less critically aware and more art-atelier-oriented than those of more recent years—a time of mutilating change. It is hard to put it down to any particular aberration of the art of photography, since there are as many potential images of the world as there are eyes and minds to frame and interpret them. There is virtually no such thing as uncolored observation, or objective documentation, as long as there is an intelligence behind the camera. The so-called documentary photography of the 1930s consists not of objective records, but of some of the most impassioned polemics in the history of art. Those sagas of the Federal Works Programs burn with the sense of the land and its people in desolation and the city in neglect and despair. They are magnificent commentary.

The classic landscapes of Edward Weston, Walker Evans, and Ansel Adams, and the classic cityscapes of Alfred Stieglitz, Charles Sheeler, and Berenice Abbott, with other equally impressive examples of the period and style, have taught us a way to look at the world, and in turn, we see the world their way.

And that is the rub. The curious thing about images of the environment is that they inevitably structure reality. Our perception is trained by them. What we have been given by these photographers of the American land and the American city—which most people call up for their definition of both—is exquisitely observed and romantically unreal. Even the so-called "realism" is restrictively romantic—set pieces of patterned perfection—the farm furrow, towers in mist, the shining skyscraper in the shadowed street. There is so much more. Does not the depth of interpretation relate directly to the quality of art?

In both literature and art, the image of the city has always been subject to philosophical and emotional manipulation. American literature has traditionally treated the city as ugly and evil, the country as beautiful and good. American photography treats them equally as art objects. Everything was grist for the popular mill of abstraction. It never was quite enough.

This is important because in architecture and urbanism the photograph has become as valid as the thing itself. Our urban concepts are defined by certain key photographic images. Thus Andreas Feininger fused for us in the forties the sense of the city's multidimensional complexity with his use of the telephoto lens in such studies as the legendary "Rush Hour, Fifth Avenue" of 1949. He said it again about space and humanity in "Coney Island Beach." Those pictures in the exhibit that turn urban experience into a revelatory pictorial expression are the catalytic documents of environmental vision.

The process is still going on. Elaine Mayes's "Autolandscapes" of 1971, views seen from the moving car, perform a similar innovative function. Bill Arnold's "Lower East Side" of 1972 says as much about the trauma of today's urban scene as it does about the subtleties of pictorial composition. It probes reality instead of merely settling for extracted esthetic effect.

But the photographer who saw the city most truly, and whose work is still unequaled in the field, is Berenice Abbott. She sought not one selective aspect, but the city whole. Her views of the 1930s and 40s never lose meaning—if anything, they gain. This is because they do not stress the romantic or abstract surface as their overriding aim; they are primarily and penetratingly real. There is an extraordinary sense of the urban essence, of the entire physical and human conurbation rather than of something skimmed off the top. "Changing New York," the Federal Works Project of the thirties, is no set of decorative arrangements or evocation of passing mood. These pictures give you New York, the city's cycle and substance, magnificently observed.

The architects are the form-givers and the photographers are the image-makers, and the relationship is more incestuous than one would think.

November 25, 1973

PERSPECTIVE ON THE CITY: THE PHOTOGRAPHER'S EYE, II

The exhibition at the New York Historical Society (1974), organized by Mary Black, called "Manhattan Now" and subtitled "14 photographers look at the form of the city," revealed the form of New York as a special kind of alchemy. These are the pictures of New York that I have always wanted to see, or to know existed, somewhere except in my own mind's eye. This is a New York that would tear me apart if I were to see it far away from home. It is primarily an architectural New York, the city as stone and steel, but it is so much, much more.

THE PRESENT—CITIES

Here is the city's sense and presence, its joint physical and emotional message, through its structure and substance, in the telling details that counterpoint its overwhelming mass. The score as art, while uneven, is high. But the special New York sensibility—a particular prideful sense of place that non-New Yorkers rarely understand—is the constant theme.

In these photographs, the city sits for its formal portrait—the great vistas from the air, the skyline and bridges—and its informal likeness in roofscapes, streets, and historic survivals. Andreas Feininger's subjects reaffirm a singular vision of the city's masses and contrasts formidably organized and established for eternity. His view of Park Avenue to the Pan Am Building is totally perceived urbanism that makes other efforts look like architectural pedantry.

In contrast, Mark Feinstein offers a catalog of extraordinary details —parts of walls, patterns of windows, doors and dormers, the texture of old paint and stone, the visual accident of fire escapes, a cast-iron column, a metal shutter, a storefront—all photographed from silent, empty streets with the tangible feel of Sunday morning sunlight.

Evelyn Hofer evokes the architectural rhythms of cast-iron and brownstone facades with definitive artistry. Sidney Kerner adds a mosaic of parts: stone-workers' heads in a tenement arch, the steel understructure of a bridge. Adelaide de Menil matter-of-factly records the city's fairytale skyscape: the top of the American Telephone and Telegraph Building as cloudborne mausoleum at Halicarnassus, the surreal, spiky chateau-style crown of the 40 Wall Street tower. Sam Falk shows a dormered, doomed Peck Slip. And then the vision enlarges, to the official panoramas of Dimitri Kessel and the views of Manhattan from the air—the city caught at sunrise, doubled in gilded water, by Robert Campbell, an airplane pilot.

But it is in the work of André Kertesz that it all comes together. He possesses the city, and gives it back to us again with the special genius of those who have mastered all of the difficult, complex insights and responses that add up to recognition of the city's soul. Kertesz's roof landscapes of chimneys, ventilators and water towers, sooty or snow-topped against skyscrapers, inhabited by a few New York birds or a woman tending plants in a window, his decaying piers and solitary pigeons, the big, anonymous buildings that somehow suggest all of the nuances of New York light and seasons, strike the inner eye and mind like a proclamation. These images go far beyond the abstract patterns that satisfy most photographers. They seek out and find the reality that is also the poetry of this town; they deal with the spirit that is the truth.

138

Except for some night views that get dangerously close, the show is almost without a cliché. It is also virtually without people. There are a few shadowed figures, but the avenues are empty except for cars. And there is no sociology, no shocking squalor or slums. The focus, is on sheer physical substance; the vision is of the city exclusively and overwhelmingly as a built phenomenon.

And yet the city is all there. The viewer is alone with it in deserted streets or birdseye views, and this, too, is right, because the ultimate truth is the solitary nature of the relationship between the city and each one of us. New York is a city in which we are always alone. Real city fear is the lonely terror of self-discovery; real city hope is the promise of private fulfillment in a thousand small or spectacular ways. The inanimate details become the touchstones of existence and reality. They are all superbly, sensitively, here.

June 2, 1974

NEW YORK: DEAD OR ALIVE?

The conventional wisdom about investment construction—tear down the old and put up the new for maximum return on the land—is taking a beating. And so are cities, in terms of some of the things that the real estate recession is doing to the urban environment.

In New York, in particular, with tight money, inflation, cost overruns, and a decade of commercial overbuilding, the traditional development pattern has bombed out. And so have a dismaying number of big new buildings. In an almost unprecedented situation, paralleled only by the great depression, completed skyscrapers stand empty or near-empty, deep in the red. Eerily silent sites attest to the fact that construction has stopped on important buildings. Costs have escalated beyond the possibility of satisfactory returns, and the money—in a business where virtually every penny is borrowed—has run out. Crisis has quietly turned into catastrophe, and not the least effect is the damage being done to the city itself.

The most cautionary tale comes from Chicago, where nothing could illustrate the problem more forcefully than the story of the Old Stock Exchange. In a casebook adherence to investment practice, Adler and Sullivan's landmark structure in Chicago's Loop was demolished for new construction in 1971. Critics and preservationists bled profusely in print before it came down, and even New York's Metropolitan Museum lusted after the 76-year-old Sullivan terra cotta ornament and rusticated ground floor arcades. Arguments about quality, style, and the Chicago heritage were to no avail. The fate of the building, which stood on prime commercial land, was sealed with the statement that it was "economically unviable."

And so it was bulldozed, and a 43-story glass and steel replacement, called the Heller International Building, went up at 30 North LaSalle, backed by astute investors undeterred by art or sentimentality or anything but the higher truths of the real estate process. Sound business practice, as defined and revered by the development community, prevailed.

Ready for the big switch? The *new* building has proved to be "economically unviable." According to a report by Rob Warden in the *Chicago Daily News*, the structure is in serious financial trouble. Among the gruesome details listed by Mr. Warden: the developers were unable to meet the $400,000 monthly payments on their $41.3-million first mortgage, a deal for a second mortgage fell through, and cost overruns sent the building's price tag soaring beyond the $48.3-million in total financing to $51-million.

Anyone who keeps score on life's large and small architectural ironies has hit the jackpot on this one. What is economically unviable now is a big building barely distinguishable from any of the other $50-million jobs anywhere, and what was economically unviable before was a unique work of art and genius. Rehabilitation might have been considerably better. There is a bitter lesson here in economics and environment. Sound business practice turned out to be both unsound investment and destructive urbanism.

The Chicago tale has a clear application—and warning—for New York. The obvious parallel is Penn Central's determination to build a large new office tower making use of the air rights over Grand Central Terminal, or on the site itself. When the landmark designation of the terminal was overturned in a recent court decision, Penn Central and the developer won the right not only to use the air rights for new construction in this fashion, but even to demolish the existing building. Fortunately, the decision was reversed on appeal.

There is virtually no doubt that such a project, at this time, would run into the same kind of economic unviability in New York that the developers of the Stock Exchange site have suffered in Chicago, if not greater. The prognosis is resounding financial failure, in addition to the architectural impoverishment of the city. But no astute developer would be dumb enough to build under these circumstances, you say? Probably not. But the fact is that some of New York's major new buildings, put up by astute developers in the 1970s, are currently huge money losers; they went right ahead, like the Stock Exchange developers, even with storm signals flying. The more conspicuous New York disasters include 1166 Avenue of the Americas (untenanted), Two New York Plaza (empty until sold recently at a huge loss), 1500 Broadway and 55 Water Street (running in the red). Their astute developers have taken an awful shellacking.

The situation is worse than anyone except real estate insiders realize. In addition to those ghostly, untenanted or partly filled new towers, construction has actually been halted on more than a half dozen major new buildings in New York. There is simply no action on the sites, which may range from gaping excavations to partial structures. Some are luxury apartment buildings. The Citicorp Building, a 46-story tower projected a year ago as one of New York's more eye-catching skyscrapers, luckily has its own bank, Citibank, to fund it.

The disaster is taking still other forms. Sound buildings are being destroyed not for new construction, as has always been the case in New York, but for that particularly blighting form of non-investment, the empty parking lot. The demolition is a hard-nosed way of saving taxes when the properties cease to be profitable, and no buyers or investment builders are in sight. It is a vicious form of disinvestment.

In New York, the size of such mutilated sites makes bomb damage look puny. The Cities Service Company, which moved from New York to Tulsa, has defaced the Wall Street area by destroying six adjacent buildings that it owns on Wall and Pine between Pearl and William Streets. To pull out the jobs—and then add insult to injury by pulling down the buildings and the tax base—is, by any measure of social responsibility, unconscionable. The Cities Service sabotage has produced a vacant lot of more than an acre and tax savings for the company of $280,000 a year. There are times when sound business practice becomes the business of wrecking cities.

The W. R. Grace Company tore down a fine Renaissance-style structure at Pearl and Water Streets, at Hanover Square, for the inevitable parking lot, rather than maintain it and pay taxes on it. The Franklin Savings Bank further weakened the shaky West 42nd Street area by demolishing a landmark quality building—for parking and taxes. While there is no investors' market, these eyesores will remain and increase in number as old structures become unprofitable due to inflation and recession, with diminishing rental returns and rising fuel and operating costs. The possibility of demolition of Grand Central Terminal for tax savings—even without building a replacement—undoubtedly occurred to the business minds involved. It is a terribly expensive blitz for the city not only in terms of taxes lost, but of sound buildings destroyed and devastating damage to the city's architectural and environmental quality.

The tax structure, of course, rewards unimproved property and demolition, giving benefits in inverse order to the owners' positive contributions to the city. And except for the device of tax relief in landmarks law, it works against preservation. (Under New York's landmarks law, it is impossible to give the only form of relief—tax abatement—to already tax-exempt institutions, which makes all landmarks owned by charitable or non-profit organizations hopelessly vulnerable.) A belated national study of the effects of assessment and tax policies on a city's planning, growth, and preservation has been undertaken by HUD.

And so the ultimate shaper of cities turns out to be, for better or worse, so-called sound business practice, or economic viability. That this often distorts or destroys more than it contributes is becoming perilously clear. If there were no other way than to let sound business take its course, there would be little hope for the urban environment.

The planners have their role, however, which is to deal with these financial and legal realities, turning them into constructive tools in the service of an environmental vision. Among the tools are tax policies, zoning regulations, land use codes, and design and legal controls, tied to the incentives of profit and loss. These devices not only profoundly affect the builders' bottom line, they guide the city's life processes toward desirable or undesirable patterns of growth and development. This is a kind of planning that New York needs more than ever, if it is to survive.

April 6, 1975

Houston

DEEP IN THE HEART OF NOWHERE

This is a car's-eye view of Houston—but is there any other? It is a short report on a fast trip to the city that has supplanted Los Angeles in current intellectual mythology as the city of the future. You'd better believe. Houston is the place that scholars flock to for the purpose of seeing what modern civilization has wrought. Correctly perceived and publicized as freeway city, mobile city, space city, strip city, and speculator city, it is being dissected by architects and urban historians as a case study in new forms and functions. It even requires a new definition of urbanity. Houston is *the* city of the second half of the twentieth century.

But what strikes the visitor accustomed to cities shaped by rivers, mountains, and distinguishing topography, by local identity and historical and cultural conditioning, is that this is instant city, and it is nowhere city.

Houston is totally without the normal rationales of geography and evolutionary social growth that have traditionally created urban centers and culture. From the time that the Allen brothers came here from New York in 1836 and bought the featureless land at the junction of two bayous (they could not get the site they really wanted), this city has been an act of real estate, rather than an act of God or man. Houston has been willed on the flat, uniform prairie not by some planned ideal, but by the expediency of land investment economics, first, and later by oil and petrochemical prosperity.

This is not meant to be an unfavorable judgment. It is simply an effort to convey the extraordinary character of this city—to suggest its unique importance, interest, and impact. Its affluence and eccentricities have been popularly celebrated. It is known to be devoutly conservative, passionately devoted to free enterprise and non-governmental interference. It is famous, or notorious, for the fact that, alone among the country's major cities, it has no zoning—no regulations on what anyone builds, anywhere—and the debate rages over whether this makes it better or worse than other cities. (It's a draw, with pluses and minuses that have a lot to do with special local conditions.)

Now the fifth largest city in the country, Houston has had its most phenomenal expansion since the Second World War. At last count, it covered over 500 square miles and had a population of 1.4 million, with a half million more in surrounding Harris County. A thousand new people move in every week. This record-setting growth has leap-frogged over open country without natural boundaries, without land use restrictions, moving on before anything is finished, for a kind of development as open-ended as the prairie. It has jumped across smaller, fully incorporated cities within the vast city limits. The municipality can legally annex 10 percent of its urban area in outlying land or communities every year, and the land grab has been continuous and relentless.

Houston is a study in paradoxes. There are pines and palm trees, skyscrapers and sprawl; Tudor townhouses stop abruptly as cows and prairie take over. It deals in incredible extremes of wealth and culture. In spite of its size, one can find no real center, no focus. "Downtown" boasts a concentration of suave towers, but they are already challenged by other, newer commercial centers of increasing magnitude that form equally important nodes on the freeway network that ties everything together. Nor are these new office and shopping complexes located to serve existing communities in the conventional sense. They are created in a vacuum, and people come by automobile, driving right into their parking garages. They rise from expressway ribbons and seas of cars.

Houston is all process and no plan. Gertrude Stein said of Oakland that there was no there, there. One might say of Houston that one never gets there. It feels as if one is always on the way, always arriving, always looking for the place where everything comes together. And yet as a city, a twentieth-century city, it works remarkably well. If one excepts horrendous morning and evening traffic jams as all of Houston moves to and from home and work, it is a lesson in how a

An exciting and disturbing city. *The New York Times/Star Black*

mobile society functions, the values it endorses, and what kind of world it makes.

Houston is different from the time one rises in the morning to have the dark suddenly dispelled by a crimson aureole on a horizon that seems to stretch full circle, and a sun that appears to rise below eye level. (New Yorkers are accustomed to seeing only fractured bits and pieces of sky.) From a hotel of sophisticated excellence that might be Claridge's-on-the-prairie, furnished with an owner-oilman's private collection of redundant boiserie and Sevres, one drives past fountains of detergent blue.

Due north on Main Street is "downtown," a roughly 20-block cluster of commercial towers begun in the 1920s and thirties and doubled in size and numbers in the 1960s and seventies, sleek symbols of prosperity and power. They are paradigms of the corporate style. The names they bear are Tenneco, Shell Plaza, Pennzoil Place, Humble, and Houston Natural Gas, and their architects have national reputations.

In another paradox, in this country of open spaces, the towers are increasingly connected by tunnels underground. Houston's environment is strikingly "internalized" because of the area's extremes of heat and humidity. It is the indoors one seeks for large parts of the year, and that fact has profoundly affected how the city builds and lives.

The enclosed shopping center is Houston's equivalent of the traditional town plaza—a clear trend across the country. The Post Oak Galleria, a $20-million product of Houston developer Gerald Hines and architects Hellmuth, Obata and Kassabaum, with Neuhaus and Taylor, is characteristically large and opulent. A 420,000-square-foot, 600-foot long, three-level, covered shopping mall, it is part of a 33-acre commercial, office, and hotel complex off the West Loop Freeway, at the city's western edge.

The Galleria is the place to see and be seen: it is meeting place, promenade, and social center. It also offers restaurants, baubles from Tiffany and Nieman-Marcus, a galaxy of specialty shops equivalent to Madison Avenue, and an ice-skating rink comparable to Rockefeller Center's, all under a chandelier-hung glass roof. One can look up from the ice-skating to see joggers circling the oblong glass dome. The Galleria is now slated for an expansion larger than the original.

These enterprises do not require outdoor settings; they are magnets that can be placed anywhere. In fact, one seeks orientation by the freeways and their man-made landmarks (Southwest Freeway and Sharpstown, West Loop and Post Oak Tower) rather than by reference to organic patterns of growth. Climate, endless open topography, speculator economics and spectator consumerism, and, of course, the car have determined Houston's free-wheeling, vacuum-packed life and environment.

For spectator sports, one goes to the Astrodome to the southwest, which has created its own environment—the Astrodomain [sic] of assiduously cultivated amusements and motels. Popular and commercial culture are well served in Houston. There is also high, or middle, culture, for which the "brutalist" forms of the Alley Theater by New York architect Ulrich Franzen, and the neutral packaging of Jones Hall for the performing arts, by the Houston firm of Caudill, Rowlett, Scott, have been created. They stand in the shadow of the downtown oil industry giants that have provided their funding.

Farther south on Main are the Fine Arts Museum, with its handsome extension by Mies van der Rohe, and the Contemporary Arts Association building, a sharp-edged, metal trapezoid by Gunnar

Birkets. They cling together among odd vacant lots in a state of decaying or becoming, next to a psychoanalytic center.

Because the city has no zoning, these surreal juxtapositions prevail. A hamburger stand closes the formal vista of Philip Johnson's delicate, Miesian arcade at St. Thomas University. Transitional areas, such as Westheimer, not only mirror the city's untrammeled development in ten-year sections, but are freely altered as old houses are turned into new shops and restaurants, unhampered by zoning taboos. (Conventionally zoned cities simply rezone their deteriorating older residential neighborhoods to save their tax base and facilitate the same economic destiny. The process just takes a little longer.)

Houston's web of freeways is the consummate example of the twentieth-century phenomenon known as the commercial strip. The route of passage attracts sales, services, and schlock in continuous road-oriented structures—gas stations, drive-ins, and displays meant to catch the eye and fancy at 60 miles an hour. There are fixed and mobile signs, and signs larger than buildings ("buildingboards," according to students of the Pop environment). Style, extracted as symbols, becomes a kind of sign in itself, evoking images from Rapunzel to Monticello. There are miles of fluttering metallic pennants (used cars), a giant lobster with six shooters, cowboy hat, and scarf (seafood), a turning, life-size plaster bull (American International Charolais Association), and a revolving neon piano. The strip is full of intuitive wit, invention, and crass, but also real creativity—a breathtaking affront to normal sensibility that is never a bore.

Directly behind the freeways, one short turn takes the driver from the strip into pine and live oak-alleyed streets of comfortable and elegant residential communities (including the elite and affluent River Oaks). They have maintained their environmental purity by deed restrictions passed on from one generation of buyers to another.

Beyond these enclaves, anything goes. Residential development is a spin-the-wheel happening that hops, skips, and jumps outward, each project seemingly dropped from the sky—but always on the freeway. The southwest section, which was prairie before the 1950s, is now the American Dream incarnate. There is a continuing rivalry of you-name-it styles that favor French and Anglo-Saxon labels and details. If you live in Westminster, authentic-looking London street signs on high iron fences frame views of the flat Texas plains. You know you're home when you get to La Cour du Roi or Robin Hood Dell.

Because Houston is an urban invention, this kind of highly salable make-believe supplies instant history and architecture; it is an anchor to time and place where neither is defined. All of those values that accrue throughout centuries of civilization—identity, intimacy, scale, complexity, style—are simply created out of whole cloth, or whole prairie, with unabashed commercial eclecticism. How else to establish a sense of place or community, to indicate differences where none exist?

Houston is a continuous series of such cultural shocks. Its private patronage, on which the city depends for its public actions, has a cosmic range. There is the superb, *echt*-Houston eccentricity of Judge Roy Hofheinz's personal quarters in the Astrodome, done in a kind of Astrobaroque of throne chairs, gold phones, and temple dogs, with a pick-a-religion, fake stone chapel (good for bullfighters or politicians who want to meditate), shooting gallery, and presidential suite, tucked into the periphery of the stadium, complete with views of the Astros and Oilers. At the other end of the esthetic scale there is the Rothko Chapel, where the blood-dark paintings of the artist's pre-suicide days have been brought together by Dominique de Menil—a place of overwhelming, icy death. One welcomes the Texas sunshine.

Houston is not totally without planned features. It has large and handsome parks and the landscaped corridor of the Buffalo Bayou that are the result of philanthropic forethought. There are universities and a vast medical center.

But no one seems to feel the need for the public vision that older cities have of a hierarchy of places and buildings, an organized concept of function and form. Houston has a downtown singularly without amenities. The fact that money and population are flowing there from the rest of the country is considered cause for celebration, not for concern with the city's quality. This city bets on a different and brutal kind of distinction—of power, motion, and sheer energy. Its values are material fulfillment, mobility, and mass entertainment. Its returns are measured on its commercial investments. These contemporary ideals have little to do with the deeper or subtler aspects of the mind or spirit, or even with the more complex, human pleasure potential of a hedonistic culture.

When we build a new city, such as Houston, it is quite natural that we build in this image, using all of our hardware to serve its uses and desires. We create new values and new dimensions in time and space. The expanded, mobile city deals in distance and discontinuity; it "explodes" community. It substitutes fantasy for history. Houston is devoted to moon shots, not moon-viewing. The result is a significant, instructive, and disquieting city form.

HOUSTON

What Houston possesses to an exceptional degree is an extraordinary, unlimited vitality. One wishes that it had a larger conceptual reach, that social and cultural and human patterns were as well understood as dollar dynamism. But this kind of vitality is the distinguishing mark of a great city in any age. And Houston today is the American present and future. It is an exciting and disturbing place.

February 15, 1976

Salem, Mass.

RENEWING IT RIGHT

I am not one for silver linings or Panglossian optimism; I deal too much in the darker sides of people and cities. I am as aware as anyone that the world, or a good part of it, is teetering on the brink. It may even seem odd at such a time to suggest that a few things are going right. One small thing that is going very right, very quietly, and that will have noticeable long-term effects, is the consciousness that cities have developed about themselves. This self-discovery, brought about by calamitous renewal and the recognition of something called the environment, is barely ten years old. It has been a largely unheralded urban revolution. But it is now generally acknowledged that an active awareness of a city's character, amenity and style, of its cultural and architectural tradition, of its ambience and quality of life, are as essential to its prosperity and health as the tax base.

In some American cities, drained by the automobile, suburbia, and social change, this awareness has been linked to survival. Salem, Massachusetts, is such a city, a small, encompassable community of 40,000, particularly rich in history and architecture. It is the quintessential example of the older American city that must "renew" itself to keep itself alive.

Salem has had all the problems of the aging physical fabric and the slipping economic base that unite failing metropolises of every size, plus the special concern of how to deal with a substantial national heritage. The difference between this city and others is that Salem is

150

carrying out its renewal successfully and sensitively. It was not done without some disastrous backing and filling and radical changes of signals in the last twenty years, but that is illuminating too. And it still has a long way to go.

The message beginning to come out of Salem is that it is just those "uneconomic" assets of history and style that must be used as the basis of rebuilding to achieve the kind of quality and interest that attracts the sort of money and activity that add up to the elusive creation of an attractive urban life.

The city's core of handsomely recycled old buildings complemented by excellent new buildings, united in an inviting network of green pedestrian passages, puts its emphasis on the human dimension and the highest standards of urban design. Its economic base is being reestablished on restored streets and in landmark buildings containing an emerging kind of personalized, specialty store with which the ubiquitous, standardized shopping center cannot compete. Salem's results promise to be a stunning rebuke to every community that has ever thought the only way to revitalization lay through imitation of those shopping centers or by mutilation of what was often a unique identity for shoddy-slick, newly jerrybuilt anonymity.

But it was not always thus. I might as well confess here that I was the original witch of Salem. In 1965, I wrote a passionate indictment of Salem's then-proposed rape by renewal. Traffic and construction were its blind priorities and demolition its hallmark. That first plan was the product of the bulldozer mentality of the previous decade and of early federal renewal policies which ignored or penalized conservation. The article brought national notoriety to Salem, and a visit from the National Advisory Council on Historic Preservation. It also prefaced a drastic change in course.

Preservation, rehabilitation, and reuse became top requirements; to date, over $3-million in public and private funds has gone into redoing old buildings. Developers were invited to submit schemes for preservation-related new construction that they were willing to build; Mondev International of Montreal, collaborating with architect Nelson Aldrich of Boston, won this critical assignment. Robert Kerr was hired as resident planner, and John Barrett, who has headed the Redevelopment Authority through all of its swings, coordinated some outstanding teamwork.

Particularly high marks must go to Nelson Aldrich and his firm and Mondev's subsidiary, the Salem Corporation, for their part in planning and design. Also notable is the work of the Collins, Dutot Partnership of Philadelphia, who have detailed and landscaped the pedestrian-park framework that sets so much of the style and amenity standards for the whole. Credit must be given to Bob Kerr, a planner-preservationist of persuasive sensitivities, who died before he could see the results, and to the banks and business community who have backed the process.

I shall not go into the technicalities of the unconventional devices such as historic and scenic easements that were manipulated as creative financing tools. Or of the intelligent planning that is putting the automobile where it belongs (in a convenient and compatible parking garage and strategic open areas) while providing the servicing of stores through courts and alleys behind streets. These are all ingenious and sensible solutions.

Nor shall I quibble about degree and kind of restoration, or inevitable errors or miscalculations, or the complexities that dictate compromise. The lovely brick and granite buildings of a pedestrianized Front Street, restored by James H. Ballou, have evidently been held for too-high rentals in a sluggish economy, slowing the renewal process. The rebuilt public market facing a beautifully reinterpreted Derby Square with its Bulfinch-style Town Hall of 1816, now successfully reunited with the surrounding brick vernacular buildings (they were

In Salem, Massachusetts, no pratfalls to the past.
Laurence Lowry/Salem Redevelopment Authority

to be torn down in the first plan), has simple new market sheds bridging past and present. But it will need subsidies to bring back the produce merchants, and it clearly runs the danger of an artsy-craftsy fate.

The point is that the rebuilding is all being done well, with a strong and yet delicate balance between centuries. What the visitor experiences now in the 40-acre central business district is still a tentative mix. There is a lot that is seedy, and one neither wants nor hopes for a total prettying up. Salem never promised anyone a Williamsburg, thank heavens, and the restoration of a fine, abused historic fabric has been a rational tool of contemporary reuse.

There are no design bows, or pratfalls to the past, just proper relationships and details. A new office building called One Salem Green, for example, by Campbell, Aldrich and Nulty, is sleekly modern and still a perfectly calculated foil for surrounding eighteen- and nineteenth-century structures, including the restored Lyceum Building (site of Tom Thumb's wedding and now a fine French restaurant). The new offices are the focus of a small City Hall Plaza, a pocket park where before there were only the shabby backs of buildings behind a main traffic street.

The central parking garage, also by Campbell, Aldrich and Nulty, is one of the few genuinely attractive, non-jarring structures of this type ever to be dropped in the middle of a historic commercial district. There are handsome brick and patterned concrete pavements, sharpened vistas, and trees and seats everywhere.

When Mondev starts the new shopping block on the central commercial spine, Essex Street, the linchpin of the plan will fall into place and everyone will breathe a lot easier. HUD has committed an "urgent need" grant of $1,470,000 under the Community Development Act to complete the pedestrian network by turning Essex Street into a landscaped mall. This promising commercial project, another by Campbell, Aldrich and Nulty, would create a functional and delightful East India Square at its heart.

Also at that heart are the Peabody Museum and the Essex Institute, two of the country's most distinguished institutions, forming a wonderfully rich blend of commercial and cultural activities. The exterior of the Peabody's new wing is a bit bleak and brutal, something that might have been ameliorated by more design finesse, but its urban intentions of street scale and placement are impeccable. The Peabody alone is worth anyone's Bicentennial visit, as one of the world's most enchanting and absorbing collections of Americana and Orientalia, mined from the exotic maritime history of early New England and the China trade in which Salem starred.

THE PRESENT—CITIES

To those who treasure the ship captains' homes with their delicate McIntyre doorways on Chestnut Street, the spacious Common with its elegant bandstand, the Bulfinch Custom House on the harbor, the rewarding streets of bowdlerized but real architectural history, the news out of Salem is good. And for all who consider the culture and continuity of cities surpassingly relevant, the Salem plan signifies a country come of age.

September 7, 1975

Chicago

A PRIDE OF BUILDINGS

Chicago and New York have something basic in common: no matter how great the toll taken by development and politics (the classic spoilers), immense power and distinction remain. Call it charisma, machismo, vibes, or the culture of cities. But there is a force and drama tied directly to the forms and nature of the physical environment that is the quality of metropolis itself. It is, ultimately, style.

To say that style is important for a city, that it may figure as much in its destiny as the human factor, is a statement that flies in the face of today's more sociological concerns. But this is the city's essence that endures as conditions change. And so I am writing unapologetically about style—the Chicago style—with full awareness that the proper Chicago story must deal also with the conditions of its unredeemed slums, the tenuous health of a rebuilt but urbanistically unreconstructed central business district, the dislocations and pathologies of its functions, and the failure of municipal government to come to grips with the past or the future. That the middle holds in Chicago is no one's fault; that the city has style and life is almost an accident.

What it amounts to, in the narrowest sense, is that Chicago is a city of architectural excellence, which New York is not; it is probably the best city in the country for building quality. That statement, of course, needs to be hedged with all kinds of qualifications about where and how that quality works as environment, and where it does not. But the good buildings, past and present, still override the bad, and they have

In Chicago, soaring twentieth-century nonchalance and spectacular
nineteenth-century space in the Sears Tower and the Rookery lobby.
Ezra Stoller © ESTO and *Cervin Robinson*

a unifying power. Chicago does not, like New York, depend on sheer, overwhelming mass and the life force that represents for effect. A visit to Chicago, prompted in part by a desire to see the latest entry in the world's-tallest-building-derby, the Sears Tower, turns out to be a richly rewarding experience in the Chicago style—or as the scholars call it, the Chicago School.

The Sears Tower is there, all right, presiding over the city with an almost nonchalant understatement, if that can be said of a 110-story skyscraper containing five million square feet of space. And Big John, the tapered and cross-braced John Hancock Building, is there too, now cuckolded with a pair of television spires. But Sears indulges in a curious self-effacement that is not unattractive. Beyond its exceptional height and unusual shape—it is made up of a cluster of square "tubes" rising to different levels—it makes no aggressive call for attention. Personally, I think this is fine, but it seems to be a disappointment to those who look for a more monumental "statement."

The structural formula, an ingenious and precedent-setting one in engineering terms, by Fazlur Khan of Skidmore, Owings and Merrill, is notable for its economy and strength. Considering that quite enough, the architect, Bruce Graham, partner-in-change for SOM, has sheathed the structure in the simplest, cleanest, flattest glass and metal skin. This is the sleek curtain wall so elegantly defined by Gordon Bunshaft, of the New York office of SOM, at 140 Broadway in lower Manhattan. The skill and finesse of the well-done, sheer skin wall are today vastly underrated.

Mr. Graham has an architectural philosophy which holds that there is no point in overreaching (except in height), overcomplicating, striving for dubious originality, or going gratuitously beyond what amounts to an unbeatable basic solution. He thinks that good is good enough. There is no straining for effect. This is a principle that should be pasted in a lot of so-called creative hats. And if that makes for the paradox of an unpretentious tall building, so be it. God is still in the details, and SOM has a direct line to heaven.

The interior lobbies at ground and mezzanine level also eschew theatrics for simple, undramatized solutions: plain, beautifully fitted metal and glass rails, smoothly curved travertine wall corners (they will not chip), flat white surfaces and incandescent lights. The 75-foot square proportions of the nine bundled "tubes" are handsome, although they are generally ignored by the tenants.

This is offhand, throwaway quality, without side. And for such a behemoth, the public spaces seem to function surprisingly well, with a casual and cheerful air, immensely enhanced by one of the liveliest, wittiest, and most colorful Calder compositions around. Sculptural movement works with people movement in a natural orchestration of activity.

The building is not as successful outside at ground level, with a conventional plaza and a dead rear end, and the philosophical and functional questions about buildings on this scale remain unanswered. Whether the architectural and engineering exhilaration of stunning structural advance and drop-dead size, which delivers a few extra problems such as downdrafts, vertigo, and environmental isolation, is offset by the kind of economic and spatial efficiency that modern industrialization and urbanism increasingly require, is an endless subject for inquiry and debate.

But there is no debate about the technological achievement. Or the fact that it is in the Chicago building tradition that combines technology and money, art and business for an expression that has created almost a century of architectural history. The skyscraper has a fascination beyond environmental price, and most of its development was written on Chicago's streets.

There is a direct line from William LeBaron Jenney's Home Insurance Building of 1884 (demolished) to Louis Sullivan's turn-of-the-century Carson Pirie Scott store (still magnificent in its succinct skeletal definition and extraordinarily lush bronze ornament) to the Mies van der Rohe-inspired SOM postwar work and Mies's own galaxy of buildings of the 1960s. Mies settled in Chicago in the 1930s and dominated its architectural life with his personal style and standards—so perfectly attuned to the Chicago product—for 30 years. This master of the modern movement built naturally on the Chicago past and assured talented successors in the same spirit. The local preoccupation has always been with skeleton and skin in its most brilliantly functional and expressive use.

Two of the finest building and open space complexes to be found anywhere are in Chicago: Mies's Federal Center and the Mies-influenced Civic Center, both on Dearborn Street. The Mies buildings are at once assertive and subtle. Their walls of glass and black steel on a surprisingly delicate module are pure poetry; they have the kind of tension and lyricism that one feels facing Bernini or Michelangelo. Against these dark, reflective rhythms, the scarlet Calder on the plaza is a perfect counterpoint.

The Civic Center is by C. F. Murphy Associates, Loebl, Schlossman and Bennett, and Skidmore, Owings and Merrill. Here the Miesian esthetic is expressed on a different scale, in huge, 87-foot bays of truss construction in rusting Cor-ten steel, with a fine Picasso head to match on the plaza. The geometric structural drama of the building is superb, as is the understanding of monumentality and space. Between the two, the First National Bank Building offers another plaza with fountains, flowers, and a Chagall wall.

Now there is talk of more plazas—pious talk about continous public open space that sounds more like a rationalization for destruction of the Chicago heritage. The real point seems to be to make up profitable land parcels under zoning that gives plaza bonuses when the assemblage is big enough. There is a scheme to demolish Holabird and Roche's Marquette Building of 1895 for another plaza on Dearborn Street where it is least needed. In fact, Mies had counted on the Marquette's containing wall.

There is an object lesson in another kind of public space—the lobby of the handsome, historic Rookery by Burnham and Root. The Continental Bank recently restored the 1886 interior in the form in which it was remodeled without trauma by Frank Lloyd Wright in 1905, surrounding it with shops and offices. This is a spectacular, semi-public skylit court with an airy, elaborate tracery of white cast-iron and white plaster ornament and a cascade of graceful stairs. It is one of the finest of all nineteenth century commercial interiors, and it has also been used for concerts and a ball. In Chicago's inclement climate, interior courts, covered spaces and passageways are an appropriate, untried alternative to the open plaza.

But Chicago is currently caught in the trap of backlash zoning and economic expediency and a City Council that is on the one hand loathe to designate landmarks or explore remedial zoning, and on the other unwilling to buck the developers' version of manifest destiny. The Council is much quicker to assist depressing new developments like the 83-acre Illinois Center where Mies meets Hyatt in total infelicity. But that, too, is the Chicago style, politically, and it can make or break the city now.

June 8, 1975

Atlanta

Atlanta is Instant City. Downtown Atlanta has been built in the last ten years. What you see in the mile-and-a-half of Atlanta's business heart is what you get: a concentration of totally new office towers, hotels, shopping facilities, landscaped streets, plazas and parks that are a product of the sixties and early seventies—an incredibly unified achievement in an unbelievably short time, when other cities were struggling with piecemeal renewal.

In the seventies, Atlanta stands as the new American city in microcosm, still rising from the rubble of demolition and the dreams and determination of its business leaders. It is a twentieth-century urban phenomenon. In addition to Peachtree Center, where $200-million in related office buildings, shopping, and the much copied Regency-Hyatt Hotel with its roof-high atrium and glass capsule elevators have already set the city's image, there are enough finished, in process, and announced and financed new projects to make any Chamber of Commerce swoon. Like most other cities, Atlanta is having financial and administrative problems, but its physical renewal is a fait accompli.

Peachtree Center's ultimate price tag will be $700-million, with design, development, and ownership by architect John Portman, another twentieth-century phenomenon. Mr. Portman is the first of a new breed of architect-entrepreneurs who match design with a stake in the financial action and a vastly increased power over urban planning. Among his other city-changing projects, based on Atlanta's successful

161

example, are the Embarcadero Center in San Francisco and Renaissance Center in Detroit, the former completed, the latter slowed by recession and inflation.

Atlanta developers have been quick to follow the Portman effort. A new sports center, the Omni Coliseum, is being joined by a 10.5-acre, 14-story, $65-million Omni International "megastructure" with a hotel, office space, an "international trade pavilion," 10 movie theaters, a swimming pool, ice skating rink, tennis courts, shops and restaurants, and, for some curious reason, the world's longest escalator.

Seven more hotels appear to be approaching reality, including Portman's $50-million, 71-story Peachtree Center Plaza and a 35-story Hilton that will be part of more shopping and office facilities called Atlanta Center, Ltd. All will be served by a projected World Congress Center, less euphemistically known as a trade exhibition hall, to rise nearby, not far from the all-new Merchandise Mart.

The $150-million Peachtree Summit office, shop, restaurant, and garage complex will be a multi-level development integrated with Atlanta's new rapid transit line, now in the design stage. Its first structures are on the way up.

Farther north along Peachtree Street is the $100-million Colony Square group, well under way, which will have another hotel, office buildings, condominium apartments, skating rink, and heaven-knows-what. Not to mention a clutch of individual office buildings with heavy emphasis on mirror glass, and three downtown university campuses. Delegations of architects, planners, and urbanists keep coming to see what Atlanta hath wrought. The Old South was never like this.

But Atlanta was never the Old South. Its business center, Five Points—now marked by a brand new park—was the spot where the Zero Mile Post was driven into the ground for the end of the Western and Atlantic Railroad in 1837. From that point the town grew, and the railroads arrived, until four met in the 1860s. It was a bustling, brawling, railroad frontier city that was totally destroyed by Sherman on his celebrated Civil War march to the sea. What rose out of the ashes in the late nineteenth century was poor and not very beautiful; Atlanta did not make its fortune again for many years.

In fact, Atlanta has not been a typical Southern city at all. An unusual economic and social structure has made the new Atlanta possible. The rebuilding is a completely private undertaking. It is the work of a privileged group of the city's moneyed, white bankers and merchants, with their roots in the business community and their feet (until recently) in City Hall, able to move with unopposed, concerted action.

These men formed a surprisingly visionary and somewhat incestuous coalition dedicated sincerely, if purely economically, to the city's future. They provided that nebulous quality called leadership. Today the white power élite is being joined by a black power élite, with a black mayor. The power structure is changing, and more of the community is being heard from, but the building phenomenon goes on.

This private rebuilding has admittedly been a commercial rather than a sociological achievement. It has emphasized the downtown business base, and if the buildings on Peachtree Street are strange, so are the faces. Atlanta is now the number three convention city in the country. Its hotels, shops, and restaurants are predicated on still more convention business, and apparently no one is asking when the glut will set in. The new office buildings cater to more out-of-towners in regional headquarters.

Atlanta has its own image. It is not made up of the dropped-in, anonymous, interchangeable parts that characterize so many other cities. The Atlanta style is recognizable, and it has been sparked by one man, John Portman, the architect who not only started the boom but set the design standards. This style combines a kind of Buck Rogers flash with an extremely astute and experienced sense of urban design. ("Architecture," he says, "is an old man's game.")

Portman's most characteristic buildings are totally Portman. There are the razzle-dazzle Regency-Hyatt Hotel with its counterparts now in Chicago and San Francisco and imitators everywhere, and the soaring glass silo of the Peachtree Center Plaza billed as the world's tallest hotel along with New York's Waldorf-Astoria and Moscow's Ukraina, an appropriately surreal comparison. Its features are a lagoon ground floor with cocktail islands, exterior glass elevators with city views, and trapezoidal rooms.

A projected apartment house, also for downtown, is designed with cantilevered "arms" in a star-like geometry. At first glance, all this seems a jazzy, nostalgic try for the twenty-first century, or some of the "dream building" producers' literature of the 1940s come true.

But when one is tempted to call these designs the stuff of which adolescent architectural fancies are made, one is drawn up short by their expertise as well as their showmanship. Their effects are shrewdly calculated in both architectural and functional terms. The efficiencies of prefabrication and other technology, the skillful dramatization of space, the knowing manipulation of both the structure and the street, the way they are joined together in a pattern of bridges, plazas, promenades, and shopping connectors on several levels with water, plants, trees, cafés, stores, and (unfortunately) a little too much dubious art—all serve to create unusually good relationships of use and amenity.

Not many people know how to put a city together, or have the opportunity to do it. Portman does, and he is making downtown Atlanta an object lesson in people-spaces and people-pleasures. The demonstration involves extreme sensitivity to the human passages of urban design, and what happens is often a delight.

Unusual among architects and planners, Portman understands both the scale of the big building and of the pedestrian on the ground. The heart of Atlanta is a pedestrian enclave. The reservation is that his big buildings are sometimes more readable as objects, or things (Zippo lighters and gift-wrapped cylinders not too far from the Popvision of Claes Oldenburg) than as structures of human purpose—an element of his architecture that is still, for this viewer, unresolved. But he knows exactly what to do when he gets the building to the street, and everywhere in between.

With other city-size projects proceeding in other parts of the country, the Portman style is becoming an established part of American urban culture. Superficially, it means that more and more hotel guests will be whirling around in double-decker roof-top flying saucer cocktail lounges. Much more significantly, he is teaching developers—by being one—how to give the city an essential connective tissue of use and amenity, to make it workable and attractive in function and design. This has been the missing element in both speculative building and bureaucratic renewal.

Without denying this success, there are those who claim that Atlanta's rebirth has left poverty and misery untouched. The city's leaders point to their latest undertaking and first foray into housing and urban renewal, a 78-acre housing complex planned by consultant David Crane. This housing, however, is designed primarily to bring middle- and upper-income Atlantans back from the suburbs to support the downtown core. At the same time, it is expected to bolster and provide services for neighboring low-income communities. The rapid transit line is also meant to benefit this group.

There is no doubt that big business and big buildings came first in Atlanta. But it is equally clear that financial success can be harnessed to social efforts, and that is the kind of vision that will insure the city's future now.

May 5, 1974

New Orleans

A small, overboutiqued section of the hundred-odd blocks of the French Quarter is about all the tourist ever sees of this remarkable city, except for an occasional foray into the garden district. Fanning out around the Quarter are seemingly endless neighborhoods of uncommon stylistic richness, in various stages of regeneration and decay. The sheer architectural quality here is astounding.

But it is not all as safe and sound as the visitor—lulled by the protected and publicized Vieux Carré—believes. The central business district right next to the Quarter, a treasury of noteworthy structures, is currently fighting for its historical life. Rows of Greek Revival commercial buildings, of the kind New York ruthlessly demolished in lower Manhattan in the 1960s, still stand, often enhanced by the characteristic iron filigree galleries added from the 1850s on. But many are gone and more are being knocked down almost daily, as are the later Italianate, Renaissance, and cast-iron structures nearby, that make up the nineteenth century commercial city.

What has happened is that delayed "development," sparked by the new downtown Superdome, is currently hitting New Orleans like Hurricane Camille. Without the Quarter's legal district protection—incredibly, this is all that has protection in the city except for some National Register listings—the historic commercial area is now being savaged by speculators. The "demolition derby," as it is billed locally,

166

goes on virtually within eyeshot of the waiting lines of pilgrims to Antoine's.

One out of every five buildings that stood in the central business district in 1970 no longer exists. Fifty-five new parking lots have been created, largely through old building demolition, and 42 percent of the district's land is now either vacant or used for parking. Except along Poydras Avenue, a central artery of the area where the "Manhattanization" of New Orleans is now taking off from the Superdome, building owners seldom have construction plans when they bulldoze, and are merely gambling on rising land values.

A Growth Management Program has been studied by the Philadelphia firm of Wallace, McHarg, Roberts and Todd for City Hall and the Chamber of Commerce. The consultants have indicated that there is more than enough vacant land to accommodate any future development needs. It is just a step across Canal Street from the Quarter to the gaping holes.

Pending completion of the study, a nine-month moratorium on further demolition was put into effect. When the moratorium hearing was held by the City Council, it drew an immediate and overwhelming rash of before-the-deadline demolition requests from landowners. In a desperate and commendable response, Mayor Moon Landrieu called a special Council meeting and imposed a temporary moratorium on all demolition permits until the formal proposal could be acted upon. But enough permits had already been granted to blitz some of the best remaining blocks.

Curiously, while this tragic destruction takes place, other New Orleans neighborhoods are being spontaneously salvaged. In-city residential districts, each one a marvelous potpourri of characteristic regional housing styles, are coming back spectacularly. Just beyond the central business district is the lower garden district, stepchild of the neighboring garden district. Almost every street there seems to be undergoing extensive restoration. The antebellum houses, ranging from modest to quite grand, are mixed with later Victorian houses and industrial and commercial buildings.

The restoration boom is solidly entrenched in New Orleans' older residential sections, which seem to go on mile after fascinating mile. The old house revival is due partly to the execrable quality of the city's suburbs and the New Orleanian conviction that New Orleans is a fine place to live.

Success, however, breeds uneasy questions. How does the city propose to keep already mixed neighborhoods integrated as they are

In New Orleans, a demolition derby
on Canal Street. *Garth Huxtable*

upgraded? How does one balance the problematic equation of poor and black displacement against rescue and revival of sound housing stock? Some answers are being sought in a neighborhood conservation study by the New Orleans firm of Curtis and Davis.

On the other side of the French Quarter are two very old districts as fascinating as the Quarter itself, but without any of the creeping preservation slickness. In Tremé, to the northwest, and Marigny, to the east, buildings range from the oldest house type, the dormered creole cottage, to the raised cottage and the post-Civil War "shotgun" dwelling (railroad plan flat) with limitless lacy jigsaw filigree and brackets.

Then there are the long avenues, such as the incomparable Magazine Street, with its vital commercial mix in modest structures sometimes arcaded or galleried for the length of a block or more, and Tchoupitoulas, with its miles of cotton and other warehouses along the river. And there are also, of course, St. Charles, where the streetcar has been placed on the National Register, and Esplanade, and farther afield, Bayou St. John.

The tourist sees little of all this unless he has city-proud friends or family. New Orleans as a whole can only be sampled in the average visit; it cannot be fully seen or savored in weeks, months, or even years. And so New Orleans is not at all what it seems from the souvenir shops of the Quarter's Chartres Street or the antique shops along Royale (moving out to Magazine as the fashionable rents get too high)—but something vaster, more complex, and infinitely more varied and real.

Not that the Quarter isn't real; its charm is just somewhat glossed. It is a rare and genuine slice of cultural and urban history. But at this moment there is some recognizable handwriting on the wall. It is more than the commercial veneer of tourism. The Morning Call—traditional home of French coffee and beignets for generations—has left to move to an improbable suburban imitation called, equally improbably, Fat City. The open French Market is being prettily glassed in to house still more candle shops. There has been such a rash of hotel construction—the real Trojan horse within the gates—that new ones are no longer allowed to be built in the Quarter, although they can still be assembled out of old blocks.

With hindsight it is obvious that hotels should never have been added to the Vieux Carré or even placed at its immediate edge, as witness the visual bomb of the new monster highrise Marriott. The city's mistake has been in treating the area primarily as a business bonanza rather than as an environmental trust, something not achieved automatically or guaranteed by esthetic restrictions. It would draw tourism just as profitably without building it in. There are more ways to destroy than with the bulldozer.

But this is quibbling in the face of the demolition crisis in the adjoining business district. The new skyscrapers do little to curb one's distress. One Shell Square, a properly pristine tower by Skidmore, Owings and Merrill, must be credited with the unlikely achievement of looking totally deserted day or night. There is no visible life behind its obscure, dark glass windows or on its equally blank and formidably formal stepped plaza, graced only occasionally by a casual wino.

Philip Johnson and John Burgee are scheduled for another highrise directly next to it on Poydras Street—already being called Park Avenue—the Pan American Life Insurance Building. Considering the sensitive urban and esthetic nature of their recent work that sounds promising. But it is less promising when one realizes that the architect and the client have knowingly destroyed one of New Orleans's irreplaceable "alleys" at the rear of the site, in spite of local pleas to save it, with the intention of "replacement" street level activity. For those who have walked the intimate alleys with their humanly scaled old structures, there is no replacement for the real thing, even in the most suave big-city style.*

Beyond that, there are the conventional horrors: a Hyatt House supercomplex scheduled to tie in with the Superdome; a 56-story office building and hotel grouping to zoom past everything for the site of the historic and handsome St. Charles Hotel, recently demolished. It is possible under existing zoning to build a larger structure on an equivalent piece of land than is permitted in Manhattan right now and someone is obviously about to do it in a no-win game of can you top this. The sad irony is that recent technical innovations have made the sky the limit in spite of marshy soil.

What price New Orleans? Only a few hundred million in local, Texas, and other investment dollars. *States-Item* reporter and columnist Jack Davis has raised the critical question. Does anyone really have the right to destroy a city because he owns the land it stands on?

April 21, 1974

* This building was cancelled because of the 1974 recession.

Washington

CAPITAL FAILURES

They are ruining Washington. "They" are not just the speculators with their Ivory soap structures lining rebuilt streets (many of the buildings look as if they'd lather); "they" are the usual assortment of bureaucracies, banks, government offices, and institutional headquarters.

Washingtonians know it. Residents have been complaining for years about the creeping characterlessness that has been eroding this city of wide skies and particular architectural charms. The curious thing is that so many of the crimes are committed in the name of suitability, symbolism, progressive development, and other assorted and misleading rot and nonsense. The result is always the same: one more block of exactly the same thing that adds up to even more nothing at all. The effects, urbanistically, are easily analyzed; attrition of interest, elimination of variety, including detail, period, image, and use, reduction to the redundancy of one deadly dull style and scale.

The only variations are whether windows are boxed in or out, or which particular cookie mold has been used to form the facade. What has almost disappeared is the real Washington, a city of streets with their own local look, a combination of Federal houses restored or reused as bars, shops, and restaurants, with the odd old theater or bank or office building that bespeaks the nineteenth-century Capital, and that add up to the kind of amenity and ambience that are also

171

architectural and social history. It has been a distinct, evocative, and recognizable Washington. There is less and less of it all the time.

The problem may be that Washington, the seat of history, fails to understand what history really is. At any rate, it misses the point of urban history abysmally. It is not so much the George-Washington-slept-here syndrome as the classic monument fix. By focusing on those classic monuments, observers, or non-observers, miss the essential infill, the background buildings that provide the flavor and framework that set the stage for the monuments. Without these contrasts, monuments become an unreal and colossal bore, whether they are genuine national shrines or institutional, cultural, or pseudo-commercial block-busters. Washington's "development" is so wrong-headed that it wrings the heart.

One is subject less to heartache than to serious disappointment, however, when faced with another new building in Washington that had an extremely sensitive historical and environmental problem: the new headquarters for the American Institute of Architects at 18th Street and New York Avenue. The new building has been constructed just behind the Octagon, William Thornton's 1798–1800 landmark house that the Institute owns, treasures, and used as headquarters, with additions, until it outgrew it.

In Washington, a traumatic tale of
architects' good intentions. *Ezra Stoller © ESTO*

It isn't that the new structure is not a reasonably good building. If the AIA was looking for symbols, or standards, however, it has come up only with what might be described as high-level average. It seems to function and it would be adequate enough almost any place but here. It is far from a great building, and the Institute probably couldn't swallow a masterpiece anyway, being a corporate entity. Institutional clients are happiest with conventional competence; they are uneasy with brilliance.

But this is not the point. The point is that the AIA set itself the conscious and sensitive task of designing and erecting a building to go with the Octagon. It was to be an object lesson in the blending of new and old in the particular way that Washington needs so desperately and muffs so consistently. After all, who but the architects could, and should, set an example?

It was also to be an object lesson in how to go about it. The AIA held a national competition. The solution it came up with, by the firm of Mitchell-Giurgola, promised to be exceptional. Then a lot of traumatic things happened.

There seems to be little question that some of the leadership and membership was uncomfortable with the quite unconventional Mitchell-Giurgola design, which was an outstandingly creative answer to the difficult problem of blending scale and style. It dealt in sophisticated subtleties, using what was at that time, but has ceased to be, an offbeat vocabulary, clothed modestly in compatible brick.

Complications immediately ensued. The program and the site were enlarged so that the building had to be redesigned and rescaled. This version was submitted to the Fine Arts Commission. The review process became horrendously involved in personalities and serious questions of how far an advisory body should go in "dictating" design specifics.

Ultimately, everyone fell on their faces. The Fine Arts Commission rejected the design, and the AIA accepted the rejection. They did so on the ground that the Institute felt bound to uphold the principle of design review as "the best known means of maintaining order in the face of all the pressures leading to chaos."

The AIA's reaction was either chicken or preposterous. Whatever the design's shortcomings may have been, and whatever the Commission's reservations may have been, the scheme was conscientious, concerned, and able, not a speculator's destructive, free-wheeling horror. In retrospect, the Fine Arts Commission seems to have been guilty of an overbearing misinterpretation of its role for an extraordinary and dubious imposition of its own taste. On these grounds, the AIA should, and could, have stood firm, without compromising its belief in the review board function. It could, in fact, have helped to clarify that function constructively and appropriately, and aided in the proper definition of review board responsibilities. It is understandable that at this point Mitchell-Giurgola resigned.

The AIA then started over. The Architects Collaborative of Cambridge, Mass., provided another design. This one the Fine Arts Commission approved as suitable, a completely mysterious inconsistency of reasoning. Because it does not work at all in terms of the "appropriateness" that was supposed to be the criterion—as a structure that would respect and enrich the style and substance of a historic property.

Its insistent, dominating horizontal bands of precast concrete destroy rather than preserve scale. The design is brutally insensitive to Thornton's far more delicate detail. The Octagon has lost presence; it now looks like a toy. The Octagon garden, while almost the same size as before in square feet, is unbelievably diminished by too much paving and too few trees and the heavy-handed, looming presence behind it.

But what is more subtly bad is that the new building fails conspicuously to promote a balance between past and present, whatever its declared intentions. Degrees of design quality become moot. It moves the "other Washington," the wrong kind of Washington, right up to the Octagon's back door instead of cherishing and extending the Octagon's ambience. How fine an architectural act that would have been. One remembers the old brick stables that served as a library and the handsome, neighboring red brick Lemon Building, and wonders how, and where, their obvious lessons of sympathetic materials and urban relationships were lost.

March 17, 1974

Marblehead, Mass.

It's standing room only in this pre-Revolutionary town, but then, it always has been. "Old Town's" narrow streets were built up early, a clapboard-to-clapboard sequence of Colonial, Federal, and Greek Revival houses of stern simplicity in the best New England tradition, to which little could be added or subtracted. Things have remained crowded, austere, and beautiful for several hundred years.

It seemed as if age and density were a natural protection against anything except normal, evolutionary change. But Marblehead's closeness to Boston has inevitably made it a bedroom community and suburbia has expanded its historic heart, bringing assorted domestic architectural atrocities common to the rest of the country. Density and demand have sent real estate prices zooming into the ludicrous range, with builders' banal worth $30,000 jacked up to $90,000 if it has any suggestion of a view. For $100,000 upward you can get a rather nice waterfront place. There is no shame.

If there is a handkerchief of land anywhere, people build. Streets that seemed permanently settled into a close mix of classical and Victorian suddenly sprout intruders in someone's garden; speculators seize the edges of the town dump and the cemeteries. Zoning and historic controls are fairly recent concerns. The "sold" sign goes up before construction is finished, and the only way to get a historical property is to become a close friend and caretaker to a dying native.

The old houses are beauties and the new ones are bastards. Among the latter, the precut "colonial" model with overhanging, seventeenth-

century-type second story for shooting Indians is very popular with traditionalists. For the more "progressive," there is quasi-modern. The developers' product has moved from the sinking-into-the-ground number, with a kind of half story at the bottom that looks as if its windows are just disappearing into the earth, permitting a story-and-a-half "decorative" phony pedimented entrance, to an extraordinary combination of fake mansards and lally columns.

The false mansard disease is the current epidemic in and out of town. It seems to have infected the entire northeast. It appears on everything from domestic to commercial structures, as a shingled (usually higgledy-piggledy imitation handmade) horizontal box topping supermarkets, gas stations, and homes for the aged. The ever-proliferating roadside eating places, from pancake houses to "pubs," are all fake-mansarded on the outside and real plastic on the inside, food included. Shopping centers (mansarded) split and multiply where woodland stood. Roadside farm stands (no mansards) with native produce dwindle every year.

This instant vernacular is not a builder's rational simplification of clearly understood, more aristocratic styles, as on the streets of historic Marblehead, for a result of logic and elegance. It is a builder's shrewd invention of a cheap gimmick meant to evoke the older, legitimate vernacular with consummate shoddiness of execution and intent.

While building booms, traffic increases. Marblehead's one-way, winding streets that accommodate nothing larger than a Volkswagen have always been a potential driver's nightmare. "Casual" country driving habits include wrong side of the street parking and blithe ignoring of "stop" signs. Private ways are like Route 128. Bucolic lanes have bumper-to-bumper parking. The town recommends bicycle use as an alternative to car use, and that compounds chaos.

As a gesture to order, at least for the lost and strayed, there is a travelers' information booth in the center of town. After several seasons when it was manned by students, the radical innovation was made of using senior citizens. Complaints have dropped, absenteeism on good beach days is no longer a problem, and the new staff is a mine of local lore. It may be the beginning of a trend. So much for the youth cult.

You have to be middle-aged, at least, in Marblehead to remember Abby May's homemade candies (caramels not made in damp weather). The shop gave way to a pizza parlor long ago. Cameron's local breads have been gone for many seasons, and the Bide-A-Wee restaurant, where little old ladies have come in vintage hats for luncheons of broiled scrod and grapenuts pudding since time began, has turned into a gift shop. (The signs were clear when Bide-A-Wee succumbed to cake mix.) The old hardware store, where a night-blooming cereus on the sidewalk outside was a once-a-summer Marblehead nocturnal event, is a handprint fabric shop. Boutiques proliferate.

But Marblehead is not without its bucolic aspects. There is a miniature farm next door to us, the source of neighborly contributions to our table, and animals have been depleting the vegetables. The owner, assisted by Marblehead's finest, spent several of summer's most glorious weeks trapping and shooting skunks. Try that under your window. Mornings dawned with an anxious inspection of the trap to see if an execution was imminent. The police arrived at breakfast time, lights flashing, guns at the ready. Not exactly one of your urban problems.

One suspects, from glimpses of an unprecedented influx of Beautiful People that the very worst may be happening to Marblehead: it may finally be getting chic. There is also a lot of sharing of houses in tight-packed Old Town by young Boston workers and airline employees, the congestion made worse by a car for every tenant. At the other end of the scale, the tourists who usually bypassed Marblehead are increasingly finding their way to its intimate waterfront in cruiser-size station wagons and Martian sport clothes.

They are also trekking to nearby Salem to line up en masse at the "Witch House," an over-reconstructed seventeenth-century landmark, complete with café curtains, at a corner marked by maximum heat, seedy commercialism, and an endless traffic impasse. There is little waiting at the handsome McIntyre and other historic houses in which the city abounds.

Salem, which now assiduously advertises itself as "historic Salem," just as assiduously destroyed or sabotaged a good part of its past before it saw the light. A series of demolition sites, mudholes, and dust-pockets have finally turned into a prize-winning preservation-renewal plan. The pieces are coming together handsomely.

The pieces are still intact in Marblehead; they are just being elbowed briskly. The tiny gardens bloom brilliantly, the High Victorian red brick tower of Abbott Hall tops a low skyline of Federal and Grecian graces, and sunrises and sunsets are magical over one of the most breathtaking of small harbors, bridged by sailboats from shore to shore. A stroll along the streets (never on Sunday) is a lesson in history, art, and taste, and the continuity that is genuine urban life. This is one of the wonder spots of the world, but the spoiling has begun.

September 16, 1973

London

THE SECOND BLITZ

I'm not so sure about London's cleaned-up buildings. The process made Paris a milk and honey beauty, but it hasn't worked that way here. Trafalgar Square, for example, has lost the dramatic contrasts of black and white stone that were as much a tradition as London fog. Both came from the burning of soft coal, now outlawed. Surprising that pollution should have had such extraordinary esthetic effects.

In Trafalgar Square all accent and chiaroscuro, all soot and chalky splendor are gone. The buildings are uniformly middlin' cream, flattened out, almost two-dimensional. Without those sweeping sooty strokes and gleaming white highlights emphasizing almost uncannily the architect's intention and the city's *grisaille*, you somehow notice that the National Gallery is not the greatest of buildings, that its colonnades are weak and its domes hat-like and slightly foolish, as if they'd been bought at Herbert Johnson's up the street.

Next to the National Gallery, James Gibbs's laundered St. Martin-in-the-Fields is still splendid, but naked after the bath. In contrast, Gibbs's St. Mary-le-Strand, farther on, as uncommon a little jewel as ever stood on a traffic island, has its exquisite tempieto portico and delicately curved steps still brushed with the light and dark strokes of a painterly patina that's just right. I dread the day they clean it. Still farther east, St. Paul's is scrubbed, but unspoilable.

Trafalgar Square attracts people like Piccadilly. Its bowl-like center, surveyed by Nelson at the elevated level of St. Simeon Stylites, its

179

fountains and magnificently absurd, overscaled lions always with a complement of youngsters astride them, are a focus for Londoners and tourists. It is quite clear that all grand-scale plazas and grand-scale plaza life are not in Rome or points south. Trafalgar Square has a broad, epic sweep of the human panorama.

All of this activity is girdled by one of the most persistent loop traffic jams in the world. For some reason clear to the traffic people and the Greater London Council planners, you can't get anywhere in the East End without going through here first. It is London's biggest traffic circle. Congeries of tourist buses disgorging at the National Gallery ensure chaos.

But this great space has all the urban vitality and social interchange that planners admire so in theory and always want to order and regulate and clean up in practice. British planners are possessed with ordering and regulating and cleaning up. They are intensely well-meaning, rational, and cerebral. Where they have ordered, etc., as in the replanned precincts of St. Paul's, the principles are orthodox and the results are lifeless. Surely there are some lessons to be learned?

London's planners' theories about what to do with tall buildings haven't worked at all. Again, the theory made lovely exposition: spot the towers across the long, low horizon that is the historic London skyline, as vertical accents for the city's wide-skied horizontality. They stick up, not to coin an expression, like sore thumbs. They are destructive and offensive not just because they are there, but because most of them are bad buildings.

And still the planners and the Royal Fine Art Commission worry about "outlines" and "vistas," as if everyone were viewing the city from surrounding hills. What one actually sees, and what is totally destructive of the substantial excellence that is the city's real hallmark, is at eye level: atrociously ordinary building, appallingly detailed. The grandeur, strength, and finesse that have been characteristic of the English architectural mind through all past periods have been replaced by the speculative mentality with buildings to match. This is how the real damage is being done.

The public debate—and it comes with every new tall building—seems to miss this point. It is always in terms of height, with proponents of the new structure forced to sacrifice a few top stories as ritual service to St. Paul's and the past. New Zealand House, for example, one of the earlier and better postwar "skyscrapers" just off Trafalgar Square, should have been higher; the drama would have been well placed. It was amputated to ambiguity by esthetic edict.

Towers are best massed as in Manhattan; they are most effective planned in groups. In London, a lone tower is an architectural and urban obscenity. A Mies masterpiece could backdrop even St. Paul's. No one debates the real issue—the quality of design.

In exasperation, one wonders if the Royal Fine Art Commission has the taste or conviction to turn down a building on design grounds, instead of just viewing from afar. It accepted the city's tallest building, the National Westminster Bank, after niggling about height—a design that I wager would have been laughed out of the planners' councils in New York. Gentlemen, it is time to stop being gentlemen.

Quality is London's basic style and continuity. Every time this quality is ruptured by some massive mediocrity it is like planting insults to Wren, Gibbs, Jones, Nash & Co. in the streets. Gresham's law is in high gear; the bad is driving out the good. This time, London is being rebuilt by greed and underachievers.

June 27, 1971

HOW FAR FROM THE OCEAN?

If you think of London as a grand, gray-skied city of pomp, circumstance, and Portland stone, think again. And put on your sunglasses.

There is a new London rising and all that is missing is palm trees. It's pretty far from the ocean, as they said about Morris Lapidus's Summit Hotel in New York, but the firm of Richard Seifert & Partners is moving London closer to Miami all the time.

The correct attitude in London is to ignore Seifert buildings, which run to circles, lozenges, zippy curves, sweeping angles, and zigzag precast frames that make them look wrapped in rickrack, knitted on giant needles, or baked in piecrusts. They tend to take off from the ground on leaping crutches, tees, or bending knees. They are decorated with sunscreens, marquees, fountains, and a complete assortment of Florida transplants.

But ignoring Seifert's London is virtually impossible, since these works are among the city's newest, biggest, and most conspicuous buildings. Their imprint is already inescapable. When the 60 structures costing £200-million currently on his boards are completed—and they include London's tallest skyscraper—there will be a new layer of London architectural history.

Mr. Seifert has been called London's most important image-maker since Christopher Wren. The comparison is awful, but apt. In terms of the quantity and impact on scene and skyline, the statement is true, but the image he is making is more of the Eden Roc than of St. Paul's.

St. Paul's doesn't have to move over; it's being pushed by a 600-foot, £30-million Seifert tower for the National Westminster Bank, now in construction a half-mile away at Bishopsgate.

Because this will be London's tallest building, overshadowing St. Paul's from any vista, the Royal Fine Arts Commission spent some time negotiating the amputation of a few stories. The commission seems to have had little effect on the design, however; it will be a streamlined movie-modernistic tower appearing to erupt grotesquely from older, colonnaded facades.

A project for Southwark, on the south bank of the Thames, combines a skyscraper, a tropical resort-style hotel, and Habitat-like housing, for an exotic pudding. It is no trifle. The complex will form a major part of the south bank view. It will also provide a continuous waterfront promenade overlooking, among other things, the Bishopsgate bank.

Some Seifert buildings are already London landmarks. Drapers Gardens, built in the early 1960s, seems much higher than its 29 boat-shaped green glass and mosaic-faced concrete stories as it looms over the Bank of England and the old Stock Exchange.

Centre Point, at St. Giles Circus, has been not only a landmark, but a legend since 1963. The 37-story tower is the result of a historic deal in which Seifert and a London developer, Harry Hyams, were able to increase vastly the normal plot coverage in exchange for a road under the building that the London municipal government wanted, or thought it wanted.

The city's road patterns were changed and the dearly bought road is unused. So is the building. Because of a government freeze on London office construction, which jacks up values through scarcity, and the intricacies of capital gains and taxes, it is more profitable for the owner to leave it unrented. Empty above the ground floor, Centre Point is worth a constantly rising fortune. It is clear who won the deal.

Stylistically, Centre Point is cartoon modern. It has one of everything: stairs, balconies, sunscreens, fountains, underpasses, and bridges done up in marble, mosaic, glass, metal, and concrete for a catalog of contemporary corn. Londoners, less familiar with the genre, seem to admire it.

Erno Goldfinger, a distinguished British architect, has called it London's first pop art skyscraper. Mr. Seifert considers this an insult. But if Mr. Seifert is not praised for his art, he is respected for his commercial shrewdness. The best way to describe him is as a cross between Morris Lapidus and the New York firm of Emery Roth & Sons. Like the Roth firm, Seifert is an expert packager of commercial space.

Of the roughly 10 architectural offices that have gotten the major part of postwar speculative building in London, Seifert has had the lion's share. He has been called the king of the developers' architects. In the decade from 1955 to 1966, the number of his employes rose from about a dozen to 200.

Developers go to him because he knows how to get the most out of regulations for the biggest building at the least cost. A prominent New York architect of substantial corporate structures observes that London's developers make New York's look like the Medici.

Mr. Seifert is a master of plot ratios—the equivalent of New York's zoning—and has a thorough understanding of the legal escape hatches in favor of the builder provided by the various town planning acts. Because it is the architect who gets the necessary permission to build from the authorities—not easy to do under the office-building freeze— he plays a vital role in the developers' programs.

Mr. Seifert is offhand about his successes. "I don't think I'm any wiser than the next man who reads his textbooks," he says. But a member of London's town planning committee, quoted by Oliver Marriott in *The Property Boom*, has said: "Every now and then we had to bring in clauses to stop up the loopholes exposed by Seifert. We called them 'Seifert clauses.'"

The man who holds so much of London on his drawing board is small and dapper, wears thin, dark-rimmed round glasses, neat dark suits and narrow ties, and looks younger than his 60 years.

He speaks warmly of his buildings and coolly of his critics. He talks of his "philosophy of design": structures that "float" rather than descend heavily to the ground, textures and patterns that "make their own shadows" in a somber and often sunless city.

Two phones ring constantly on a V-shaped desk in an office of bland impersonality, the wood walls hung with renderings of his more ambitious projects. Everything is comfortably ordinary.

Mr. Seifert's only conspicuous failure has been the rejection of an application to build Europe's biggest hotel in London's West End, shaped, it was said, like an upside-down elephant with its trunk in the air. It would have been a bit too much.

In fact, Mr. Seifert's work is not all bad. His tower massing and ground planning is often good, if muddled by tasteless tricks. And he is not alone. Most new London work is consummately mediocre, even lacking the Seifert flair.

But if, as Mies van der Rohe said, God is in the details, Seifert details are blasphemy. The bases and podiums of his buildings are a claptrap of motifs and materials that look thrown together. The word is cheesy. Cheesiness is the one thing—more than ill-placed towers—that can destroy centuries of London's hallmark: substance and quality.

The critical difference between Wren and Seifert is that Wren built for the highest standards of art and public purpose, not for speculative economics. There are a lot of splendid old buildings standing in Seifert's way.

June 12, 1971

COVENT GARDEN, I

In the two and a half years since the announcement of the Covent Garden Draft Plan, opposition to the redevelopment project for central London's famous market and theater district has been increasing.*

No, it wouldn't be loverly, is the growing refrain in response to the Greater London Council's master plan for almost a hundred acres of the city's historic heart. As a result of the reaction among the public and in the press, further studies were conducted and a revised proposal has just been released. It seems certain to trigger more protest, although objections were neatly turned at the news conference held to introduce it.

The proposal was unveiled by the Countess of Dartmouth, recently appointed as chairman of the Covent Garden Joint Development Committee of the Greater London Council. She presented arguments for keeping the area's charm while turning it into a hotel and convention

---

* This was an early protest against the plan, written in 1971. The plan has been partly scrapped and partly radically revised. At present it is in limbo.

center—an exercise in contradictions at which no one turned a hair.

The plan was not actually presented; it was simply there on display, in fine multicolored graphics, for anyone who wanted to look. The essence of it was available in a handsome, super-rational brochure.

The original plan was undertaken because Covent Garden Market will trundle its fruits and flowers across the river to a new location next year. (It is hard to imagine St. Paul's Church, by Inigo Jones, or Henry Fowler's glass-topped market building without a fronting sack of broccoli.)

Because one of the dictums of planning is "think comprehensively," a 100-acre site was selected for redevelopment, including the 15-acre produce market. New roads were drawn, a hotel and convention center "spine" paralleling the Strand, and a housing "spine" at the northern edge were suggested, and pedestrian "character routes" were plotted to keep the most historic sites and buildings.

Less historic sites and buildings were doomed, including many from the eighteenth and nineteenth centuries, as were the wonderful street-scapes that England is still so casual about and Americans are beginning to wrap in cotton wool.

There were only a few problems in the way: a large colony of elderly low-income people who had lived their lives there; small, low-rent businesses of remarkable cultural and artistic variety; and a passionate sense of community. There is also the fragile social and economic balance of a fluid, lively, mixed-use neighborhood of a specific and valuable nature, combining people, arts, entertainment, shops, business, and industry with the spontaneous preservation of the past.

These last factors are valued highly now by American urbanists, who have learned from grievous planning error and who see the Covent Garden district as an exemplary case of healthy self-regeneration. Such matters as toilet facilities can be corrected.

Changes in the revised plan include a reduction to 96 acres, with housing and open space constant, but with present housing doubled. Shopping space would be reduced from the first plan, offices increased marginally and hotels increased considerably.

The convention center, a calculated magnet for tourists and transients, has drawn the most fire. The public seems more aware than the planners that nothing short of a bomb will change neighborhood patterns and character more totally than massive tourism.

The key to the plan is not so much "humanity" or "amenity"— words dropped constantly in discussion—as it is "economic viability." The belief is that "economic," or high, commercial rentals and land uses will support more public and humane functions, including housing. In practice, the principle usually sends the best intentions down the drain.

"We cannot carry high holding charges on the land or conjure money," says a "valuer" for the Council. "We need developers."

Knowing that, any developer worth his speculative spurs calls the tune. Developer pressures have already raised the original 10 million square feet of floor space contemplated for the area to 30 million.

As a result of the protests, a larger proportion of older buildings will be retained in the new plan. But at the end of the project's three-phase development, in 1985, a third of the area will be new construction. The character of the new, from other London examples, is as predictable as porridge.

The rationale for planned redevelopment is not only the moving of the market but the fact that the Covent Garden area is some of central London's most expensive land. The Government has clamped a lid on private development in the last decade, pending a comprehensive plan, in the hope that the wholesale destruction and tenant removal that go with uncontrolled speculation could be avoided.

The damage will be done instead by gentlemen's agreement, based on a set of planning principles that are all wrong. This is a plan resting on the fact that land values have gotten too high to permit a healthy, historic, irreplaceable, spontaneously regenerating neighborhood of proven social uses and attractiveness to exist—because it is "economically undeveloped." That anachronism has not been resolved or even faced by the Council.

Through a process of double-think, no attention is paid to the fact that the "contemplated improvements" would either destroy or sterilize exactly what the plan promises to conserve.

Pressures for redevelopment are intense. The planners' intentions are pious. The Greater London Council "hopes" for quality design from developers. It "hopes" for a balance between profitable and unprofitable enterprises. It sees compatibility and compromise. American observers who have been through the same planning wringer see disaster.

The Council is still indulging in a kind of paternalistic, centralized planning that has gone violently out of style in other places. It may get its body blow in London through the unpopular Covent Garden proposal. Questions from the press seem politely antagonistic. Council members looked a little grim.

To queries about the role of community participation—there are no community members on the planning team—Lady Dartmouth, who has been in public life since 1954, replied by explaining the democratic process according to Council procedures.

When a hirsute young man wearing a "Stuff the GLC Covent Garden Plan" button identified himself as a community spokesman, he was resolutely cut off. To a member of the press who suggested that the young man might be allowed to speak, a determined Lady Dartmouth explained, later, that the protester, James Monahan of the Covent Garden Community, was an unrepresentative outsider who had been "unconstructive" in a previous meeting.

"I may have curls here," she said, pointing to one of London's smartest coifs, "but I have steel here," putting a finger to her brow. "I will not be bullied. He thinks we should start all over."

He may be right.

June 14, 1971

COVENT GARDEN, II

If everyone will hold on for a fast ride on the environmental roller coaster, we will examine some of the cumulative ironies and inconsistencies of which the plans of men and the world they live in are made. The point to remember is that each step seems reasoned and logical, but the ultimate result is absurdity. This might be called the First Planning Law.

A prime example is the relocation of Covent Garden Market in London, a process that was masterminded by professionals in a city of notably rational men. (That means the British sit still for an awful lot.) In a planning decision that goes back to 1957, with a study of all of London's food markets and a recommendation for their coordination, it was decided that Covent Garden Market should be moved. In its crowded, picturesque, traffic-jammed, chaotic setting in London's heart at the portal of St. Paul's and the Opera, it had served Londoners from Inigo Jones to Eliza Doolittle with fruits, vegetables, and flowers.

After the appropriate number of feasibility studies and reports, a new market site was selected in 1964 at Nine Elms, a short distance across and along the Thames. The move was full of ineluctable planning logic, even if the first objective of total market coordination had been lost along the way. London's major produce market was therefore replanned without too much consideration of other London markets' placement and practices. (If you embrace the "kiss of death" theory of large-scale plans, this may even have been a good thing.)

The new and greatly enlarged site would provide plenty of room for the mammoth trailer trucks that were turning Covent Garden's historic streets into a nightmare of congestion. The location included both rail and water facilities, which it was believed would reduce truck traffic. The old market area in the center of London would be released for extremely profitable redevelopment. That redevelopment would then pay for the new market. And, of course, there would be the latest facilities: acres of modern sheds, forklift trucks instead of barrows, color-corrected lighting for the flower hall. A neat set of planning syllogisms.

So what happened? Planning logic—as well as the plan—got stood on its head. The market moved, all right; it was recently installed in its new quarters at Nine Elms. It has parking and 400-yard-long warehouses. It will undoubtedly work as a market because it will have to. But British Rail, beset with economic problems, has refused to date to build the railhead for servicing the market, although the presence of the railroad was one of the prime reasons for site selection, and trains hurtle right through its center without stopping. As a result, the trucks now converge on the populous residential areas of Lambeth and Wandsworth. This is driving the good people of Lambeth and Wandsworth (appropriately) bananas.

The redevelopment plan proposed for the Covent Garden area turned out to be an ambitious casebook of planning horrors. It was recognized as such, not by the planners, but by the people. A rising wave of citizen sophistication and participation aborted the scheme. Enough speculative redevelopment had already taken place in London —often with the planners' conscientiously calculated blessings—to make both the delicate nature of the urban fabric and the destructive results of reordering it ominously clear.

The proposal called for keeping monuments and some historic streets in a really appalling form of tokenism, while the rest was to be bulldozed for a much-argued mix of hotels, convention center, offices and/or what have you. This was all to be serviced by the kind of through roads that planners love to draw on maps. It was a formula guaranteed to eliminate the magic life and quality, human scale and style that had made Covent Garden such a special place for so many centuries.

By pulling out the market, the city of London virtually pulled the plug on the Covent Garden community that had actually been preserved by its messy presence. (Too hard to redevelop.) With the area's less than logical but patently irreplaceable urban values belatedly recognized, and the community protesting, the comprehensive plan was called off. ("Comprehensive" is the key professional word, implying rationally coordinated objectives. Anti-planners react to it with Pavlovian terror.)

This also pulled the plug economically; all the anticipated revenues of land disposition and new building went down the drain. And so did the funds for paying for the new market and the move to Nine Elms. Now the yawning gap left in Covent Garden by the move threatens what was a uniquely creative, colorful, and successfully integrated urban entity. The heart is gone. Sterilized museums or artsy-craftsy boutiques are depressing prospects.

Why did each logical step lead to an unexpected and ludicrous result? One explanation is that there seems to be some vengeful god with a dark sense of humor watching those who attempt to impose intellectualized order on the complex and subtle accretions of urban civilization. Multiple disasters have become the familiar fallout of assiduous tidying up.

Another explanation, supported by an increasingly sensitive and far less sanguine approach to the difficult business of dealing with the urban organism, is that planning has been through the fire and is in a revisionist phase. Experience and empiricism have been the painful teachers, with a notable assist from such critics as Jane Jacobs and the Venturis. Mistakes are bound to be built into the complexities involved, but planners are humbler and more cautious about monkeying with people, places, and profits and centuries of urban culture. They have learned a lot.

Still another point of view would have it that planning at best is a kind of necromancy. The omen of absurdity was there in the Covent Garden affair for anyone with an instinct for clairvoyance. Nine Elms had no elms. What clearer sign and signal to all subsequent absurdities? According to *The London Times,* the Central Bureau of Fruit and Vegetable Auctions in the Netherlands has donated nine sapling elms to the completed market. According to observers, they look dead. According to the experts, they are fine. But look what the experts did to Covent Garden.

January 12, 1975

The Past

Pleasures

For some, champagne and foie gras, or even simple grass. For me, the pleasure of Hawksmoor's London. For immediate reassurance that genius is eternal, a special pilgrimage to Christ Church Spitalfields.

And there, in the neat and inevitable sign on the steps, was the neat and inevitable notice: "Christ Church Spitalfields, built in 1729 by Nicholas Hawksmoor, considered one of the finest buildings in the country. £67,000 ($160,000) is needed to restore it to its former glory, and gifts, no matter how small, will be gratefully received at the Rectory, 2 Fournier Street." The church was closed.

The first time I saw Christ Church I wasn't looking for it. I wouldn't have known it if I fell over it, which I did. A tourist visit to Petticoat Lane on a Sunday morning, a turn into the deserted Spitalfields market, a sudden view of that looming ecclesiastical ghost at the end of the street, and wham! the shock of Architecture Power.

A strange church, unlike any English baroque I had ever seen before. A sure massing of unorthodox parts into an unconventional, overwhelming, haunting whole. Great hollow scoops in the tower's sides that play brilliant tricks on solid form. A bravado Palladian arched portico that makes correct Palladianism look puny. The structure is not composed, says Ian Nairn in *Nairn's London*, "it is transmuted somewhere right down in the blood so the whole building becomes a living idea."

The unfashionable eighteenth-century Spitalfields streets around the church are shabby, and winos are draped against the iron fence on a warm spring day. A small white lilac blooms in the churchyard, like hope. And yet, these Spitalfields streets are doomed, Nairn says, by lack of love.

"Even now, this could be one of those living areas in the heart of cities over which so many words are spilt at conferences. Charity is far away and compassion even further." If slow death by neglect overtakes Hawksmoor's masterpiece, he warns, "the church might as well present a banker's order for 30 pieces of silver. For this is the faith, manifest."

I was haunted by that building until I discovered what it was. Finding out was as gratifying as knowing that one had recognized a great vintage wine at a blindfold tasting. I joined the Hawksmoor buffs.

Christopher Wren's London is the London of guidebooks and histories—better known than Hawksmoor's London and easier to see. St Paul's is Wren's great orchestration; his smaller churches are grace notes that have set London's style for 300 years.

Nicholas Hawksmoor was Wren's "back-room boy," first apprentice and later associate, before he became an independent practitioner. With Wren's and Vanbrugh's, his work spans the late seventeenth and early eighteenth centuries, a time—one of many—when England demonstrated its peculiar genius for building with art and grandeur. (London has always survived its planners; what it may not survive in this century is its architects.)

Hawksmoor was a thorough professional, something the British have traditionally treated with condescension. The gentleman-dilettante was always preferred; he cut better butter and got better jobs. There have been some superb ones, including Wren.

Hawksmoor died in 1736, when the Georgian Palladian style was making Wren and Vanbrugh unfashionable. Wren's reputation had to be "rehabilitated" by Sir Joshua Reynolds and the brothers Adam. Hawksmoor's has waited until now.

For all this and more, there is a properly passionate and scholarly book by Kerry Downes, *Hawksmoor*, published in New York by Praeger in 1970, based on his monograph and catalogue raisonné of the architect's production. It is one of those rare, readable works, soundly grounded in knowledge and sensibility.

By the standards of the later eighteenth century, Downes points out, Hawksmoor lacked "the supreme virtue of Taste." The Baroque, by way of Italy and France, was out; the Renaissance, by way of Palladio, was in. Refinement was admired; delicacy supplanted robustness. Hawksmoor's work seemed gross and incomprehensible and "the age of Taste could make little of it." The nineteenth century lost view of

him, involved as it was in everything from Regency Classic to Ruskinian Gothic and Butterworthian Victorian blowouts. (As Nairn says, in
cataloguing churches, there is more than one way to reach God.)

Hawksmoor is very much the taste of today. For twentieth-century
eyes, he is example and mentor. An age that deals in pure form, that
sees architecture as organic mass, that no longer deals in the wall as an
inert surface to be decorated, is bowled over by Hawksmoor's sophisticated complexity in which style and form become a sculptural and
architectonic whole. This is architecture that has what Vanbrugh defined as the "Solemn and Awful Appearance" of greatness. That's
what gets you at the end of a Spitalfields street.

Hawksmoor's London is in unfashionable places: St. Alfege Greenwich, St. Anne Limehouse, St. George-in-the-East Wapping, Stepney.
It is in the City, too, at St. Michael Cornhill, an essay in unacademic
Gothic with a churchyard tucked behind it bright with spring tulips
and serene with that quality Londoners call amenity. It is near the
Bank of England, where the twin towers of St. Mary Woolnoth, on
the tightest of sites, fuse onto walls that teach every lesson about
plane, mass, and decoration an architect needs to know. Small church,
much art.

It is at St. Mary Bloomsbury, where the steeple puts George I atop
a Roman altar crowning a stepped pyramid on columns with lip
service to the Mausoleum at Halicarnassus. Surprisingly, it is at
Westminster Abbey, in the towers, "familiar to the world, but recognized by few," says Downes. "It is surely a fitting but also ironical
conclusion to so brilliantly obscure a career as his that his last executed
work should be the self-effacing completion of a great medieval
monument."

At St. James Garlickhythe, where a steeple that may be Hawksmoor's or may be Wren's tops a restored Wren church that fairly
bursts onto the narrow slope of Garlick Hill, there is another notice.
But this one, unlike that at Spitalfields, does not call for salvation.

It calls for three "poor, honest young women" to share in the
eighteenth-century bequest of one Signor Pasquale Favale, who left
dowries for deserving London girls about to be married, or married in
the past 12 months, to be given each year. This year's applications are
invited by June 30. Signor Favale married a London girl, it seems, and
was very happy. There is salvation of all kinds.

June 13, 1975

PIRANESI'S ROME

There are four Romes of powerful and enduring imagery: ancient Rome, Renaissance Rome, modern Rome, and Piranesi's Rome.

Piranesi's Rome is the least and most real of all. It is a Rome of phantasmagoric romanticism, of enormous, overscaled buildings and vast panoramas, of heroic, ancient spaces inhabited by dwarfed and tattered humans, of gnarled, giant trees sprouting from ruins, of huge classical monuments and shadowed cisterns, an epic cross between accurate archaeology and surrealist vision, of eternal grandeur and decay.

It may be a Rome that never was, according to A. Hyatt Mayor, who calls the artist's eighteenth-century Vedute di Roma "the most obsessive illusion ever dreamed of any city to cast a spell on man." But the world has seen Rome through Giovanni Battista Piranesi's eyes ever since.

One of the last of the line of buildings that grew out of that vision— the marbled and colonnaded rotunda of McKim, Mead and White's Low Memorial Library at Columbia University, an ornate space in which grandeur and uselessness have finally fought it out to a stand-off—is the setting for a show of Piranesi drawings and etchings. The display includes 23 superb drawings seen for the first time in two centuries.

These drawings, studies for the completion of the church of San Giovanni in Laterano, are the newly acquired property of the Avery Architectural Library at Columbia, from which all of the exhibition's 101 items are taken. In contrast to Piranesi's profligate production of etchings, his drawings are extremely scarce.

His design for the sanctuary to complete the Borromini church was never carried out. The drawings disappeared after their presentation to Cardinal Rezzonico in 1767. Nothing is known of them from that date to the 20th century when they were found through a passing scholarly reference to their presence in a European family collection.

Also in the show is a rare first-impression set of Piranesi's 14 Carceri etchings (the "new" drawings and the Carceri are both a gift of Dr. and Mrs. Arthur Sackler), those strange, troubling prisons so progressively darkened and distorted as Piranesi reworked the plates that they have been called landscapes of the mind.

There are plans, elevations, and sections for five projects for the church sanctuary. Done in ink and wash, they are either totally in Piranesi's hand or executed by the master in their major parts.

Most spectacular are four designs for a papal altar and baldachino of Borrominiesque splendor. Freehand details have a breathtaking immediacy of touch and eye. There are suggestions of Venetian lightness and trompe l'oeil and the sheer beauty of drawing that made Venice, and the drawing as an end in itself, central to the eighteenth-century art scene.

There is a passionate intent to build in these wonderfully detailed and richly ornamented designs in the scenographic northern tradition of Palladio and Longhena. But except for Piranesi's remodeling of the Aventine church of Santa Maria del Priorato in 1764–65, the "architetto veneziano," as he consistently signed himself, was an architect manqué.

Those who have looked through the famous keyhole of the garden door of the Aventine church to see St. Peter's framed beyond—a tourist staple—have looked right past Piranesi's single architectural achievement.

The rest remain those "sublime dreams," as Horace Walpole called them "as savage as Salvator Rosa, fierce as Michael Angelo, and exuberant as Rubens, scenes that would startle geometries and exhaust the Indies to realize." They are today, as A. Hyatt Mayor reminds us, "a part of the lens of every cultivated eye."

March 22, 1972

JEFFERSON'S VIRGINIA

The University of Virginia, built from 1817 to 1827, is probably the single most beautiful and effective architectural group of its kind in this country, or in the history of American building. And since it is a work so distinctly from the heart and mind of Thomas Jefferson, the great statesman and humanist whose art and politics shared a common philosophy and culture, a trip to his "academical village" is a fine way to touch base with the beginnings of the new nation.

PLEASURES

I paid a first visit on a day in late winter, in soft rain. For February, the temperature was mild, and the even light and gray sky set off the Jeffersonian formula of red brick and white colonnades with a singular clarity and serenity. The wet weather enhanced the color of clay-red earth; the green of the grass was pre-spring muted.

As it was conceived and still stands, the heart of the University of Virginia consists of two rows of continuous, connected pavilions and colonnades facing each other on the east and west sides of an approximately 750-foot-wide lawn. Called the east and west lawns, these rows are backed by a second, arcaded row of dormitories known as the east and west ranges. There are gardens between the rows, enclosed with serpentine brick walls. At the center of the main axis of the group, at the north end, is the Rotunda. The complex is set on a ridge, so that the modern university recedes below it.

The three-sided rectangle was meant to be open ended, for a spectacular view of the valley and mountains beyond. With a sublime stroke of insensitivity, the vista was closed with new construction in the 1890s by McKim, Mead and White. If the vista were open now, however, the view would be of motels, shopping centers, gas stations, and the random signs that are the totems of the twentieth-century environment. To get to the world of Jefferson one must go through the world of Venturi—a traumatic, time-tube trip from the pop landscape of the twentieth-century to the neo-classical architectural elegance of the early nineteenth century. Motels to Monticello, it might be called, or, subtitled, how the rolling hills and rocky ridges of the beautiful Piedmont, sweeping to the Blue Ridge Mountains and the rim of the sky, became the world of the schlockbuilt fast buck.

The University's heart is literally centuries away. The classical pavilions, of which there are five on each side, are joined by the colonnaded student dormitories between. They were used originally for instruction and the professors' residences. Although the effect is unified, each one is different, as is frequently pointed out, because Jefferson wanted the various classical orders illustrated to serve also as teaching models. They range from the Doric of the Diocletian Baths and the Ionic of the Theater of Marcellus to the orders as found in Palladio.

The colonnades between pavilions gradually grow longer from one end to the other, a fact that is noted less frequently. The one exception to the Roman or Palladian orders is a maverick pavilion with a recessed arch that seems to derive from the latest thing in France at that date—the work of Claude Nicholas Ledoux—a not surprising architectural adventure for Jefferson the Francophile. This use of the new French style was as avant-garde as some of the other sources were doctrinaire.

But there is nothing doctrinaire about this architecture as a whole, and that is the reason for its beauty and importance. Although it gives the appearance of uniformity in the classical totality of its composition and details, it is still rich in calculated variety. There is something in man that loves order and unity; they are virtues that induce serenity. But the unity of this complex is never static, because of the differences in its never-identical parts and the subtle device of the changing measure. The architecture is a kind of paradox: at once didactic and free, monumental and humanistic, aristocratic and pragmatic, romantic and rational, formal and hospitable. It combines an intimate human scale with controlled, universal vistas. The result is consummately lovely, with a quality of grace lost to our age. These are lessons that have escaped the modern monumentalists.

But it was far from perfect. Roofs leaked, chimneys smoked, the orientation that produced such handsome effect also exposed the rows to burning western sun in summer and driving east winds and rains in winter, and cut off southern breezes in the heat. The pavilion lecture rooms were inadequate and the professors' quarters didn't work for family life. The proximity of the students to faculty was a cause for complaint. But whatever is, or was, wrong seems to be forgiven today for the impact and pleasure of the whole. Students compete avidly for

A quality of grace lost to our age. *Israel Shenker*

the cell-like rooms with their (unchanged) outdoor facilities. Firewood stands neatly stacked outside the doors.

It may be somewhat ungrateful to examine the role of Jefferson more closely in this design. The concept was clearly his; it had surfaced shortly after 1800 in earlier proposals. And his adjustment of the plan and relationships of the parts are sensitive responses to site, function and form. But there is a tendency to magnify the considerable talent of a man who was essentially a gifted amateur.

Jefferson was "fixated" on books and on "fishing" his designs out of them, according to Benjamin Latrobe, his friend and America's outstanding architect at that time. Latrobe was a man of sophisticated professional training and taste. Jefferson turned to Latrobe for advice on the Virginia scheme, and the suggestions he got from both Latrobe and from William Thornton, the first architect of the Capitol, are exactly what turned the design from a skilled amateur concept into a professional masterwork.

He must have been a bit of a nuisance, as so many well-intentioned amateurs are. To both Thornton and Latrobe he wrote for "a few sketches, such as may not take you a minute . . ."—a request that always makes the pros groan. But Thornton suggested columns instead of piers for the arcade, which adds much to the power of the scheme. And Latrobe crystallized that power with the proposal for "something grand" at the north end, in the form of a great dominating building, where Jefferson had just intended to continue the rows. This gives the composition its full force and definition. And Latrobe anchored the plan with the pavilions at the corners. These changes were catalytic improvements. Jefferson chose the Pantheon as the model for the rotunda, and made able adjustments in scale.

When Jefferson worked alone, as at Monticello, he produced an extraordinary, eccentric, half-failed building. It is not a really beautiful house, inside or out. There are splendid starts and inept stops and passages that mismatch intention and result, demonstrating at every unresolved turn how his spatial and structural knowledge failed to keep up with his ideas. Architecturally, that house is in trouble everywhere, but the vision that comes through was exceptional. More than a cultivated classicist, more than an expert Palladian, Jefferson had already embraced the bold "new" expressionistic neo-classicism of Soane in England and Ledoux in France. The two-story-high rooms, the strange second floor disguised as part of a single story, all grope passionately for the new spatial expression.

Jefferson experimented and overreached magnificently—another characteristic lost to our cautious, computerized time. He never played safe and he avoided, in the words of the historian William Pierson, "the sterility of the absolute." His architecture reveals him as a "humanist and poet concerned with the goodness of life."

The Jefferson design for the. University of Virginia suggests the whole range of values to which American democracy aspired: unity in variety, the subordination of the parts to the whole, a humanistic order and the dignity of the individual. Delight was also there; where has delight gone in 150 years? What has happened to the values that infused the life, art, and politics of the new nation?

March 9, 1975

THE SORCERY OF GAUDI

Even at the small scale of the show held at the Spanish Institute (1973) Gaudí is overwhelming. Genius always is. The display was the work of Nieves Peris and Janet Lauren, and the text offered about as succinct a summary of Gaudí's work and style as one would wish.

Born in Catalonia in 1852, the Spanish architect was a genuine eccentric. A dandy in his youth, he never married, and eventually dropped all secular commissions for church work, although no one quite knows why. In later years he begged alms on the street for work on his masterpiece, the Church of the Sagrada Familia in Barcelona, an incredible surreal structure in which molten dream imagery joins with precise structural design. He met an Ionesco-type end when he was struck by a streetcar in 1926.

His late work is almost fearful in its ingenuity. One can see the thin dividing line between his wildly talented expression of Art Nouveau pushed to dazzling tour de force extremes and what would easily reduce, in lesser hands, to a whiplash horror show. Here floor plans undulate like snakes and furniture writhes with tortured life behind sinuous facades and wrought iron grilles of piercing virtuosity.

Never has Art Nouveau been more brilliant and contorted, more rational in its pursuit of irrationality, more provocative in its calculated distortions of conventional esthetics, more ugly-beautiful. It is work that seduces the imagination until normalcy seems flat and dull; each venture must be more outrageous than its predecessor. It becomes a special taste and obsessive addiction. The viewers' minds and responses are totally co-opted.

Gaudí's furniture progresses from "spiky medieval to an image of generalized organic growth," in the words of George Collins, whose excellent monograph on Gaudí in the Braziller series of 1960 still stands as an authoritative account. The work is full of astounding vitality, not the least element of which is its firm dependence on basic structural principles, even at its most far out, which is very far out indeed. "There is a madness here that Gaudí shared with a number of Modernista designers," Professor Collins writes.

The delusory obsession with so-called organic or natural form, in which nothing is allowed to be straight or static, appeared early in Gaudí's work, before it briefly engulfed the arts everywhere at the turn of the century. There is, for example, the extraordinary Art Nouveau dressing table that appears to be walking off in all directions at once in a Groucho crouch, done in the 1880s for the Palacio Güell.

Gaudí's earliest work, labeled eclecticism in the exhibition, is strong in Gothic references, with a kind of Moorish recall breaking through in the smoking room of the Casa Vicens (1883–88) with its carved grotto ceiling. Nature is already the theme in panels of birds and leaves.

The next stage, here called revisionism, is marked by two handsome and disparate examples, the Palacio Güell (1885–89) and the Convent

God, or the devil, is in Gaudí's details. *Amigos de Gaudí, U.S.A.*

School of the Order of the Teresas (1888–90). Güell, with its superb parabolic entrance arches, is lush, elaborate and quasi-historical in its interior references. The spaces are open and free-flowing. By comparison, the convent school is austere, dependent for effect on contrasts of tile and brick, with a matching stricter geometry for its furnishings. The structural artistry of Catalan brickwork can always be found in the attics and underpinnings of Gaudí buildings.

Modernismo, the Spanish Art Nouveau, appears full blown in the Casa Calvet of 1902. The next step, which the show calls a transition from modernism to functional expressionism, is marked by the famous Parque Güell, a project in landscape and urban design in Barcelona that remains one of architecture's most remarkable products.

Radical functional expressionism appears in the last two houses, Casa Batlló (1904–06) and Casa Milá (1905–10). The sheer creative brilliance of Casa Batlló is breathtaking. What is barely implied in interior photographs is the incredible molding of space, not only through sculptured walls and ceilings that suggest a sorcerer's, rather than an architect's manipulation, but also through the subtle, shifting and shaping element of illumination through skylights and light-wells, with fluid shafts of white and colored luminescence.

For Disneyland, one need go no farther than a Gaudí rooftop, where everything breaks loose. A garden of whimsical chimneypots in a riot of colored tiles shows the architect as sculptor, colorist, and craftsman. These rooftops, the Parque Güell, and above all, the clustered towers and pinnacles of his crowning work, the Church of the Sagrada Familia —for all the world like some giant confection but totally without wedding-cake innocence—appealed strongly to the later surrealists. They were more intrigued by the church's strangeness than by its structural mastery, but every unique form grew out of engineering studies conducted in Gaudí's workshop.

Strange the work surely is, and compelling. Even a bench for the Casa Calvet has a sinister kind of fascination, with an armature more like a polished skeleton than wood, and arms like jawbones. Only the rather pedestrian floral punchwork on this piece is disappointing. With Gaudí, God, or the devil, is in the details.

In his later years, Gaudí's work, totally directed to the completion of the Sagrada Familia, became a complete fusion of the structural and the esthetic. His style, his energy, his flamboyant personal sense of beauty, have never been surpassed. He was, as they say, an original, in the finest meaning of the word.

November 11, 1973

THE CHAIRS OF MACKINTOSH

The chairs of Charles Rennie Mackintosh are spectral. They are presences. They upstage people. They have more strength and identity than anyone in a room. At the Museum of Modern Art exhibition, they are lined up, dramatically backlit on platforms, with an impact so far beyond the simple statement of "chair" that they are curiously exhilarating and unsettling.

That is exactly as it should be. These chairs are overwhelming both as art objects and as indicators of a talent of such absolute pitch that each line and curve is a revelation of grace and reason. Emilio Ambasz, who has directed and installed the show, uses drawings and photographs of Mackintosh's buildings and interiors to make the point quite clear. There is no way to overstate the quality of a Mackintosh design.

What the chairs are not able to indicate in their isolation is how their startling and sensuous forms and motifs were the focus and full expression of the rooms in which they were set—rooms unique in the history of art. Nor can they indicate, in turn, how these interiors were tied to the buildings that Mackintosh designed in the period between the 1890s and the first World War—that time of esthetic transition and revolution.

Actually, very little of that work remains. The Glasgow Art School (1897–1909) is a landmark of proto-modern architecture. Some houses still stand. One of Miss Cranston's celebrated tearooms (1897–1912) is functioning, in part, in Glasgow; others have been demolished; and one, dismantled and saved, has been promised reconstruction by the Glasgow Corporation.

Some of the originals of the 20 chairs in the museum's lineup still exist—one can be seen in the next gallery in the museum's permanent collection—but all on view in the show are careful reproductions. These "re-creations" have been lovingly crafted under the direction of Professor Filippo Alison of the University of Naples; three are in production by Cassina of Milan, with royalties to the University of Glasgow. These three are available in New York to anyone who happens to have a spare $1,000 to $1,600.

The work of Charles Rennie Mackintosh (1868–1928) transcends what has come to be known as "Scottish Art Nouveau" or "the Glasgow style" of the turn of the century. The creative activity that centered around the Glasgow School of Art at that time, led by such architects as Voysey and Mackintosh, involved all of the arts of design. Mackintosh's wife, Margaret MacDonald, was a superb practitioner of Art Nouveau. But his own work went significantly beyond any established style.

His influence was enormous. Exhibitions at the Vienna Secession in 1900, in Turin in 1902, and in other European cities established his reputation on the Continent. He was much admired by Hoffmann and Behrens and the architects of De Stijl. His contribution was surely known to Frank Lloyd Wright. The Glasgow Art School is one of those buildings after which architecture is never the same.

His work combined rigor and poetry to an extraordinary degree. Mies van der Rohe called Mackintosh a "purifier of architecture." He seemed to give both structure and decoration new meaning. According to Andrew McLaren Young, "the decoration was clothing for new ideas—new ideas on the role of function and the geometry of architectural space." Nikolaus Pevsner calls his art a "fusion of puritanism with sensuality." But there is nothing ambiguous about his attitude toward structure and ornament; both are thoroughly understood as mutually reinforcing in art's richest tradition, a process lost to the later modern movement.

These chairs are not for sitting. Their purpose is to state structure lyrically; struts, slats, and supports become esthetic absolutes. Nonstructural elements—backs and headrests—are enhanced by exquisite ornament. They were meant to stand against a wall in breathtakingly precise relationships to the spaces of a room, or to act as space dividers —far more important than conforming to human physiology. Their lines and motifs were devised to complement other elements in the setting. The whole interior composition was an orchestration of geometric and decorative parts.

Thus a sky-high ladderback was meant to fill a space between two closets, and the squares at its top repeated squares in the closet doors and squares in the pattern of a rug. In the tearooms, exaggerated height gave privacy and stated boundaries. A latticed, overscaled, curved cashier's chair was a cage against the room. But each chair is superb by itself. The parts are delicately related with the intensity and finesse of abstract art—which, in a sense, they are.

Mackintosh's color is as important as his forms. The floating clarity of pure white interiors, the dramatic impact of black-based schemes shot with mauve and silver, the incredibly romantic range of the grays, pinks, and violets of his personal palette, must have supplied a *frisson* in grim, gray Glasgow. He could make lavender a piercing climax to a milk-white room. Violet light glowed through a climactic prism of glass. A spot of red became a crashing chord in a wall of geometric black, white, and gold. (Unfortunately, this color cannot be experienced in the present show.) How much we have lost with the modern movement's resolutely limited range of primary colors, its denial of the ambiguous or strange, its betrayal of the capacities of the senses through reduction and oversimplification.

But beyond color, Mackintosh understood space. Pevsner notes that "neither Frank Lloyd Wright nor Le Corbusier brought internal space more boldly to life." The magic spell of the spaces and artifacts of a Mackintosh room has been described impeccably by Friedrich Ahlers-Hestermann:

"These rooms were like dreams: everywhere there are small panels, gray silks, the slenderest vertical shafts of wood, small rectangular sideboards . . . that look as innocent and serious as young girls about to receive Holy Communion—and altogether unreal. Here were mysticism and estheticism . . . with a strong scent of heliotrope, and a feel of well-cared-for hands, and of delicate sensuality. Two upright chairs with backs as tall as a man stood on a white carpet, looking at each other over a slender table, silently, like ghosts."

Today, Mackintosh has a new importance for those who seek enrichment of life and art. "He was," says Emilio Ambasz, "the unique figure who reconciled the seductive ornamental powers of Art Nouveau with the modern movement's redemptive passion." The word genius is appropriate.

November 24, 1974

ART AND NOSTALGIA
AND THE GREAT WORLD'S FAIRS

Whether you deal in first-hand memories or trendy revivalism, a small show called "1930s Expositions" (New York Cultural Center, 1973) is an enchanted bit of nostalgia. It memorializes an innocent and romantic world that idealized past and future on the pleasure principle in an art form of equal innocence and romanticism that reached its apogee in a single decade.

The display, which consists of enlarged photographs, reconstructed models and wonderful campy souvenirs from the collection of Lawrence G. Zimmerman, was organized originally by Arnold L. Lehman for the Dallas Museum of Fine Arts.

These were the American World's Fairs of legend, illusion and fantasy, spawned by the London Crystal Palace of 1851 and spun off by Chicago's white plaster extravaganza in 1893. There was a Century of Progress in Chicago in 1933, the California-Pacific Exposition in San Diego in 1935, the Texas Centennial Exposition in Dallas in 1936, the Golden Gate International Exposition in San Francisco in 1939, and the World of Tomorrow at the New York World's Fair in an absolute orgy of excess in the same year.

I came in at the end of the decade for the last one, as a schoolgirl, so my responses are both personal and academic. But the sight of the Trylon and Perisphere and the Futurama brought memories crowding back of fireworks-illuminated Courts of Honor, sleek, levitated soap statuary and color-washed fountains on summer evenings, with the particular bittersweet poignancy of lovely, lost times.

It is an historic era now, and the style it embodied was pure futuristic fairy tale, made of the hopes and dreams of hard times, when many needed hopes and dreams to stay alive. There was no cynicism. There was no black humor. The human condition, or one's awareness of its problems and inequities, had not reached the point where a sense of the absurd became salvation. It was an absurd world, in its own way, but we loved its flashy, streamlined promises of better things.

These glorious, overreaching efforts, Mr. Lehman's exhibition text tells us, were "all eagerly anticipated and intensely debated during the planning years, enormously successful in terms of attendance and all generally financially unsound. Like the movies and baseball, fair-going became a recognized American pastime. In a decade of economic depression, fairs offered an escapism similar to but more tangible than Hollywood palliatives [that] easily outdrew the reality of contemporary life. . . . Great, white, magical, temporary cities thrilled millions of awed visitors."

And no wonder. Chicago's three-and-a-half-mile lake-front site in 1933 was committed to "advancement through technology" in theme and style. Its plywood and plaster buildings owed much to the *moderne* mode propagandized by the Paris Exposition of 1928, with its flat, faceted and striated surfaces, shallow ornaments of Art Deco inspiration, and smoothly curved and striped vertical and horizontal forms.

It was all style, even its technology, and it reached its peak in the

PLEASURES

Travel and Transportation Building by E. H. Bennett and Hubert Burnham, where ostentatiously cable-hung, dark and light prismatic panels and a stunning Art Deco sunburst entrance were obviously the impeccably modernistic *dernier cri*. (Modernistic, we remind our non-historian readers, is not a synonym for modern; it specifically identifies this 1920s–30s style, currently adopted as fashionably high camp.)

The Federal Government had a Busby Berkeley special of three triangular, striped, concave-sided towers rising suavely from a globular base sprouting stepped projections and heroic statues like department store dummies wrapped in carefully folded napkins, theatrically flood-lit from below. The whole fair was bathed in brilliantly colored light by Joseph Urban. Raymond Hood and Paul Cret were on the architectural commission.

San Diego in 1935 devoted the 1,400-acre Balboa Park to an orgy of Spanish-Colonial *modernisme* in its California-Pacific Exposition, based on the remaining Bertrand Grosvenor Goodhue buildings of the Panama-California Exposition of 1916. Stylized and imaginary Aztec and Mayan motifs were flattened into friezes and borders and all-over patterns on massed and pyramided structures. The automobile companies added their characteristic white stuccoed facades.

Dallas in 1936 orchestrated a monumental celebration of Texas under six flags, and 60 percent of the buildings were permanent, to serve as exhibition halls for future state fairs. A contemporary description of its style serves best: "Severe and monumental, interpreted as modern, flavored with the condiments of Egypt and Archaic Greece, and finally seasoned with the warmth and sunshine of the southwest."

Again, this supereclecticism relied on bold, modernistic massing and formal geometry. The entrance was an enormous Lone Star, and the searchlight-striped sky at night over the huge, symmetrical Esplanade of State and its central reflecting pool must have made a stage-set Hollywood couldn't match. Sculpture, in all of the fairs, was universally unsurpassed trivia. Here archaic-visaged maidens with pastry-horn Greek hairdos and smoothly inflated bodies trailed cut-paper draperies over extruded cactus plants and other native flora.

San Francisco in 1939 exploited its Pacifica motif for a kind of orientalized modernistic fantasia on the 400-acre, man-made Treasure Island in the Bay. The high-points were "elephant towers" of stepped, abstract geometry on soaring pyramidal bases and fountain courts where oversize plaster goddesses dangled stars.

The combination of futurism, exotica, and streamlined classicism, in various formulas, was Everyman's vision of tomorrow. It was the last gasp, in Mr. Lehman's words, of the grand space-making schemes of

Symbols of romantically remembered pleasure.
Chicago Architectural Photographing Company

the Beaux Arts planners and the adolescent excesses of the industrial designer's art.

Apart from its evocative delights, this show is a conscious departure from the approved art-historical way of looking at exposition archi- tecture. Superficially, it is a bow to high camp, an ode to kitsch, and an example of the current fashionable preference for period corn. It breaks with the tradition of Sigfried Giedion, which traces exposition building as a series of dramatic exercises in progressive technology, from the glass and metal of the Crystal Palace to the increasing spans engineered for various Machinery Halls. This led finally to the circuses of tortured experimental techniques in recent years.

The approach was valid and the structural history it taught was real; it was just hopelessly one-sided. The pictures in the history books are carefully selected for timeless technical details and the taste of the time is just as carefully finessed.

There is now a new and rising art historian's view of the inter- national exposition as a catalyst of taste and style. Its function as a prime cultural indicator has been passed over for real or imagined cosmic significance. It tells about society at a certain moment, which is the role art and history play best.

And so there is more to the sudden passion for the memorabilia of the recent past than mere nostalgia. Nostalgia is a sadly desperate game, an instinctive gut reaction to the fact that we have gone through, and are still going through, a period of shattering change, a destructive, antiheroic, anti-beautiful phase of smashing beliefs, idols, and ideals, in a world that offers none of the certainties and standards that kept earlier generations stable in adversity.

It is a clutching at the symbols of romantically remembered pleasure —we forget the boredom or pain—for those who experienced it, and a kind of cultural role-playing for the young. It is the regret, conscious or visceral, for a simplicity and optimism that can never come again. Art is part of this, and today life and art are complex and anguished, and you can't go home, or to the great World's Fairs, again.

October 28, 1973

THE SKYSCRAPER STYLE

The Art Deco avalanche is on. The period and its products are being flirted with by the popular press, puffed by dealers in nostalgia, and apotheosized in a series of books. Finch College's exhibition (1974), called "American Art Deco Architecture," has put the movement into proper focus in the broad terms of American building of the 1920s and thirties with emphasis on what is increasingly called the Skyscraper Style.

No style has been more neglected, undervalued, misunderstood, or camped up. No style has been more vulnerable to the bulldozer, egregious remodeling or the disdain of contemporary scholars. In the peculiar terms of the growing popularity of Art Deco (named after the Paris Exposition of Modern Decorative and Industrial Art of 1925), kitsch is being given equal standing with high art. And so the selective scholarship and qualitative standards imposed on the subject by Elayne Varian, who organized and installed the exhibition and wrote the catalogue, are exactly what is needed at this moment.

It is as easy to be entranced by this style as it is to miss its genuine substance. There is immense visual pleasure in its fantasy world of ziggurats, sunbursts, zigzags, waves, stepped triangles, stylized machines, abstract suggestions of energy and speed, and the exotic natural wonders of waterfalls, tortoises, condors, and doves. One marvels at the superb craftsmanship in marble, bronze, glass, bakelite, monel metal, plastics, and rare woods.

The appeal of this vintage modernism—naive, romantic, and upbeat —is enormous. The American work is a sizeable production by men of notable talent, among them Eliel Saarinen, Paul Cret, Raymond Hood, Bertram Goodhue and others who have not yet received their due. But what is most clearly and heartbreakingly revealed in any presentation is that the buildings shown represent the last great period of decorative art. We are struck with the poignant reality that it will never be possible to do this kind of work again.

Art Deco, or Style Moderne, is primarily the art of the skyscraper age. As such it is extraordinary that these structures have been systematically excluded from the modern architecture textbooks, or relegated to footnotes. They are among the biggest and best buildings in a country that has earned its place in architectural history in large part through skyscraper development.

Taking technology for granted and embroidering the result. *The New York Times/Paul Hosefros*

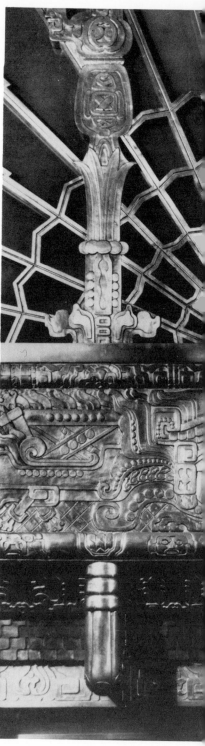

Because they failed to conform to the tenets of the International Style—a rigid "functionalism" with a "technological" esthetic that equated ornament with "crime"—they have been blacklisted by the official historians of the International Style, which had a valid claim and stake in the twentieth-century architectural revolution. The International Style is, in fact, correctly perceived as the prime base of modernism, but to make the point propagandistically its promoters were rigidly exclusionistic. These exclusions, particularly with hindsight, have become ludicrous.

The essential difference between the International Style skyscraper and the Art Deco skyscraper (and there were hybrids, such as Raymond Hood's 1931 McGraw-Hill Building in New York) is that the International Style struggled to reveal the expressive visual power of the structural frame, and Art Deco simply took the technology for granted and embroidered the result.

It is quite possible to read structure and function in the column and spandrel facade of the 450 Sutter Building of 1930 in San Francisco by Timothy Pflueger and James Miller. But beyond that the spandrels are decorative fantasies, and both glass and metal are angled for a richly plastic facade. One of the least recognized factors of these Art Deco skyscrapers is the extremely successful plasticity of the building as a whole, aside from the applied ornament; there is a great preoccupation with planes and volumes and sculptural effect. Such effects are further dramatized with light, often in the form of lit glass tubes—another element of the Deco vocabulary. The Niagara Mohawk Building in Syracuse, New York, is a spectacular example.

Most of these characteristics aim at a frankly surface appeal that is highly suspect within the puritan ethic (esthetic?) of modernism. To International Stylists, this approach, tied as it is to tradition, is original sin. Still, the ornament is often extremely beautiful. It is perhaps hard to grasp the fact that elevator lobbies can be historic interiors; Art Deco turned them into incredible twentieth-century art forms. These examples are disappearing, however, persistently destroyed by marble-slab "modernization." A radiator grille, a mailbox, or a doorknob can be, and is, a collector's item. When a building is torn down or remodeled, the discarded parts are so prized that the vultures close in.

It is worth noting that Art Nouveau and Art Deco have much in common: they both emphasize the primacy of a new vocabulary of ornamental forms of a remarkable creativity and strong sensuous pleasure, bypassing structural innovation. If one style is valid, so is the other. And yet the former is accepted as part of the official twentieth-century esthetic and the latter is not.

These buildings are rarely designated as landmarks, and even their documentation has only begun. So far, their fate is in the hands of speculators. Los Angeles's Richfield Building of 1928 by Morgan, Walls and Clements was demolished in 1967. The Cities Service Company, which moved from Wall Street to Tulsa recently, has torn down an assortment of its Wall Street properties in spite of New York's official pleas to save them, leaving only Clinton and Russell's 60 Wall Street tower built for Cities Service in 1932. It faces an uncertain future. In a more welcome move, Oakland, Calif., has converted Timothy Pflueger's Paramount Theater of 1931 into a home for the Oakland Symphony.

Those who can should take a few field trips in New York and other cities. The elevators in the Chrysler Building, for example, are a special esthetic experience; each cab is an elaborately different marquetry and metal Deco garden of delights. The best exhibitions of the art of architecture are still in the streets. It will be tragic if these buildings end up as fragments in a museum.

November 17, 1974

BEAUX ARTS BUILDINGS I HAVE KNOWN

Many of my earliest and most persistent architectural memories are of the Beaux Arts in New York, but I was unaware of it, like Molière's bourgeois gentilhomme who didn't know he was speaking prose. When I did become aware of it, I found out I wasn't supposed to like it. Alas, it was too late. Those buildings were as much a part of my life as my family, and I could neither dismiss nor neutralize my feelings toward them, which were intimately involved in the process of growing up.

By a curious coincidence, one of the institutions that taught me that they were all wrong now tells me that they're all right, and I'd be confused if I weren't delighted. The Museum of Modern Art, in a scholarly reversal of its own tradition as keeper of the flame of modern architecture, has featured a large and beautiful show of nineteenth-century French academic drawings called "The Architecture of the Ecole des Beaux Arts." The Beaux Arts style, in its variations from ornate French classicism to cool Roman and Renaissance revivalism, is to be found in this country's major monuments from 1890 to 1910 and later. The Architectural League has prepared a tour list of some of the best local Beaux Arts buildings, available at the Museum. In connection with these activities, I would like to present my own list. It might be called Beaux Arts buildings I have known and loved (or hated) in New York.

I grew up, all unwittingly, in a Beaux Arts structure called the St. Urban, whose style and substance were light years away from today's architectural con-game known as the "luxury" apartment house. All the milestones of my childhood and adolescence are colored by Beaux Arts experiences. I think of Grand Central Terminal, not in its present grimy state, battling for its life, but as I remember it on Friday afternoons when we would take the Merchants' Limited—crisp white damask and roses in silver bud vases in the diner—to visit family in Boston. The trip began in the Grand Concourse, which seemed to hold all the nameless promises of pleasure and adventure of travelers' past and present in its constantly moving, muted rhythms beneath the great sky-blue vaulted ceiling with its illuminated constellations. (Tomorrow, the universe.)

Grand Central's monumental richness and superb efficiency were accepted without question by New Yorkers; in fact, it was fashionable only to question its style, considered inferior to European models and somehow tainted with American utilitarianism. I can see now that it is absolutely one of the best things of its kind anywhere in the world. The facade from Park Avenue South is quintessential Beaux Arts— immense arched windows and paired, fluted columns rising building-height above the girdling roadway like a triple triumphal arch, fronted by a bronze Commodore in his astrakhan-collared coat directing taxis to the other side. It is hard to imagine New York without Mercury, Hercules, and Minerva atop Jules Coutan's monumental clock; it is part of the city's essential image and remaining elegance.

There were trips from Penn Station, too—McKim, Mead and White's Roman extravaganza of 1910 in cream travertine and pink granite, later soot-darkened, where the traveler debouched into the tepidarium of the Baths of Caracalla. It was demolished in 1966. "One entered the city like a god," Vincent Scully has written, ". . . one scuttles in now like a rat."

When I was allowed to roam New York by myself, I went first to the Museum of Natural History, where I spent spellbound days in the

Promises of pleasure and adventure beneath a vaulted sky.
Courtesy of N.Y. Public Library,
Astor, Lenox and Tilden Foundations

old J. C. Cady wing of 1877, a dark, blackish-brown pile later cleaned to a surprisingly frivolous pink. The blue whale suspended from the entrance ceiling became my friend. So did the building. When the Museum built its new centerpiece in 1936, an archeologically correct Roman monument in retardataire Beaux Arts by John Russell Pope, I hated it, and still do. Not because anyone told me to hate it (by then I knew), but because those pompous, forbidding, overscaled steps led to huge, cold, tomblike halls, vast, dim, dead spaces in which one felt depressed and diminished. This is a kind of building totally devoid of joy. I cannot make myself go there now, but I am glad that lots of other people do.

The world really opened for me across town, at the Metropolitan Museum. It was true-blue Beaux Arts (Richard M. Hunt, Richard H. Hunt, and McKim, Mead and White, successively, from 1895 to 1906) and its grandeur worked. The steps invited rather than repelled, in that formal Beaux Arts *marche,* or moving progression of spaces, that invited one into the high-ceilinged hall with its tapestries, chandeliers, and stray knights in armor or oversized antiquities. (I have never been able to reconcile myself to its current "restoration," a slick cross between IBM and I. Magnin glamor.) In the best Beaux Arts fashion, these spaces either beckoned you up the grand stairs (if you were young and supple) to the painting galleries, or led you left or right, to the worlds of Egypt, Greece and Rome. It is no exaggeration to say that this building shaped my life.

So did the 42nd Street Library (Carrère and Hastings, 1898–1911), when my art studies began to take me there for research. Another beautiful Beaux Arts building became a friend. It made no pretense at chumminess; it was intended to impress, but again, it worked. A sense-expanding spatial sequence from the arched and colonnaded portal to more marble and massive stairs and richly detailed rooms inside provided both grace and grandeur and suggested that man might be noble, after all. Or at least that he knew quality from junk.

Walks around town left indelible impressions. There was the New York Yacht Club on West 44th Street (Warren and Wetmore, 1889), a baroque extravaganza with flowing water carved below galleon-shaped windows—what child would not adore it? I was a post-post graduate student before I knew that this was *architecture parlante,* defined in the Architectural League's guide as "architecture whose function is literally articulated by its form and decoration"—here ships and sea in stone.

A woman still does not enter New York's great Beaux Arts men's clubs, except as a pariah through designated areas. I remember visiting the University Club (McKim, Mead and White, 1889), a Renaissance superpalazzo, and making an instinctive, architecturally propelled rush for the great, gutsy marble columns visible from the door. None of that, now. I was peremptorily turned aside into a pusillanimous "ladies" dining room. The insult was as much architectural as personal.

At the Battery, I found the U.S. Custom House (Cass Gilbert, 1907), 40 giant columns around its sides, embellished with dolphins, rudders, tridents, and winged wheels, guarded by Daniel Chester French's Four Continents. Farther along, on Liberty Street, was James Baker's 1901 Chamber of Commerce Building, a particularly rich fruitcake of dormers and bulls-eye windows, colonnade and copper-crested roof, frosted with garlands. Delighted by their outrageous assurance, I adopted them both.

From my office window, as I write, my constant companion is a small Beaux Arts skyscraper directly across on 42nd Street. It is elegantly composed and decorated, with three elongated, vertical bands of round-arched windows dominating a delicate, five-bay arrangement, topped with a crown of carved stone. The street at its feet is porn-country; the neighborhood around it is a disaster area. But the finesse with which the building proposes that skill and order are not only justifiable but desirable, is somehow reassuring. I raise my eyes for an architecture-break in a city that is as heartbreaking in its beauty as it is in its poverty and decay. It is still a city of dreams—promised, built, and broken.

November 9, 1975

A HARD ACT TO FOLLOW

I have had two continuing love affairs with Beaux Arts buildings in New York, the Metropolitan Museum and the Forty-Second Street Library. Both institutions have opened doors to the discovery of the wonders and beauties of the universe for me as a child and an adult, something the big city is supposed to do—and does.

High school, college, graduate work, and professional research have led me to the library's elegant French classical pile of Vermont marble on Fifth Avenue, past Mr. E. C. Potter's lions of 1911, through the Corinthian columns of the triple-vaulted entrance and the rich, bronze doors to the noble foyer, up the monumental stairs into the half-acre vastnesses of the reading rooms as gently sounding as trees by the sea.

One can, of course, rise directly to the treasures of the third floor by elevator, now efficiently if somewhat banally automated, but I remember the open bronze cages run by autocratic ladies in sweaters on stools who took grim delight in closing the doors in your face. When you missed them, you waited, and waited, and waited. You walked, then, along corridors as wide and splendid as ballrooms lined with displays of rare prints on the way to the imposing stairs and the skylit silence of History and Genealogy and the Fine Arts.

I can do it blindfolded, but except for the section of the second floor where the addition of ugly fluorescent lighting fixtures strikes a harsh, false note, I wouldn't want to. I'd hate to miss that prime example of sentimental Victorian pictorial history by the yard, Munkacsy's Blind Milton Dictating Paradise Lost to his Daughters on the second floor landing. But it is not for nostalgia or memorabilia that I sometimes detour to Fifth Avenue. It is for substance, style, and quality in a city and world that are hard put to provide such commodities today and hardly know how to evaluate them. I am not weeping for the past; I am concerned for the future.

For me, the building has always worked well. I have found it an excellent tool, and much, much more. I could not be persuaded to admire a monument that does not work, not even the beautifully detailed elegance of Carrère and Hasting's Beaux Arts masterpiece of 1902–09. No building is admirable that abuses function.

Some turn-of-the-century commentators thought the library forfeited claims to architectural greatness because its classical grandeur had been fitted to function as the designers' primary concern, with some sacrifice of approved monumental formulas. Later it was fashionable to admire only the rear of the building, where plain, vertical slit windows light the stacks and lighten the structure's mass with proto-modern simplicity. How temporal are the standards of critics!

It must be remembered that this is one of the last of the great nineteenth-century buildings. It was actually conceived and planned in the 1890s. Still, it has consistently filled twentieth-century needs. In spite of its formal grandeur, the experience of the building is intimate and emotional. In spite of its scale, it is never cold or tiring. For me, it is always like going home.

PLEASURES

The New York Public Library receives support from two sources. The city-wide circulation system is paid for by public funds from city and state. The research collections, of which the 42nd Street branch is the heart, are sustained by private funds from the Astor, Tilden and Lenox Foundations, the three sources united in 1895 to create the New York Public Library, plus gifts and annual fund-raising.

The Mid-Manhattan Library, an addition across the avenue, increases the availability of general research and circulation material. The new facility represents a careful jigsaw of city, state, federal, and public and private funds and it is wonderful to have it. But did it have to be so depressingly ordinary in design? The trip across the street was all downhill. It makes one hope that the furniture of the mind is what really counts. I don't, of course, believe that for a minute; you can't be literate, or educated, and non-visual at the same time.

Across the street, Messrs. Carrère and Hastings keep their backs politely turned. Mr. Carrère is in bronze by Jo Davidson and Mr. Hastings is in marble by Frederick MacMonnies. Both are in niches at the foot of the north and south stairs.

They got the commission by competition in 1897, a process that has produced some of the country's best public structures. The building was authorized by the city on the site of the old Croton Reservoir in the same year.

The completed structure cost $9-million and is virtually unreproduceable at any price. Pressed for a description, Mr. Hastings called it a modern building. It was meant to serve the needs of its day, he explained, by an evolutionary use of the Renaissance forms that he believed most suited the tastes of Western man. He was rumored to be less than satisfied with the Fifth Avenue front. Some thought the building overly rich in decorative detail. That was before craftsmanship died.

As urban planning, the library still suits the city remarkably well. A stepped terrace on the Fifth Avenue side offers a balustraded, tree-shaded space skillfully separated from street traffic. An "esplanade" at the rear, between the building and Bryant Park, from 40th to 42nd Streets, arched over by giant trees and bordered with ivy, is one of the best and earliest examples of the block-through pedestrian passage now stressed by New York's planners. Compare this gentle monumentality and knowing humanism with the pompous aridity of the new street treatment of the library's sister Beaux Arts monument, the Metropolitan Museum. Someone should have looked 40 blocks south.

The library's white Vermont marble, cleaned in 1950 and hosed down early Sundays, is mellowing to a pale Athenian gold. "It is one building in the spring morning with the new green of the lindens," wrote David Gray in *Harper's Monthly* of March, 1911, "another in the autumn rain, another in the snow-suffused winter twilight, and others under the moon or the night sky, or under the low-hanging yellow mist tinged with the city's lights." That is the enduring magic of New York.

January 24, 1971

THE FUTURE GROWS OLD

The near-legendary, radical modern house that Walter Gropius built for himself in Lincoln, Massachusetts, in 1937—the revolutionary architectural shot heard across the country—is being acquired by the Society for the Preservation of New England Antiquities. The architect's widow, Ise Gropius, is giving it complete with original Bauhaus art and furnishings, views of hills and apple orchards, and an incredible complement of birds.

It is an occasion for pleasure and a few gentle reflections. There is, first, the lovely, subtle paradox of the Gropius House, that clarion call to the future, as an authenticated antiquity. How inexorably time turns the avant-garde into history! And how much delicate irony can be obtained from the fact that this house marked the conscious rejection of history in terms of emulation of past styles (indigenous tradition was the superbly rationalized substitute) and the declaration of a new esthetic and a brave new world. Thirty-eight years later, the revolution has become commonplace, and there is revolution against the revolution. The new esthetic is the norm, and the brave new world grows old. The landmark takes its place as part of the history that it has spurned, and the movement that rewrote history becomes history. Always, history wins.

Nor are there any clear-cut definitions of art or antiquity. All those made-in-the-Bauhaus furnishings of the 1920s—a rare collection that any first-rate museum would covet jealously—were only 50 years old at the time of Walter Gropius's death and were therefore classified by

A landmark of a simpler and more innocent time. *Damora*

the IRS, under inheritance tax laws, as "obsolete." When does obsolete become antique? In 100 years, by true-blue, Red Queen, IRS logic. Brought out of Germany in the 1930s, first to England and then to America when Gropius came to Harvard to head the Graduate School of Design, they have already run the gamut from radical to camp to classics of the minor arts.

The art history books will tell you that Gropius's arrival was the signal for change, both through example and architectural education. The school had been languishing in the Beaux Arts stereotype with design exercises for regal casinos and Hôtels de Ville while the vanguard of modernism was shattering the intellectual barricades in Europe. Gropius's house, designed with Marcel Breuer, who followed the same escape route from Germany, was an instant landmark when it was completed in 1938. And the generations Gropius taught at Harvard from 1937 to 1952 went out to build and teach in turn, transforming the American landscape—to an extraordinary degree—in the image and philosophy of the master. The fact that a revolution won is a revolution lost by the very nature of victory compounds both irony and history.

A trip to the Gropius house today, whether one knew it personally at the time of its greatest impact or as a standby of art history courses, is a sentimental journey. The neat, white structure sits on a hill, in a proper New England landscape of fields and woods—both timeless and a period piece. On a recent visit a reluctant spring had barely greened the grass over the stony earth; an almost invisible cloud of yellow and russet suggested buds on bare branches.

It is hard to remember that the house was built as a daring object lesson in the compatibility of twentieth-century technology and art —an ardent polemic as well as a home. To anyone expecting a doctrinaire, Teutonic, textbook exposition of functional purity and rebellious doctrine, it can only be a surprise. This is a conventional house now, familiar, lived in, *gemütlich*. The scale is intimate, the ambience informal. Plants run riot in the light rooms, there is all the impedimenta of accumulated family living, and the birds—the amazing birds—dart, fly, and feed beyond the glass window walls that frame huge tree trunks and distant views.

The famous innovations are all standard practice now; you must look closely to see them: the fireplace stripped of traditional mantel trim and frame that became a modern cliché and embattled anachronism (the argument raged for years about the romantic vestigial hearth versus "honest" mechanical heat); the wall of bracket-held bookshelves; pictures not hung, but placed casually on shelves and surfaces; the lightweight, movable, casual furniture with emphasis on function; rooms that flow into each other; and of course, the glass walls with panel heating and exterior overhangs that both let in, and regulate, enormous amounts of seasonal light and sun. It is a handbook of the new rules of twentieth-century domestic architecture, grown old gracefully.

The famous Bauhaus furnishings of tubular steel, canvas and wood are comfortably shabby now, and some of the chairs have achieved their original objective of mass production. The tables of curved tubes connected to wood surfaces with carefully visible screws no longer have the conscientiously handcrafted machine look with which they came out of the Bauhaus workshops. To the uninitiated, they would look a little like something put outside of a thrift shop as a come-on bargain. To the knowing, they are a delightful historical curiosity: esthetic morality (the implied honesty of modern materials and machine manufacture) married to an elitist industrial art.

Is it unsuitable to say that the house is charming? The delightful guest bedroom with its toe-to-toe beds in white, black, and red, and the small master bedroom with its glass-walled dressing room, liberated forever from "bedroom suites," were startlingly different in their day, but are extremely comfortable and inviting now. The downstairs and upstairs porches that united indoor and outdoor living areas with such novelty seem routine. The use of the horizontal wood siding of traditional New England construction in the inside hall is suitable, not startling. And what was most unconventional at the time—the selection of all hardware and built-in accessories from standard catalogs and frequently from industrial sources—gives a distinct nostalgic flavor, although they were among the most radical of the house's modern features.

The building was not only not custom-made, in this sense, but it was constructed rapidly, from spring to fall in 1938. The cost, $18,000, was financed by a Lincoln sponsor, Mrs. James J. Storrow, because the Gropiuses had no funds. They paid rent until they could buy the house from Mrs. Storrow's estate after her death.

There is a strong scent of Art Deco and Industrial Style in such details as door and cabinet handles and lighting fixtures, including a fine torchère. An angled glass-brick wall, in spite of its pleasant logic as a light conductor and divider, cannot escape the stamp of camp. The famous outdoor industrial steel spiral stair that was almost a symbol of stark new esthetic drama against the flat white wall plane is now a pure 1930s touch.

Taken in its entirety, the house is as much a period statement as any Bulfinch treasure. It meets the same standards of style, significance, and authenticity. The rationale of its acquisition by the Society is incontestable.

The Gropius house is, in a sense, a symbol of a simpler and more innocent time; it was a moment when esthetic rebellion was seen as a social need and as "the puritanical devotion to truth which characterized everything Gropius did," according to G. Holmes Perkins, a former Harvard colleague. Truth was so much more easily perceived then; right was so clearly distinguishable from wrong. The angels were an identifiable band. If the results, with the hindsight of years, seem more complexly shaded, they are no less remarkable. This is indeed the kind of history that changed the world.

May 18, 1975

FRIENDS IN PUBLIC PLACES

I am not the person to judge the statues in the Metropolitan Museum's show on "New York City Public Sculpture" (1974) as art, because they are all my friends. Besides, my competence runs more to how public art affects public space.

I have been a street wanderer since childhood, and most of these heroic bronzes and marbles are familiar individuals for whom I feel a surprising warmth. It wasn't until I developed "taste" and studied art that I found I wasn't supposed to like them—not really. The Union Square equestrian statue of George Washington by Henry Kirke Brown is not the Colleoni, and Bernini would have laughed at the Maine monument. The standards of verisimilitude and representation of virtues larger than life had become esthetic unmentionables.

And so the reviewer of this nineteenth-century public sculpture by American artists is in trouble. He can have a ball with it as camp or a problem with it as art, since it is impossible now to approach it in terms of its original intentions. It is hard to accept it philosophically and grossly unfair to judge it any other way, even while applying the absolute yardstick that the critic must carry. Skills serve philosophy, and the simplistic promotion of heroic ideals and the perfectable nobility of man as beloved by the Victorians and considered the perfect accent for city spaces has succumbed to the realities of the age of the anti-hero.

That is why attempts at representational heroic sculpture today are instantly doomed; without belief there is no art. And it is therefore a wrenching effort to evaluate the success or failure of these nineteenth-century monuments as sculpture alone. Even though it has become fashionable to admire and admit the emotional impact of the Lincoln Memorial—we now acknowledge the moving quality of Daniel Chester French's giant seated figure within Henry Bacon's classical temple—few fully embrace the genre, the period (which extended well into the twentieth century), and the product.

This step has been taken wholeheartedly, however, by the director of the museum's show, Lewis I. Sharp, who is also responsible for the commendable catalogue (produced with a grant, quite properly, from the Plaza Hotel, on whose doorstep both Augustus Saint-Gaudens's General Sherman and Karl Bitter's Pomona, Goddess of Abundance, stand).

PLEASURES

This most sensitive and delightful presentation of 22 examples of New York statuary ranges from the handsome totality of the architecturally planned space at the entrance to Brooklyn's Prospect Park by Stanford White, with the collaborating effort of a galaxy of sculptors, to John Quincy Adams Ward's Horace Greeley brooding over City Hall Park in a fringed chair.

In some cases, the public spaces were designed or carefully considered at the same time. In others, the statue was placed almost arbitrarily, with much debate over site. In almost all instances, the architect was commissioned for the base as carefully as the sculptor was commissioned for the figure and was a man of equal reputation.

Saint-Gaudens, for example was consistently partnered with Stanford White, and Ward and Richard Morris Hunt were a repeated team. And until you've seen a really bad base, like the awkward highrise of the equally awkward Daniel Webster in Central Park (whose pomposity affords a certain delight), you may not be aware of the difference this can make.

To consider this work in terms of urban design is a distinct relief. Although I must confess to an increasing admiration for Saint-Gaudens, whether it is inspired by his ladylike "Victory" leading Sherman appropriately toward Bergdorf Goodman's, or by any number of his masterful figures and friezes.

The Plaza, properly called Grand Army Plaza, just south of Central Park at 59th Street and abutting Fifth Avenue, is a close-to-perfect city space. Even the unpardonable mutilation provided by the General Motors Plaza across the street, an object lesson in a plaza in the wrong place and in contrasting commercial banality, has failed to destroy its integrity.

Bergdorf's now stands in place of the Vanderbilt mansion, but its classily unpretentious modern style is a fine backdrop for Bitter's Fountain of Abundance, with its serene Renaissance basins. To beat a marble horse, the General Motors building, with its provincial posh, is the only fall from grace. It replaced the Savoy Plaza.

The fronting plaza itself is the work of the architect Thomas Hastings, of Carrère and Hastings, who completed it in 1916. He united the concept of the sculptor, Karl Bitter, and the presence of Sherman. The result is eloquent proof that excellence and elegance—élitism if you will—can also be popular. No public space in New York City has more universal appeal.

The monuments count as much as the spaces. They create the ambience, the character and sense of place. People flock to them. At the least, they are places to sit down; for the more thoughtful, they are places to contemplate change. They also offer certain kinds of enduring human presence and intimations of glory and pleasure. It does not matter if the glory is hollow (Sherman left the South in ashes, after all) or if the pleasure is evoked in stone (abundance may only be in Bergdorf's windows). One does not live by art alone.

Today's plazas are made as much by zoning regulations as by the architect's creative impulses. And what the architect puts in—for he almost universally controls the urban and esthetic product—may elevate those voids to fine public spaces or be gratuitous decoration. But that was true in the nineteenth century, as well.

The difference now is that the vision is coolly abstract and the philosophy rests on the beauty of geometric elementals rather than with the evocations of natural form. There is no warming recognition, no identity of human purposes. Sometimes, however, the result is excellent, full of the absolute power of successful spatial and sculptural relationships.

The scale and style of the plaza of Gordon Bunshaft's sleek 140 Broadway, with its dramatic accent of Noguchi's upended red cube, is a fine example of architect as patron. Bernard Rosenthal's large work at Astor Place elevated its ordinary "found space" setting from mere traffic flow to public space. Louise Nevelson's handsome piece is meaningless on upper Park Avenue, because it neither creates nor complements space worthy of the name.

When the pool in front of the Vivian Beaumont Theater at Lincoln Center has water, the Henry Moore provides that essential, fulfilling element of style and definition that raises the whole complex to urban art. Not least is the strong, evocative sensuosity of the work, as opposed to geometric abstraction. There is an extra dimension of implied human reference that does much to make people relate to the space. That all-important result must usually be achieved in the modernist esthetic by finesse of proportions and scale.

The use of space and sculpture is traditionally one of man's most creative contributions where it counts most: as a three-dimensional part of the functioning city scene and of the activity of life. More people experience art here than in galleries and museums. The art of the city is the most pervasive art of all.

September 15, 1974

Where the Past
Meets the Future

Successes

Peter Cooper was a self-made man with a fortune gained from glue and iron rails, and a passionate attachment to New York. He founded and endowed the Cooper Union for the Advancement of the Arts and Sciences, a tuition-free school open to anyone of "good moral character," and housed it in the Foundation Building constructed at Astor Place in the 1850s. At the time, the building stood for the most advanced nineteenth-century technology and style, in the structural use of early steel beams and in the Italianate chic of Fred A. Petersen's rather stolidly arcaded facade.

One hundred and fifteen years later the building had experienced a number of changes, including the addition of some extra stories that give a rather awkward proportion to the original scheme, and the gradual transformation of what must have been fairly straightforward interiors into a shabby maze. The cylindrical elevator shaft that Cooper so prophetically included for the future (he was sure that elevators would be round) had been given a rectangular cab, and visitors milled through a boiler room to get to the basement Great Hall, the setting of Lincoln's famous "Right is Might" speech. The building had been designated a city landmark and listed on the National Register of Historic Places.

The School of Art and Architecture continued to occupy the Foundation Building, although the School of Engineering had gotten a dumb and ordinary (no compliment intended) new building across Seventh Street in the early 1960s.

A decade later, the Trustees, with President John F. White, decided to renovate the Foundation Building and commissioned the head of the Architecture School, John Hejduk (a Cooper Union architecture graduate) and Professor Peter Bruder (a Cooper Union engineering graduate) to do the job. The first intention was simply to clean it up and bring it up to code but that involved so much work that logic dictated a more extensive and creative solution. The rehabilitation took two years and the operation was a success.

That success is notable on interlocking philosophical, esthetic and functional levels—in a way that comments significantly on the values implicit in the act of preservation. Mr. Hejduk has done more than present New York with a refurbished landmark and the school with efficient new quarters. He has asked some serious questions about use, history, and art, and he has answered them visibly, with logic and style. The Cooper Union renovation is an outstanding example of the real meaning of preservation at a time when the "recycling" of older buildings of architectural merit is becoming increasingly common.

These are not simple questions, and Hejduk's thoughtful answers range through an assortment of strengths and subtleties. What he has done, in essence, is to put a new building in the old shell. The programming of that new plan is conceptually and spatially elegant. It is a modern solution that still manages to evoke the past even though literal conservation has been sacrificed in many places. Compliance with current codes has hidden the fine, foliated cast-iron columns in sleek, fireproof plaster, and the original plan is recalled but transformed for contemporary uses. But what no longer exists is still suggested in spirit. Calculated new-old contrasts add an extra dimension to the building appropriately expressive of its twentieth-century life.

A good old building should develop layers of esthetic meaning like the rings of a tree, continually enriched, rather than violated, by contemporary functions. This process does not include the abortive accretions of expediency, but the appropriate revisions of space and use. Pickling à la Williamsburg, or restricting restoration to the limited doctrine of "accurate reconstruction," is actually an evasion of history. (There are some buildings of museum caliber, of course, where only this process will do.) That kind of preservation is a form of mercy killing.

In the new Cooper Union plan, studio spaces and "cells" are virtually where they were in the northern sector; the south end is still used for formal circulation. But there are significant differences. The space has been opened up for greater simplicity and a contemporary esthetic. What was dark is now flooded with light. What was closed and fragmented is now an expanded spatial geometry. Where stairs and walls have been moved, the round elevator shaft stands virtually as abstract sculpture, played against the light-filled drama of the Victorian windows.

The counterpoint of new and old is constant. The first two floors, housing the library and exhibition and administration space, are now treated as an intricate construct of volumes and planes no older than De Stijl and Le Corbusier. A play of partially opened and closed spaces is viewed from above and across through interior windows. Trompe l'oeil vistas appear flat and painterly at first, and then resolve themselves progressively in three dimensions. On the top floor, one wall of the "Peter Cooper suite" is the floor-to-ceiling translucent glass face

Asking questions about use and history, and answering them with logic and style. *John Hejduk*

of the building's old clock, with the nineteeth-century works poised like freestanding art in front of it.

"It's a tough old building," Mr. Hejduk says with obvious affection. "I wanted to keep the feeling, which ran from Palladian to industrial, from bottom to top. It was good, solid stuff." It also has extraordinary scale and an unreproducible generosity of proportions and ceiling heights. This amplitude is emphasized by bright, white loft spaces dimensioned by forests of columns on their original modules.

The structural work, by the Fuller Construction Company, was an engineering spectacular. The south end of the building was gutted, and the exterior walls were temporarily braced from outside. For a while this "cathedral" space "found" inside was astounding. (The cast-iron columns discarded from the reworked south end disconcerted a number of watchful observers unaware of the total scheme.)

On the north end, two floors of bearing walls were removed to accommodate the library. The original framing above these walls was literally jacked up to remove the load while new structural steel was inserted. Then the old cast-iron columns on the upper floors were realigned. The building still rests on the original granite arches and cast-iron columns of the restored and updated Great Hall.

Cooper Union is now the best of both worlds. Its "Renaissance" shell is intact. And the clarity and detail of the consciously sophisticated modernism of the interiors speaks of the creative continuity of history and art. Almost symbolically, Peter Cooper's round elevator shaft is finally fitted with a stainless steel tube. "My joy is boundless," says Mr. Hejduk.

December 8, 1974

SPRUCING UP THE BANK OF TOKYO

The Bank of Tokyo has a particularly fine location, just above Wall Street, facing Trinity Church and its historic churchyard, which includes among its markers and pleasant greenery a row of cherry trees given by the bank some years ago. The Bank of Tokyo has occupied offices at 100 Broadway as a rental tenant since 1952, first as an agency of the parent bank in Japan, later as the New York State-chartered Bank of Tokyo Trust Company.

At one point in the building boom of the 1960s, the bank arranged to put up its own new building, a bit farther down Broadway, but the plans fell through. When the 100 Broadway lease came due in 1973, the bank decided on a long-term lease based on renovation, with costs to be shared by owner and tenant. The owner improved all basic services, and the bank embarked on total remodeling of the interiors as well as exterior renovation, with its own architects, Kajima International, Inc., under the direction of Nobutaka Ashihara. (Mr. Ashihara, who had worked for Roche, Dinkaloo Associates, credits Kevin Roche with sympathetic advice about respecting the old building's style and integrity.)

At present, the Bank of Tokyo occupies 13 of the 21 floors, with options for the rest of the space in the next ten years, and it has tailored all of its floors to its specific needs. As Jiro Ishizaka, general manager of the main office, says, "Where would we get a better address?"

Nor could they easily find a better building. One Hundred Broadway is one of those sleeper landmarks (undesignated) of which New York has so many more than anyone realizes—an outstandingly fine early skyscraper built from 1894–1896 as the American Surety Building by Bruce Price, one of the better known architects of the time.

Price called his Beaux Arts design a "rusticated pillar," and it followed the popular esthetic conventions of the day. The new, steel-framed tall building was treated as a classical column on a vastly enlarged scale, its height divided into proportionate approximations of base, shaft, and capital. The white marble facade, newly cleaned and extraordinarily rich, features a row of two-story, attached Ionic columns at the base, a shaft of 12 rusticated stories, and an increasingly ornate top of seven stories with pilasters, pediments, and a coda of cornices. Above each of the ground floor columns is a full-scale, sculptured classical figure, and two more figures rise above the first of the cornices to embrace a central window with a fine French flourish.

This facade has been beautifully cleaned and restored. The visible changes are new windows and a modernized ground floor. Where the front of the building was originally flush with the backs of the columns, it is now set back a few feet to create an arcade. This passageway is a genuine amenity in Lower Manhattan's congested streets.

A studied and stunning transition from nineteenth to twentieth century.
The New York Times/Jack Manning

It also represents a sacrifice of store space for a civilized urban gesture. The new, setback front is of clear glass, without mullions, its crystalline modernity a striking contrast to the classical marble columns. The space behind the glass has been completely opened up for a stylishly contemporary banking floor in stark white marble, with accents of black, dark brown, and emerald green. This 320-foot-high banking floor is surrounded at its periphery by a mezzanine and second floor, open to view through dark gray glass.

But the most spectacular contrast is where part of the former lobby area has been retained as a kind of central "court," in the all-white open space, marked off only by immense, round, brownish-gray marble Corinthian columns, which rise the full 32-foot height to an intact, elaborately coffered bronze-gold ceiling. Suspended from this ceiling, in a deliberate contrast of style, is the sharp geometry of a large brushed aluminum sculpture in the form of a warped rectangle, hanging point downward, by Isamu Noguchi. It is a studied and stunning transition from nineteenth to twentieth century. The total effect is of a dramatically successful counterpoint of new and old.

The separate office entrance, at the south end of the arcade, is a long, narrow space that retains a superbly ornate, black and gold coffered ceiling and upper walls; the lower walls are now faced in more of the pure white marble, with elevator doors of mirror-finished aluminum. Above these plain, polished, light-reflective surfaces are the gilded masks, putti, acanthus motifs, wreaths, and arabesques, theatrically illuminated on a dark ground.

Strict preservationists will probably cavil at the loss of all but selected parts of the original ground floor interior and their calculated combination with starkly contrasting surfaces, rather than more faithful restoration. I find the result a model of a sensitive, sophisticated, rational solution for contemporary use and the bank's particular needs, with maximum architectural and cultural impact and a heightened sense of past and present. It works, and so does the building. The floors above are simple and standardized, with lighting designed for energy conservation.

There are a few unfortunate touches and design uncertainties; the newly gilded and incised exterior lettering, for example, is not as good as the former signs, although the building directories inside are elegant graphics. But what counts most is that the Bank of Tokyo has opted for a handsome, recycled structure rather than the standard anonymity of most new buildings. The combination of the tastes, crafts, and uses of two different eras has resulted in maximum stylistic drama. The bank has gained a sense of quality and identity. It has made a gesture of art and urbanity that reflects well on both the client and the city.

December 28, 1975

ALBANY: A HAPPY ALLIANCE
OF PAST AND PRESENT

If you turn your back on the $1-billion worth of high camp on the Albany Mall, you will face one of the neatest architectural achievements in the country. Just beyond the State Capitol, fronting Academy Park on Elk Street, is the new headquarters of the New York State Bar Association. This $1,626,616 center for the 22,000 members of the State Bar is an object lesson in civilized urban architecture.

In a happy alliance, the lawyers and the architects, James Stewart Polshek and Associates, have preserved a row of handsome nineteenth-

The words that come to mind are imagination and taste.
George Cserna

century town houses on Elk Street and incorporated them, not as a false front, but as a working part of a completely and strikingly contemporary complex built behind them. The words that come to mind are skill, imagination, and taste, qualities not encountered too often on the urban scene.

On Elk Street, you are still in the Albany of Henry James—sedate, small-scaled, with high-stooped houses, ornate window lintels, and evocations of a more leisurely world.

You enter the Bar Center through No. 1, its substantial period door flanked by colored glass sidelights. Nos. 1, 2, and 3 have been retained to the depths of their front parlors, for meeting, conference, and dining rooms.

No. 4, on the corner, collapsed during construction and had to be demolished—something like shooting a horse with a broken leg. It leaves a grassy side plot leading to the pleasant open court that joins the new and old sections of the building.

The three historic houses are connected at their rear by a glass-walled corridor that opens to the outdoor court. Entrance to the new section is either through the court or through a corridor from the nineteenth-century front hall.

The new part of the center is divided into three parallel, skylit sections filling the rest of the sloping site to the next street. They increase in height toward the back. The first is for reception, the second is a Great Hall, and the third contains office space. Topping the office space is the Grievance Hearing Room, where questionable legal practices are investigated. They don't shoot bad lawyers; they disbar them.

The relationships of the various parts of the structure in terms of useful and beautiful spaces provide changing pleasures for the eye. The calculated vistas and contrasts, the logical movement from public to "quiet" areas, the measured views and effects demonstrate a good deal of what more-than-merely-competent architecture is about.

The Great Hall is the focus of the building. Serving as library, lounge, and formal social reception area, it is a spacious 40 by 66 feet and soars the structure's full 41-foot 6-inch height. Its natural stucco-finished walls are washed with light from a skylight, narrow vertical glass on one outside wall, and a window wall on the court. Opposite the window wall is a library wall of law books, with the exposed balconies of the tiers of office floors rising visibly above. A bit of trompe l'oeil with glass and mirrors helps.

Emphasizing the space are flaglike banners by Norman Laliberté, one 6 feet wide and 28 feet long hung most of the height of the hall. This nonstop representation of world legal systems in every sweet and hot color of the spectrum is a glowing blend of deeply serious symbolism and gentle wit. Law and order becomes law and joy.

If the lawyers are heroes today, just a little over three years ago they were looked on as villains. In their first plan, Nos. 1 to 4 Elk Street were to be demolished for the new headquarters.

Instant outcry from preservationists followed the announcement. The legal profession is trained to reason, if not to urban esthetics. Reasonably, the Bar Association reconsidered the project.

The architect agreed to seek a real use for the old buildings that could combine with new construction without sacrificing the Bar Association's modern needs. The solution is a national model.

It would have been cheaper not to care. Demolishing the house that crumbled and rehabilitating the historic buildings added about $80,000 to the basic budget. Another $204,553 went for foundation changes due to poor soil, the work made more difficult by the fragile old structures. Other concessions to quality raised the price nearly $70,-000 more.

Combining new and old was a delicate and costly task. But you get what you pay for. The result, says Mr. Polshek, "brings the profession into the twentieth century gracefully."

The building clearly says that continuity, tradition, and art are part of life and law, tangibly expressed in the turn of the corner from Elk Street to Eagle Street, from the nineteenth to the twentieth century. This is excellent image-making as well as excellent architecture. Smart, these lawyers.

September 25, 1971

BOSTON: A SENSITIVE SUCCESSION

In the curious mess that is Boston's Back Bay around Copley Square —a series of striking new construction projects connected, to use the word loosely, by sloppy disorder that cannot even qualify as messy vitality—there are some outstanding buildings. But the new Boston Public Library by Philip Johnson and John Burgee would be outstanding anywhere. It poses, and solves, a number of functional, structural, environmental and esthetic problems with mastery, and represents the kind of unity of program and solution that is what the best architecture has always been about.

The building was ten years in planning and construction, with requirements and budgets turned inside out, and it is fortunate that it took that long. Ten years ago Philip Johnson was not the architect he is today. Other cities have his learning pains; Boston has his best work.

The new central library addition, as it is called, is a $24-million, 10-story structure that provides 170,000 square feet of public space, and currently houses more than 600,000 volumes.

The new facilities accommodate 1,200 people at one time, offering prints, films, music, and audio-visual aids as well as books, and they have been judged functionally excellent in their initial operation. Since the opening, user figures have risen, at a time when libraries are fighting for attention and survival.

The new structure abuts the original McKim, Mead and White library of 1895, which is one of Boston's most proper, elegant and cherished landmarks. Although the new wing is larger and in a totally different style, the two buildings relate reasonably well. The addition upstages the old library with its bigger and bolder themes, but it does so with impeccably good architectural manners. It does not diminish the original structure except in scale.

It is also abundantly clear that this is a major, contemporary Philip Johnson work, just as the nineteenth-century palazzo is distinctly a McKim, Mead and White classical gem. The new wing takes no back seat to its distinguished predecessor. Mr. Johnson has had the good taste to indulge in no false modesty.

He has built a complicated structure of outwardly deceptive simplicity. For classical, arcaded refinement, it substitutes the assertive scale of 60-foot bays between massive piers and the bold plasticity of large lunette windows with canted facades and heavy, cornice-like projections above.

Compatibility with the McKim building was a primary condition of the assignment. Different structural systems almost a century apart dictated changes in span and appearance. But the original roof line was to be held, with maximum space to be provided within those restrictive height limits.

The same Milford granite that served McKim, Mead and White was to be used, and for this the original quarries were reopened. The structures are connected on two levels.

Posing and solving a number of functional, structural, environmental, and esthetic problems. *The New York Times/Joyce Dopkeen*

Beyond that, the relationship rests on no superficial decorative recall other than barely suggestive forms and the uniform rooflines; it is based on a very sophisticated visual expression of an unusual structural system that is an essential part of the design and uses of the new building. This is extremely well worked out, technically and esthetically. The solution is therefore much more than skin deep.

The building has to be read inside out to grasp its skill and understand the full measure of its success. At its heart is a 60-foot-high court that slices through its center. The space is washed in natural light from nine skylights that recall the building's plan of nine equal squares.

The entire structure has only 36 supporting columns. They are placed at the perimeter and in groups of four around the great hall. From these columns, the architects and consulting engineer, William Le Messurier, have hung 16-foot-deep trusses at the seventh floor, from which the third through sixth floors are suspended. Both space and flexibility are gained from this device, which eliminates forests of smaller columns and heavy floor slabs.

A post-tensioned concrete slab forming the second floor gives the same advantages of openness. The first and second floors are thus also column-free working areas. Mezzanine bridges appear to float, supportless, due to a highway type of construction, over the ground level.

All of this creates totally flexible, uninterrupted space, more floor area than conventional systems would provide, and incomparable spatial and esthetic drama. This is an almost grimly handsome building. But its quality is incontrovertible.

Floors that literally measure an acre in size are clear as far as the eye can see, except for equipment and furnishings. Programs have unaccustomed freedom of plan. And there is a complex interplay of the spaces as seen from the great hall that is quietly spectacular.

This focal hall and its ceremonial stair are also faced with Milford granite. There was an unhappy time when budget problems eliminated its use, but it was restored largely through construction efficiencies and economies of the contractor, Vappi and Sons. The Architects Design Group of Cambridge are the local associated architects.

The McKim structure is in the process of being converted for research uses. Its fine, golden marble and Gustavino tile vaulting preserve the quality and technology of another era, although a kind of informational vandalism of signs and showcases has had a disquieting effect. The famous murals are sooty and invisible. The open garden court remains a soothing oasis.

The library's director, Philip J. McNiff, whose concern for computerized catalogues is matched by his ease with the art of architecture, has said, "The lifting of the spirit and the lifting of the mind are related." The best buildings in Boston have a tradition of playing that dual role.

September 24, 1973

WASHINGTON: VICTORIANA LIVES

Victorian taste is still as exotic and unfathomable to most Americans as the puberty rites of far-off tribes, but the Smithsonian Institution's Renwick Gallery, a restored nineteenth-century structure, is a noble preservation success. In a classic struggle for survival, it is nice to report that the good guys have won.

WHERE THE PAST MEETS THE FUTURE

Formerly the Court of Claims, and originally the first Corcoran Gallery, the building was scheduled for demolition in 1958, when shards of disintegrating ornament threatened passersby and the kindest word in a Congressional bill of particulars calling for its demolition was firetrap.

One hundred years earlier, the red brick and sandstone structure, commissioned in 1858 by William W. Corcoran, the banker and art patron, and built from 1859–61 at Pennsylvania Avenue and 17th Street, burst on classical Washington like an ornate Technicolor pastry. It was the city's most avant-garde expression of the arts.

Today it is a $2.8-million restoration miracle, an example of the civilized reuse of the past to enrich and inform the present, and the nation's official showcase for the arts of design.

Between, it was sold to the Government when Corcoran built his new gallery in 1897, stripped, partitioned, thrown to the judges and the pigeons, and abandoned to the General Services Administration and general decay.

Demolition of the building was to be part of a gigantic renewal booboo that would have gutted Lafayette Square and its environs of art, charm, and history. In place of the old court and Federal houses there were to be matched marble mastodons.

Under the Kennedy administration, the plan was scrapped, and architect John Carl Warnecke began the restoration and rebuilding of Lafayette Square and the rescue of the old structure. In the Johnson administration, it was given to the Smithsonian. In 1969, Hugh Newell Jacobsen, the Washington architect, took on the completion of the interior.

The refurbished building, which will be used for public functions as well as providing display for American design, crafts, and decorative arts, is named for its distinguished nineteenth-century architect, James Renwick, Jr. Renwick also designed the Smithsonian's first building, the turreted proto-Disney structure on the Mall.

Renwick's design for Corcoran was in the latest French taste, modeled after Lefuel's addition to the Louvre in Paris under Napoleon III, known stylistically in this country as Second Empire. It was complete with monograms and portraits of Corcoran in friezes and cartouches. Humility hadn't yet been invented for the rich.

Corcoran sat out the war in Paris with his gallery unfinished and his money in gold bars, and did not open the building until 1871.

What the visiting awestruck public saw then was a giant staircase leading to the main picture gallery, which contained Corcoran's choicest paintings, hung in tiers on a plum-colored wall. They rose to a

SUCCESSES

24-foot high cornice, below an elaborately decorated ceiling that soared to a 38-foot-high skylight. A "modern" continuous gas fixture circled the room.

Below the paintings the effect was more spartan: a wood dado, wood floor and benches, and a projecting brass rail protecting the wall. Opposite was the Octagon Room, designed for the most notorious art object of its day, Hiram Powers's titillating naiad, the Greek Slave.

Today, the visitor climbs the stair to the Grand Salon, and lo, there are many of the original paintings, borrowed from the Corcoran collection, "tiered" on plain walls.

The ornate ceiling is gone. The dado, wood-grained in the nineteenth-century fashion, has been rebuilt. The magnificent room—this is actually a small building of great spaces—is now furnished with velvet island settees topped by gigantic urns from the Philadelphia Centennial Exposition of 1876, a pair of 10-foot eagle commodes from New York's Metropolitan Museum that obviously needed a 95-by-42-foot home, and an assortment of chairs from the Smithsonian collections.

It is all, of course, a "tasteful" reconstruction. It does not pretend to "accuracy" or "facsimile" status. Ninety percent of the woodwork and almost all of the detail was gone. The $2.8-million question was how to "restore" a building that was meant, by Renwick, to have

A classic struggle for survival. *The New York Times/ Mike Lien*

white marble with white china-gloss trim inside and was never carried out that way, served as a warehouse for uniforms during the Civil War, was completely redone in the gravy-stain-and-ormolu taste of the 1870s before it opened and was subjected to creeping G.S.A. green and toilets tucked in corners for the next 55 years.

You do it, in Mr. Jacobsen's words, "by getting it back to the spirit of Renwick," not by seeking literal reproduction. "The guy was awfully good," Mr. Jacobsen says. "He picks you up on the street, takes you into the building, there's that roll of drums on the stairs, and then you're up there—in the great space."

For exterior restoration, there were Matthew Brady photographs; for interiors there were hundreds of design pattern books of the day.

The exterior was painstakingly cleaned, patched, and repaired by the Washington firm of Universal Restoration, Inc. More than 90 percent of the original detail had to be reconstructed in a special molding, casting, and carving process using a stonelike composite with a sandstone aggregate finish.

Inside, twentieth-century technology—air conditioning, heating, wiring, and plumbing—had to be threaded through a nineteenth-century structure, hewing to the thin, dangerous line of appropriateness. Tons of G.S.A. lights, anemostats and wall clocks that had popped into place unbidden with mysterious speed had to be replaced.

But if the Smithsonian knew exactly what it was doing with the building, it seems to be totally at sea about its function as a display case for design. The exhibits suffer from ambivalence, torpor, and clichés. Given a concept, which it clearly lacks, the new Renwick Gallery can, and should be, a superb and civilized setting for the arts of design.

January 28, 1972

PHILADELPHIA: THE BIZARRE AND THE BEAUTIFUL

The Pennsylvania Academy of the Fine Arts, a quintessentially Victorian building by Frank Furness, the Philadelphia master of the style's boldest extravaganzas, opened on April 22, 1876, for the nation's Centennial year. The cerulean blue ceiling of its grand stairhall was studded with silver stars, the walls were a gilded geometry of stylized flowers on a rich, red ground above incised floral patterns on Natrona, a sandstone-brownstone blend. Ornamental bronze stair rails boasted bouquets of clustered-globe gas lights sprouting from elaborate, spiky stems. Arcades of Gothic arches surrounded the court and galleries, accented by polished columns of Pennsylvania blue or rose crystal marble. Doors and woodwork were of golden oak; floors were carpet or intricately patterned encaustic tile. Colors were plum, blue, gold, sand, and olive green. There was no brown anywhere.

Exactly one hundred years later to the day, for the Bicentennial, the Pennsylvania Academy reopened. It had been closed for two years for restoration. By the time the doors were shut, a century of neglect and renunciation of the Victorian esthetic had reduced its showy glitter to genteel mud. What had not been suppressed by changing taste had simply succumbed to grime. If the Academy had been a Furness bank or insurance building, or one of the many Furness works in the path of downtown renewal around that super-Victorian fruitcake, Philadelphia's City Hall (which proved too solid and too expensive to demolish), it would be gone. More than half of Furness's Philadelphia buildings have been destroyed, and much of the rest of his legacy has been severely mutilated. No architect has risen to higher favor in his own time or plunged to greater depths of rejection in later years.

By 1973, the fate of the Academy hung in the balance; it was saved by a vote of the Board, advised by art experts and preservationists. The reopened building is spectacular; the colors glow again, the gold glitters, and all is radiantly diffused with the light of the double skylit roofs that make the structure a giant greenhouse. A little inevitable dust will serve to dim the brand-new luster and place the building and its style more legitimately in time. But the original intent of its superb spatial organization and intricate decorative arts is revealed with clarity. This is not only the rehabilitation of a building, and of an

249

extraordinary architect's reputation; it is also a pivotal step in the reevaluation of this country's Victorian architecture.

The $5.1 million restoration was carried out by Hyman Myers of the architectural firm of Day and Zimmerman. It involved meticulous research, including scrapings, archeological-type digs, study of old photographs, and an obvious devotion to the cause. (That spread to the workmen, as well.)

Construction of the building, which housed both the galleries and an art school founded in 1805, was the last word in fireproofing in the 1870s: shallow brick vaults carried on cast-iron beams, combined with cast-iron columns, trusses, and solid brick bearing walls. New mechanical systems have been inserted into the ample spaces provided by Furness's ingenious original arrangement for heat and ventilation. There are new skylights and lighting, and some discreet remodeling has added extra levels for the school and a restorer's studio. Polychrome iron columns have been uncovered where encasing plaster was stripped away, as well as chamfered rooms that had been paneled over. Purists will find some fudging where missing, heavy cast-iron parts were replaced by lighter, modern materials. But the twentieth century has been as true to the nineteenth century as it is realistically possible to be.

The timing of the restoration, ostensibly for the Bicentennial, actually coincided with a growing consciousness of the excellence of the best nineteenth-century architectural design. The zeal of preservationists, based largely on sentiment and history, is being matched by a sharpened and increasingly knowledgeable appreciation of the virtuosities of Victorian work by both practicing architects and architectural historians.

In fact, it is not without significance that the installation of the building's opening show, "In This Academy," which included the excellent choice of temporary gallery colors from clear white for contemporary work to plum, sand, and gray-blue-violet for older pictures, was the work of the Philadelphia firm of Venturi and Rauch, simultaneously embattled for its colors and backgrounds for the Whitney's "Two Hundred Years of American Sculpture." (The Academy's refurbishing was started under Tom Armstrong, who moved on to head the Whitney, and was completed under the current Academy director, Richard J. Boyle.) The younger "Philadelphia school" architects, in today's vanguard, find much to support the Venturian theme of "complexity and contradiction" in the rediscovery of the Victorian richness that the modernists rejected.

In the past few years there has been a rising tide of interest in Frank

A rich and complex system of symbols and meanings.
The Pennsylvania Academy of the Fine Arts

Furness's work from the 1870s to the turn of the century, led by a coterie of Furness buffs. The Philadelphia Museum held a Furness show in 1973, accompanied by a fine book and checklist by James F. O'Gorman, working with George E. Thomas, Mr. Myers, and Cervin Robinson. Professor O'Gorman has characterized Furness's buildings as "among the most boisterous and challenging in an age noted for aggressive architecture." This exuberant, colorful style died of "good taste" by the end of the century, killed by the proper palazzi of McKim, Mead, and White.

The Furness oeuvre is bizarre and eccentric. He was an original, in the sense of a talent that takes the taste of his time and transforms it into an overwhelmingly personal expression. That taste, as the historian Carroll Meeks defined it some time ago, was for the "eclectic picturesque." In the work of Furness, it became, in O'Gorman's words, "a bedlam of heterogeneous parts."

Turrets, textures, polychromy, rounded and pointed arches, mansarded and decorated pavilions, dwarf columns, diapered brick patterns, strangely placed windows, warped levels, and fulsome ornament were combined in compositions of almost volcanic intensity. Deliberate oddities of arrangement and scale created explosive visual pressures. This is not the naive "bad taste" that has been so simplistically disdained by later generations; it is a deliberately manneristic style that richly rewards the informed eye. The facade of the Academy, done early in his career when the firm was Furness and Hewitt, is actually one of his more restrained works.

All of these features can be traced directly to the dominant creative strains of the nineteenth century. Furness's originality is an amalgam of English Ruskinian Gothic, Butterworthian ecclesiology, French neo-Grec classicism, the parallel urges for structural rationalism and decorative romanticism, and the elegant ornament of Owen Jones. His work fuses and transcends it all.

The point to be made is that this remarkable architecture has much to teach us—and surprisingly, perhaps, it is the younger architects who are most aware of it. The danger is that these lessons must be learned without falling into the trap of an eclectic decorative revival or of sacrificing the salient lessons of the modern movement. But those "modern" architects who work on the restoration of these Victorian monuments are particularly impressed. Hugh Jacobsen speaks respectfully of the grand stair in Washington's Renwick Gallery as "that roll of drums, getting you up to the great space." The stairhall at the Academy is clearly one of those great spaces, with involved, rewarding relationships to the rest of the building that are both striking and subtle. The plan is an outstanding example of the Beaux Arts *parti* (Furness studied with America's first Beaux Arts trained architect, Richard Morris Hunt) in which the function and progression of spaces create the architectural whole.

On entry, the stairhall is experienced on three physical levels; the eye and body and expectations are directed along the architectural *marche* up to the galleries and through them, led on by the pattern of natural light from the skylights and by the color and ornament, all as calculated as they are dazzling. (The artificial light flattens and deadens the building's contrasts and subtleties; it still needs work.) It must be emphasized that this is not decorative excess for its own sake. Each detail is used to enhance, accent, and differentiate, to create spatial flow and unity. These are tools manipulated with full awareness.

What we experience in the Academy is not nostalgia; it is architecture. The Victorian building is only beginning to be recognized as good architecture, and even, on occasion, as great architecture. Its richness is a complex system of symbols and meanings, of visual devices and sensuous effects that may have titillated a nouveau riche culture, but that also formed an extremely sophisticated and skillful, erudite and brilliant, highly manneristic nineteenth-century building art. Many of its monuments have been destroyed out of ignorance. Much of what remains is an abused and irreplaceable heritage.

The Pennsylvania Academy of the Fine Arts

Failures

GOODBYE HISTORY, HELLO HAMBURGER

See the 116-year-old historic house. See it being knocked down. See the hamburger stand in its place. Pow. America, of thee I sing; sweet land of Burger King.

The house was Mapleside, built solidly of sandstone with the classical graces characteristic of the mid-nineteenth century. It stood in Madison, Wisconsin, until it was bought and demolished by the hamburger chain, which professed to be ignorant of the building's esthetic and historical worth. Last-minute attempts by preservationists to raise $100,000 to save it failed. Good-bye history, hello hamburger. From historic home to "home of the whopper" with a swing of the wrecker's ball.

This hamburger stand got an extra onion. It was given as part of the "orchids and onions" awards program of the Capital Community Citizens, a lively environmental action group in Dade County, Wisconsin. The incident was reported in the *Wisconsin Architect* and *Preservation News*. As far as I know, there is no plaque on the hamburger stand.*

Usually landmarks are demolished for parking lots. Blacktop without onions. This is one of the most popular sports in cities. Urban renewal has drawn its demolition lines around uncounted (has anyone ever counted?) historic buildings and districts. Waterfronts, Federal survivals, Greek Revival enclaves, anything that has meaning in terms

---

* But Burger King, astounded or enlightened by the public response, set up a staff architect for environmental matters.

of the history, style, or sense of place of American communities is x-ed out first as the oldest, shabbiest, and easiest to demolish.

Within the last few years, as the nature of the losses became distressingly apparent, protests mounted. Federal legislation has been passed to amend original urban renewal law so that historic preservation can be assisted in renewal areas. Local agencies have been backed, pushed, and pulled into revision of plans by concerned citizens, with either overt or covert resistance. The struggle goes on, while the historic areas stand and rot, touched with the peculiar blight, stagnation, and decay that comes with renewal designation and inaction.

Maybe we need the gags to relieve the despair. But the humor is pretty black. Consider Newburgh, New York, for example. Newburgh is a Hudson River town in every sense: it is a product of the era when the river was celebrated in the arts and its spectacular hillside sites were romanticized by a variety of Victorian styles. Today the city has every kind of blight and problem going, and the renewal it charted for itself wrote "good riddance" across the map to its past. There is a curiously simplistic belief in troubled towns that wiping out a city wipes out its problems. Actually, the bulldozer only pushes them around, while eliminating the city's real assets.

In the midst of its difficulties, Newburgh came up with a gag that made national headlines. Demolition lines in the urban renewal plan, as usual, were drawn around one of the city's best buildings—the Dutch Reformed Church, a prime and elegant Greek Revival structure built in 1835 by Alexander Jackson Davis—now on the National Register. Right next to it was the line of the rehabilitation area. The rehabilitation area, it was pointed out by the *Times-Herald-Record* in a fine exposé, contained Big Nell's, the city's most notorious brothel. Big Nell's, listed as a single family house with 16 bedrooms, was eligible for federal fix-up funds and might even get a nice new entrance street at government cost to replace one closed by the urban renewal plan. The church was eligible only for demolition.

There was enough fuss to reprieve the church and close Big Nell's, although the renewal agency, located in a building within sight of both, did some conspicuous foot-dragging in remapping. The municipality has been backed, dragged, and pushed toward a plan to utilize the landmark constructively.*

In Hudson, New York, the same kind of senseless urban renewal plan claimed the 1837 Greek Revival General Worth Hotel. The Hudson YWCA was willing to take over the building and the Hudson

---

* In recent years, like many other cities and towns, Newburgh has changed course.

River Valley Commission, the State Historical Trust, and the National Trust for Historic Preservation urged that it be saved. But political heads prevailed and Hudson demolished its National Register property. Ready for the biggest gag of all? Read it in the *Hudson Register-Star*:

"A modern Dairy-Queen Drive-In will be constructed on the site of the historic General Worth Hotel that fell victim to the bulldozers last year. The Common Council in special session voted to sell the site for $1,700. Council President Thomas Quigley said the purchase 'was a step in the right direction to develop downtown Hudson.' "

America the beautiful,
Let me sing of thee;
Burger King and Dairy Queen
From sea to shining sea.

March 31, 1971

ONLY THE PHONY IS REAL

Country music got to be what it is in Nashville, as everyone knows, and it is equally well-known that its temple is the Grand Ole Opry House, a Nashville landmark of considerable historic and esthetic interest. The building was constructed originally as the Union Gospel Tabernacle in 1892, at a cost of $100,000 contributed by the public and Captain Thomas Green Ryman after his conversion by the Reverend Sam Jones during a persuasive sermon on "mother" or "liquor"; it's not certain which theme did the job.

From 1904, when Captain Ryman died, the building was known as the Ryman Auditorium. During the 1920s and 30s, it was host to every important dance, opera, and theatrical troupe that toured the country. Grand Ole Opry was established in 1925, and after a series of radio studios and smaller theater homes, moved into the Ryman in 1941. The rest, as they say, is history.

Although it was neither an opera house nor a legitimate theater, the

256

Ryman has one of the most star-studded histories of the performing arts in the United States. As architecture, it is a vernacular version of the Ruskinian Gothic—a style with a high casualty rate because its fashionableness in the nineteenth century is matched only by its unfashionableness now, except with the experts. Taste turns, usually, after an entire era has been destroyed. The building is a unique combination of popular architectural and cultural history. Enough so, in fact, to be listed on the National Register of Historic Places.

Well—and this won't surprise anyone—the Ryman Auditorium is expendable. In one of those glorious cultural confusions of past and present in which only the phony is real, there is a *new* Grand Ole Opry House. It has been constructed in a $26-million amusement, or "theme," park called Opryland ten miles from Nashville, owned and operated by the National Life and Accident Insurance Company, which includes among its corporate enterprises the Grand Old Opry. The new Grand Ole Opry House is a modern, $15-million extravaganza containing the country's biggest TV and radio facilities, as befits a multimillion-dollar industry based on simple little country tunes.

National Life was originally politely, but adamantly against saving the Grand Ole Opry House. This move can probably be attributed to a mixture of architectural ignorance and business astuteness. In response to considerable protest, the execution is now postponed "indefinitely," and the building stands empty. Opryland puts it all together now in one profitable commercial and tourist package. "When these good people come to Opryland and later a National Life agent calls," the company's head man, William C. Weaver, has been quoted in *Business Week* as saying, "they'll have something to talk about. We'll have ways and means of getting people's names and addresses at Opryland. I think it will be a right interesting tie-in."

A good number of people, including the National Trust for Historic Preservation, want to see the Ryman preserved. As usual, the issues are complex. The building is in a deteriorating downtown, and the neighborhood suffers, like many other downtowns, from crime. The house's discomforts are legion and facilities for modern performances are obviously inadequate. Curved wooden pews and a "Confederate Gallery" and an atmosphere that has become a country music tradition and trademark—featured in TV presentations—are no match for superelectronics. The question of the old building's reuse is problematic, and the most compelling kind of commercial economics raises its familiar head.

"We are trying to keep an open mind," Mr. Weaver has said. But

National Life has accepted no opposition reports, and it refers to preservation promotion as "agitation." Impatience, even in reply to such authorities as the dean of architectural historians, Henry-Russell Hitchcock, is thinly masked, and arguments against preservation become increasingly oblique and self-justifying. Protest is called a "media event."

In the name of reasonableness, the company has sponsored studies that have come up with the not surprising news that preservation is "economically unfeasible" due to extraordinary costs for rehabilitating the old building. This is par for the course. There is probably no landmark rehabilitation that was not called economically unfeasible before it was successfully done. And a record number have been done in the time that the Ryman has remained closed.

One study was a report by the late Jo Mielziner, who, whatever his accomplishments in the field of stage and theatrical design, was not the most qualified expert on old building renovation and reuse, to put it mildly. Mr. Mielziner concluded, comparing apples and oranges in an interesting range of non sequiturs, that because the old tabernacle served drama in a makeshift way and its design and construction are provincial rather than sophisticated, it does not deserve to be saved. The sources he quoted, such as *Antiques* magazine, refuted his inferences.

The experienced architects to call on for proper evaluation, such as Giorgio Cavaglieri, who redid the New York Shakespeare Festival Public Theater from the old Astor Library, the firm of Hardy, Holzman, Pfeiffer, the authors of a National Endowment study on the reuse of old railroad stations, Roger Webb of Architectural Heritage, or Anderson Notter of Boston, who did over the old Boston City Hall, or Hugh Newell Jacobsen, who converted the Old Corcoran to the new Renwick Gallery in Washington, have not seen a sign of a beckoning finger. Beyond saying that it will welcome any solution, National Life shows no indication of actually seeking one.

The company says that it is not concerned about competition if the Ryman continues to function. Even with its discomforts and inadequacies, it would probably continue in demand. National Life is modest about Opryland's profitability, but it is a successful national tourist attraction, and it seems odd that there should be such concern, if competition is not the question, about the costs of keeping the Ryman operable. In actual fact, the company has preferred to contribute substantial funds to a new performing arts center rather than to assist the survival of a local cultural heritage. It could probably keep and subsidize the old building if it were interested in community service and public image. It might even benefit from both.

Destroying the Ryman is more than demolishing a touchstone of Nashville's past. Pulling out means abandonment of a neighborhood that needs help, and speeding the death of downtown. That's fine for the kind of redevelopers who wait like vultures to produce sterile new urban pap. But good urban design practice would have suggested long ago that the area should have been renewed in terms of historic rehabilitation and that a most important key was the Ryman and its related economic uses. There is more than one way to kill a neighborhood.

The final indignity is National Life's well-publicized plan to use the bricks and some of the artifacts of the bulldozed Ryman to build—I kid you not—"The Little Church of Opryland" in the new amusement park. That probably takes first prize for the pious misuse of a landmark and the total misunderstanding of the principles of preservation. This travesty has convinced a lot of people that demolition is an O.K. thing. Among them are Billy Graham and Tennessee Ernie Ford, who is reputed to be waiting to sing the first hymn. Well, as I said, in today's world, only the phony is real. Isn't anyone on the side of the angels?

May 13, 1973, revised March 1976

OF LANDMARKS AND LITTER, OR THE GAMES GNOMES PLAY

The gnomes are busy in and around New York, destroying landmarks and generally lousing up the urban landscape. Gnomes, in the modern definition, are creatures specializing in acts of perverse illogic or malevolent nonsense that result in situations of consummate absurdity in which the rest of us are trapped. They are particularly active in official circles. Gnomes, for example, had the dandy idea a few years

ago of widening Fifth Avenue by cutting back the park side in order
to speed traffic; when the outcry started they crawled right back under
their manhole covers. Really professional gnomes would have gotten
the job done when no one was looking; they usually deal in the sneaky
fait accompli.

Gnomes are responsible for removing all those nice old blue and
white enamel street signs that carried both street and avenue identification on each side, replacing them at random with ugly yellow signs
that read on one side only and look as if they had been lettered by,
well, gnomes. It is part of their technique to see that an unpredictable
and aggravating number of street corners remain totally anonymous.

Halloween week was trick or treat on the Governor Thomas E.
Dewey Thruway. Assemblyman John A. Esposito complained to the
Thruway Authority that the Hot Shoppes kept their curtains drawn,
encouraging a "funeral parlor atmosphere" and blocking out the fall
foliage. Gnomes always draw curtains where there are views. That is
one of the first laws of gnomery. The Thruway Authority then ordered
the restaurants to open the curtains so the customers could enjoy the
autumn leaves with their snacks. Rest assured, the curtains will be
pulled shut again.

I have always known that gnomes design all thruway restaurants
anyway; no one else would be clever enough to select just those fixtures, fabrics, and colors that are such a perfect combination of the
dreary and the ordinary that everything is reduced unerringly to the
same hokey-deadly bargain-basement decor. Real people couldn't
possibly be responsible. There will never be any escape from the
standard vista of mechanical folds of horrid cloth, whatever cerulean
sky or autumnal hills may glow beyond. And, of course, there are
gnomes in some central commissary creating food to match.

Back in midtown Manhattan, a mural appeared on the naked walls
next to the spot where the Franklin Savings Bank razed a good old
building at Eighth Avenue and 42nd Street. It appears to be a Mural
with a Message. I don't know what the message is, but this mural
clearly has one or it couldn't be quite so belligerently unpleasant. In
the general messiness of the area, it is not clear whether the Bar-B-Q
and Parking signs are part of it. But to give credit for obvious good
intentions—it is the work of some fine people called the City Arts
Workshop—it is undoubtedly meant to heal the demolition wound.

What it replaces, sort of, is a building of notable—I'm afraid I must
say considerably more notable—artistic quality. What bit the blacktop
was a superior classical Beaux Arts structure with museum-worthy
sculptured bronze doors and solid detail and trim. The parking lot

where it stood is a dubious urban and esthetic achievement that gives the bank a less-than-civic-spirited image and a tax break. Meanwhile, at the Museum of Modern Art, there was a big exhibition of Beaux Arts buildings. There was also an Architectural League guide to the city's Beaux Arts landmarks, but it did not list Beaux Arts blacktops. I don't say the gnomes worked out this scenario consciously, although there are gnomes making tax laws and sitting on bank boards and the destructive nonsense involved is disheartening. But as a gesture to art and the city, the irony of this mural is profound.

And then there is the matter of the city's litter baskets, those 500-pound concrete bombs (esthetically and functionally) that were supposed to advance street cleanliness and curb vandalism while carrying a rainbow of profitable advertising on their sides. At last and final count—they are being phased out, although one wonders, with manpower cuts, who will be left to carry them away—the city had collected $835. And the streets have collected 2,200 of these blockbusters in assorted stages of visual pollution. The holes for trash were too small, the tops rusted while the bases became stained and discolored, the trash piled up and overflowed, and the ads failed to materialize. It was a devilishly ingenious, pre-tested debacle.

Taxitop ads are supposed to be another bonanza. Inevitably, the assault on the environment becomes a reality, but the bonanza doesn't. What we have now is taxis with pointy heads. New York's basket-case cabs, notable for their advanced condition of unsanitary decay, have been topped by Rube Goldberg. It must have been hard to find an act to follow those hand-cobbled interior partitions behind which New Yorkers crouch on broken seats in coffinlike gloom. They are surely produced by Dr. Caligari or the cottage industries of some early Triassic culture—or gnomes.

At Rockefeller Center, a lease on a nineteenth-century building with an old bar has not been renewed so that a lease could be given to someone else who will reconstruct it to turn the real nineteenth-century building and the real old bar into a phony nineteenth-century building and a phony old bar. This is happening at Hurley's, a landmark watering place of honest mien and little pretension, where a no-frills bar has existed continuously since the construction of the building around 1870. It even held out successfully as Rockefeller Center was built around it. The new lessee is going to turn it into a "real old-fashioned nineteenth-century tavern" with gas lamps and gismos and instant ersatz nostalgia. Absurdity is destiny in New York.

November 16, 1975

Dilemmas

AN EXERCISE IN CULTURAL SHOCK

A funny thing happened on the way to the new Custom House at the World Trade Center in New York. Public architecture declined and fell. The new Custom House is a seven-story glass and aluminum structure flanking the Trade Center's North Tower, part of the complex designed by Minoru Yamasaki and Associates and Emery Roth and Sons. These offices, a vast functional improvement over the old ones at Bowling Green, consist of efficient, standardized accommodations with eight-foot ceilings and all the latest mechanical comforts and conveniences. They are also a paradigm of modern commercial and institutional blandness.

Sixty-six years ago at Bowling Green, the Customs Service moved into its brand new Custom House designed by Cass Gilbert. The now-abandoned 1907 Beaux Arts structure is a fruitcake of Maine granite, a potpourri of marbles, a congeries of statuary. Comparison of the two buildings staggers the sensibilities. It is an exercise in cultural shock.

The new building, like the whole Trade Center group including the giant twin towers, is an exercise in design by reduction. This is partly the fault of the times, when soaring construction costs have led to cheapness by choice and necessity, and partly because of current building systems, which substitute the technology of the neutral grid for solid, stylish stonework.

But it is more the fault of the architect, who has trivialized the inherent drama of modern engineering, and nullified the legitimate and powerful esthetic that is its true effect. He has succeeded in making some of the biggest buildings in the world ordinary and inconsequential.

The old building is richly embellished with references to the sea. Its stone and wood carvings, bronze grills, and plaster trim flaunt dolphins, seashells, ships' prows, rudders, masts, and waves. What is not nautical is classical. Forty giant columns girdle the building's substantial and ornate stone mass.

There are masks of Mercury and the keystones of the elaborately framed windows are carved heads of the races of mankind. Tennessee marble figures in the attic represent the ancient and modern seafaring powers. Four heroic statues of the continents by Daniel Chester French flank the front.

None of this splendor could be moved to the new building's functional, featureless grid, or to the stock spaces inside. The Customs Service could not take along the huge, hanging bronze lanterns of the soaring grand hall with its rose, green, and cream marbles, nor could the service remove the Reginald Marsh murals from the vast, gloomy Rotunda that depict the stages of arrival of a ship in port, painted as a Public Works project 30 years after the building was completed. (Marsh received something like $90 a month for the job.)

But some things have been moved, among these a few of the 1907 and earlier Custom House furnishings. Before Bowling Green, the Service occupied the even more distinguished Greek Revival Merchants' Exchange by Isaiah Rogers on Wall Street. In 1906 Montgomery Schuyler, the great architecture critic, temporized about the new building because he liked the old one better. But he called the new one a valuable civic possession and a work of distinction.

What went along to the Trade Center are massive classical bookcases from the Merchants' Exchange, chairs from the original United States Appraiser's office that preceded the Customs Court, portraits of 16 former collectors including Chester A. Arthur and Theodore Roosevelt, miscellaneous tables and sofas and some wall sconces.

Their former setting was the office of Fred R. Boyett, Regional Commissioner, with barrel-vault ceiling, fluted pilasters, and mahogany doors. Their present setting is a "ceremonial" room in the new building, but the 8-foot 2-inch ceiling—a whole two inches higher than the office ceilings—will not hold the crystal chandelier that hangs close to that length at the center of the old room; it would touch the floor.

Mr. Boyett's old office was part of a main-floor suite designed for

A few things you can't take with you . . .
The New York Times/ Barton Silverman

the Secretary of State. It includes a coffered and gilded ceiling with shell and ribbon motifs, a carved wooden screen and walls and an unused, monumental stone fireplace. The new building has photolabs, projection and screening rooms, and a pistol range.

"Our people will be more comfortable," Mr. Boyett says. "We needed room for training programs and employee cafeterias and lounges that we don't have now. The Customs operation has grown and changed radically."

"But if I'd had my say 10 years ago," Mr. Boyett adds, "we'd have used the $36-million we're putting into the new building to remodel the old one to make it the show Custom House of the world."

The cost in 1907 was $5,130,000 for the building and $2½-million for the land. It stands where the original Fort Amsterdam was built, probably the most historic spot in Lower Manhattan.

Not long ago it would have been looked on only as one of the city's most valuable pieces of real estate and its scraps and shards would have been carted off to Secaucus like Penn Station in favor of a profitable, die-stamped tower. Today there is a general concern for preservation. It is an officially designated New York landmark, and a listed building on the National Register.

There are serious legal and financial problems ahead. But the sponsors point out that other cities have already shown the way. Customs may have entered the age of jet transport and the functional esthetic, but you just can't get those dolphins, masts, rudders, sails, winged wheels, and cosmic connotations of commercial glory any more.

October 4, 1973

CAN ANYONE USE A NICE ANGLO-ITALIANATE SYMBOL OF GRAFT?

The demolition of New York's notorious Tweed Courthouse, behind City Hall, never announced publicly, was an early priority of the Beame administration. It has not yet taken place because of the city's financial crisis. There is no money for anything, good or bad. But the decision was simply the ultimate extension of the conventional wisdom that the building is nothing but a shoddy piece of graft.

In recent years, there have been notable changes in attitude. There are scholars in the fields of art, history, and culture who see the Tweed Courthouse, with the blinders of distaste removed, both as a legitimate New York landmark on every level from architectural to political history, and as a handsome period building as well. It is, they point out, an outstanding example of the nineteenth-century Anglo-Italian style, extremely rare in New York—a genre introduced by Barry's Reform Club in London. Its basic esthetic is unaffected by Tweed's celebrated gravy train.

Traditionally, guides and commentaries have vied in its denunciation. Built as the County Courthouse in 1861–72, and used later as the City Court, its "Corinthian architecture of Massachusetts white marble" is described in King's Guide of 1893 as a "basis of the $10-million peculations of Tweed and his associates." The later WPA Guide ups the peculations to $12 million and calls it "one of the gigantic steals in the city's history."

All true. And the remarkable thing is that it is still a substantial and stylish building, its impressive interiors defaced with layers of mud-colored municipal paint. Its marble, carved wood, massive construction, and profligate space could not be bought today for any rational figure. Sic transit the building art. Old Tweed would have the last laugh, in perfect, and appropriately cynical, New York style.

In spite of its obvious qualifications, the Courthouse is not a designated landmark. It has been so universally repudiated for its unsavory associations that it is probably too hot a political potato for the Landmarks Commission to handle.

Ironically, public building recycling no longer represents some fantasy of the future; these reused structures are the resounding preservation successes of the present.

There are the examples of the Old Boston City Hall; historic Federal Building transfers across the country; the Old State, War and Navy Building, now the Executive Office Building, and the Old Court of Claims, now the Renwick Gallery, in Washington; and the Public Theater in the Old Astor Library and the Public Library in the Jefferson Market Courthouse, in New York—just to scratch the national list. They were all scheduled to be demolished. And they all surpass any possible replacements in style and character, with no loss in serviceability.

It was therefore suggested to the administration that the Tweed

If corruption is the measure, heaven help some Roman arches and
Renaissance palazzi. *Garth Huxtable*

Courthouse should not be torn down without a feasibility study of the
possibilities of remodeling it for the Executive Office Annex. And so,
former Deputy Mayor Cavanagh, a kind, agreeable, and reasonable
man, whose face crumples in sad disbelief when the Courthouse is
praised (he displays a letter stigmatizing it as a symbol of corruption
on which grounds heaven help a few Roman arches and Renaissance
palazzi) ordered the study.

It was made for the Task Force by the Municipal Services Administration and to nobody's surprise it called for demolition. It called for it
"in any event." In any event apparently meant in spite of the fact that
the study found that it would be cheaper to restore and remodel the
old building than to construct a new one (with a few caveats about
reduced life span and maintenance costs) and that the space available
would reasonably equal the space required. Former Parks Administrator Edwin Weisl Jr., was the lone Task Force dissenter.

It is a report (unreleased, but relentlessly bootlegged) remarkable
for its lack of preservation expertise, total absence of design visualiza-
tion, and failure to acknowledge any qualities except those of the
most pragmatic structural immediacy. It really goes back to square one.

That old chestnut "waste space" keeps rearing its head, with the triumphant observation that a new building could have the same square footage and be one-third the size of the old one. The esthetic rationale is that anything on that site should be smaller than City Hall —an argument with no validity at all, since everything turns on relationships, not measurements. The same goes for that other old chestnut, "matching style."

Two out-of-town experts have already come, been cordially received, and delivered unwanted advice. Roger Webb, of Architectural Heritage, Inc., which turned the similar Old Boston City Hall into prime new offices, found the conversion both practical and reasonable. Hugh Newell Jacobsen, restorer of the Renwick, said he would stake his reputation on the building's soundness and the desirability of remodeling and reuse, meeting all building code and operational requirements.

But the specter that keeps rising is not Boss Tweed; it is the "colonial revival" replacement the administration wants and the esthetic and urban damage it will do to City Hall.* Honest graft is to be preferred to pseudo-historical hypocrisy. Next to that Early Howard Johnson vision, the Tweed Courthouse looks like a rose.

July 7, 1974

KICKING A LANDMARK

A way has been found to save New York's landmark Villard Houses on Madison Avenue, behind St. Patrick's Cathedral, but the solution is dreadful. That could also be known as the New York paradox: anything worth doing is worth doing wrong.

There is the further paradox that everyone involved seems to want to do what is right. The owner of the beautiful McKim, Mead and White brownstone palazzo of the 1880s is the Archdiocese of New York. Since the Archdiocese ceased to use the major part of the building and Random House moved out of the north wing—the U-shaped

---

* Even near-bankruptcy confers some blessings; at the moment the project is dead.

Renaissance palace is actually a group of town houses around a court —most of the building has been empty. The Archdiocese is maintaining the structures, which were designated as a landmark in 1968, at considerable expense and sacrifice. Because this must surely be ranked as one of the most elegant and tempting parcels of prime midtown Manhattan real estate, the Church's dilemma is obvious.

The developer, Harry Helmsley, wants to build a new, 52-story hotel and office building behind the Villard Houses, utilizing the full development potential of the zoning of both the tower and the landmark sites. In fact, it appears that he will ask for still more size from the Board of Standards and Appeals. The Archdiocese has executed a lease on all of this property with Mr. Helmsley, as the Palace Hotel Inc., and the lease contains a number of safeguards for the treatment of the landmark buildings. But the actual design of the new building and the use and treatment of the old ones are Mr. Helmsley's baby.

The architect, Richard Roth, Jr., of Emery Roth and Sons, has worked hard to keep the landmark and give the developer what he wants. What he wants is very clearly a standard, money-making commercial formula that works—nothing risky or offbeat. It isn't so much that creative or imaginative or sensitive design is being minimized or downgraded; it is simply that this sort of design is totally outlawed by the formula from the start. Mr. Helmsley apparently also wants a close resemblance to his Park Lane Hotel on Central Park South, one of those (formula) travertine-clad, arcade-topped, easy exercises in spurious elegance.

The landmarks law requires the Landmarks Preservation Commission's approval for any alteration of a designated exterior. The alterations being requested are the demolition of the last 25 feet of a 1909 extension, including a small porch and tower and changes in the roofline in that area. Although there will be serious changes in parts of the interior—the rooms of the central section, which includes the handsome Gold Room, will be gutted for a hotel entrance—the Commission has no control over this part of the plan because the interiors have never been designated. The interiors of the wings, one of which is particularly fine, would remain intact.

The plan is to "connect" the soaring hotel-office tower to the Villard Houses through the central section so that pedestrians could enter the hotel through the existing Madison Avenue court and arcade. A new hotel lobby directly behind that entrance would take the place of the demolished interiors. The Villard front would thus become a false front, because the rest of the central section would simply have a wall put behind it, making it a kind of stage-drop for the hotel. (Fire requirements make this necessary says the architect, but others dispute it.) The wings, untouched but also unutilized, are to be rented out for whatever suitable tenants or purposes present themselves.

The ultimate paradox is that there is absolutely no attempt or pretense or inclination to use the potential of the beautifully crafted and detailed landmark structure in any way. It is a death-dealing rather than life-giving "solution." The superb Belle Epoque interiors—virtually all that are left in New York of the Vanderbilt-Astor era—are written off as so many square feet of "hard to use" space. The "solution" is total rejection. If the architect and developer had set out to kick the landmark in the pants, they could not have done a better job. (In fairness to the architect, his office is supposedly replete with earlier schemes that studied reuse, but evidently period salons are considered incompatible with commercial hotel functions.)

The net result is that the landmark is left standing, subject to finding tenants to use it. This is exactly the same problem that exists now, without the disfigurements of the new construction. Moreover, the threat still remains that if no tenants materialize and the building continues to be a financial burden to owner and lessee, application for demolition can be made under the landmarks law. In spite of the economic benefits that would accrue to owner and developer in this dubious scheme, the Villard Houses aren't home safe yet.

It is particularly hard to accept that continued hazard when the proposed design is so patently insensitive. The travertine-striped tower, with its cliché arches, is hokily pretentious. A Certificate of Appropriateness for this proposal would be a travesty.

Has everyone forgotten the lessons of the Racquet and Tennis Club (also McKim, Mead and White) and Lever House and the Seagram Building on Park Avenue? The modern, Miesian esthetic can be handled with basic elegance, to the benefit of both kinds of classicism. New York has a right to a design of skill and sophistication as well as appropriateness; these are the qualities of the city's style.

Add the further paradox of the promise of the interior designer to furnish "in the spirit of" the rejected, original interiors, and travesty becomes a bad joke. These interiors are mint examples of the genuine grandeur that today's hotels imitate so tackily in a pastiche of token vulgarities. It takes no effort to conjure up a vision of the depressing ersatz version that will be substituted for the real thing. It is another "successful" formula.

The reasoning behind this debacle is not mysterious. It is the reasoning of the investment mind, of which Mr. Helmsley has one of the best in the business. The investment mind does things in the guaranteed no-risk investment way. It deals exclusively in how to produce the stock commercial product, no matter what peripheral interferences may intrude. A landmark is an interference. This approach does not accept unconventional challenges, even when they would deliver dividends in beauty and ambience. This could be an internationally notable hotel of cosmopolitan grace rather than a model stamped out by computer. All the ingenuity expended has been devoted to avoiding capitalizing on the landmark or sullying the formula in any way.

Ordinarily, the Landmarks Commission could engage in a little design negotiation for improvement. But the lawyer for the Archdiocese politely reminded the Commissioners at a public hearing that if they didn't like the proposal, the Archdiocese might just begin to think about the Lutheran Church decision, which permits a non-profit institution to demolish a landmark.

The question might be asked whether an outstandingly successful investor might not, just once, think in terms of the extraordinary instead of the ordinary. It is, after all, Mr. Helmsley's city, too.

January 5, 1975

. . . WITH THE OTHER FOOT

When the first version of the Villard Houses–hotel project appeared, the Landmarks Commission sent it back to the developer for revisions. Although the interiors had never been designated, the Commission also made the suggestion among others that a way be found to save the Gold Room.

The threatened Gold Room is part of the south wing, which was remodeled by McKim, Mead and White for Whitelaw Reid in the 1890s. Brendan Gill, who is engaged in a study of Stanford White, calls this "the richest and handsomest set of rooms then in existence in New York and perhaps in the entire country." Nobody except Mr. Helmsley and Mr. Roth seems to feel that the Gold Room is expendable. The double-height, barrel-vaulted, balconied room with its La Farge murals, sculptured wall detail, and generous gold leaf is unequivocably magnificent; it is also the last of its kind in New York. It is easy to visualize the kind of impoverished design that will replace it. The decorating clichés of the modern American hotel are vacuous, pretentious, and immutable.

In fact, it is hard to figure out what anyone did in the four months between the first and second versions submitted to the Landmarks Commission. The later proposal had a new and less offensive tower, but it was far worse along the side streets, with corny, overscaled arches in fake brownstone to "match" the Renaissance Villard facades, and the Gold Room was still scheduled for demolition. By any measure except computerized investment design, the results were a wretched failure.

The New York Chapter of the American Institute of Architects, after a visit to the Roth office for a full presentation, wrote a letter of protest to the Landmarks Commission. The chapter's representatives were struck by the lack of evidence that the problem of the Gold Room had been studied with anything approaching interest or adequacy. Repeated inquiries to both the architect and the developer's representative brought the curious response that, because the Villard Houses and the hotel plan have different floor levels, no way can be found to incorporate any of the historic interiors.

Any architect worth his salt knows that this is not an insoluble problem unless someone wants it to be insoluble. Nor does the matter of protecting the old while building the new provide insurmountable costs or engineering considerations. After examining plans and elevations, the AIA suggested solutions. "How often," the architects asked, "can a new structure so easily annex so distinguished a space?"

The impression that remains is that the hotel "experts" find it easier to stick relentlessly with stock solutions than to make the different levels work within their economic game plan. There is a brand of hotel gnomes, turned out by hotel schools, supplied with a stock of cheap clichés that is currently defacing the country, and the world. The fact that the hotel might gain immeasurably in beauty, quality, and individuality, and that this could ultimately be an economic asset, is apparently beyond the comprehension or concern of anyone involved.

It might be noted in passing that the Plaza found weddings so lucrative it hired a specialist to promote them, and the Gold Room and south wing could make a superb wedding suite. As for business and style, when the Plaza returned its conventionally junked-up Green Tulip restaurant to something resembling its original Edwardian Room authenticity, business shot up.

A proposal worked out by the New York Landmarks Conservancy

How often can a new structure so easily annex so distinguished a space? *Nathaniel Lieberman*

with the architect to make the Gold Room a bar was disapproved by Mr. Helmsley. The objection quoted was that you can walk down into a bar, but not up going out of it. No one has succeeded in eliciting a better answer. At least one observer of this exercise in Marx Brothers logic has offered an escalator.

In sum, what is being given to New York in return for a hugely profitable investment package is a particularly slick bit of real estate sleight-of-hand. It is fool-the-eye preservation. The owner of the Villard Houses, the Archbishopric of New York, and the developer could, of course, simply tear the buildings down, due to deficiencies in the landmarks law, and that is their not-so-concealed trump card. But they know that this would be an extremely unpopular act that would make public villains of them both. Nor does the church deserve this, after years of conscientious, costly care of a landmark that has become a financial burden.

But this way of "keeping" the landmark, which involves some physical destruction as well as the destruction of its integrity, and no real investment in its continued life, is a spurious tradeoff. The city is being conned. For the Villard Houses are more than immensely superior architecture. Located in the city's functional and fashionable heart, they are pivotal to New York's quality and style.

One comes reluctantly to some inevitable conclusions. The architect, whatever his restrictions, has done an appallingly bad job. The developer, whatever his intentions, is inflexibly wedded to standards that he evidently will not relinquish or modify for values that he fails to perceive. He will not, in short, invest money or creativity in a superior solution. No calculations are being made in terms of image, quality, and civic pride—which can also be a profitable formula. It is, alas, a state of mind. And it determines the state of the city, as well.

June 22, 1975

A HOPEFUL TOAST

The latest chapter of the Villard Houses saga—which seemed so hopeless a cause to so many—is something to delight the believers and confound the cynics. In the curious way of New York, which wheels, deals, and compromises while managing to sustain some extraordinary standards in the face of impossible odds, a solution is being found.

After going back to the drawing board twice, against steady, mounting public pressure, the developer, Harry Helmsley, the architect, Richard Roth, and the owner, the Archbishopric of New York, working cooperatively with the Landmarks Conservancy, a private group, the Landmarks Preservation Commission, a municipal agency, the American Institute of Architects and other professional organizations, as well as the local community board, wrought wonders. They huffed and they puffed and came up with substantial improvements in interior and exterior plans. To Mr. Helmsley, for these extra efforts, we raise a glass. (Considering that the 1886 Villard Houses are mint Age of Elegance McKim, Mead and White, it has to be vintage champagne.)

It has now been found that it is possible to keep and use the Gold Room as one of the hotel's public spaces. The Library of this wing will also be incorporated. Currently, talks are continuing to see if some of the better north wing interiors can be converted to shops, rather than gutting them, as planned, to make new stores.

On the exterior of the new hotel-office tower, which will also contain apartments, the earlier cheesy design gimmicks have been dropped for a more suitable and straightforward approach. The project has gained considerably in distinction and merit, all of which can only accrue to the builder's advantage. There are possible tenants for the remaining, unused Villard interiors that the project abandoned—a still inexplicable waste of a unique resource of quality and style. But that peculiar oversight can be lived with; these rooms will stay intact, and their desirability and rental prospects will increase with the new construction.

The problem that is still to be solved is the disturbing one of the variance needed to build the tower. The developer is asking for an increase in bulk based on arithmetic that some question, a matter that usually goes before the Board of Standards and Appeals. In this case, however, the impact is so much greater and the issues so much broader than a narrow interpretation of the zoning rules would allow, and the "tradeoff" for the city involves so many critical and delicately balanced elements, from the economic boost of the new construction to appropriate preservation devices and surrounding traffic patterns, that the Archbishopric has elected to take the appeal to the city Planning Commission instead. Jurisdictionally and philosophically, this seems like the right thing to do.

In any case, it will be up to the city to decide what is proper and acceptable, probably, again, through negotiation. There is now the promise of a solution that all can abide by, that will keep the Villard Houses from demolition and in the mainstream of New York life. And that's not bad—for New York or anywhere.

The scenario relies less on heroes and villains than on increasing awareness of urban quality, a tough, sophisticated faith, and sustained cooperative effort. In the end, all of the participants are the good guys. Who can ask for anything more?

September 21, 1975

The Near Past

Immortality is conferred in devious and unexpected ways. If you're an architect, there's always hope. The latest switch in architectural immortality has come with the remake of King Kong. The producers have been running a full-page ad announcing that their first full-page ad was so popular—with 25,000 requests for full-color reprints—that they are working around the clock to fill orders. The ad shows King Kong breaking up airplanes with his right hand and clutching whoever plays Fay Wray in his left hand, standing astride—and this is the point —not the Empire State Building, as in the original film, but the World Trade Center towers.

While this may provide less of a nostalgic kick, it is vastly elevated high camp. And it also gives King Kong an infinitely superior footing. Instead of perilously grabbing the famous Art Deco spire, he has each leg planted firmly on one of the two new flattop towers.

The Empire State Building, of course, is a star in its own right, with an enduring romantic charisma. Somehow it implies every cherished legend of New York glamour, from the glittering speakeasy era to the suave luxe of the seventies. It is genuinely immortal. By contrast, and as a symbol of the city, the World Trade Center towers are consummately uninspiring. (They still sell more Empire State Buildings in the five and ten.) And whether the producers of the film are aware of it or not, the change they have made is fraught with cultural and esthetic implications.

278

Today's tall buildings are not stars. They are impersonally impressive at best, giant nonentities at worst. Another movie, *The Towering Inferno*, for example, was not about a building you could recognize or cherish. This was simply a large object to which catastrophe happened.

I could offer an intellectually seductive explanation of the change, with dithyrambs about the anti-hero and the anti-symbol and how our vision of men and monuments has been altered. This is a populist age in the arts, led, of course, by the elite, and we are tearing down symbols (symbolically) and elevating the ordinary with determined reversals of good and bad and beautiful and ugly. It is a vision that can be hopelessly counterproductive, or it can provide some rich dividends in much more complex and sophisticated ways of seeing life and the world. Anti-art is true to our times.

But the real reason for the change in the tall building is far more down to earth. It is just as rooted in culture and history, but it is less an act of philosophy than an expression of profitable pragmatism. It is a truism that today's tall building is strictly the product of economic calculations, tempered by codes and the law. Those boxy flattops that have replaced slender spires to jar the skyline and the viewer (architects and city fathers would be surprised at the amount of public concern over a city's skyline) represent the best buy in structural space.

Corporate growth and computerizing are also prime contributing factors. Today's huge corporations require huge floor areas in stacks; no builder is going to offer them a tapered tower. And no one could care less about a skyscraper version of the Mausoleum at Halicarnassus—a favorite conceit of the 1920s. Status is conferred by sheer size and the comparative quality and solidity of materials and fittings. The business of America may be business, as Coolidge said, but it has also become its art.

This phenomenon has been reinforced uncannily by the modernist architectural esthetic. The twentieth-century architectural revolution claimed the higher beauty of utility over ornament; it endorsed the look of the machine product as an artistic end. It enshrined the functional esthetic. But it is an awfully short and dangerous step from the kind of expert and delicate adjustments that turn utility into art, and from the recognition of those adjustments to the most ordinary solution, or the least design for the money.

This deterioration is sanctioned, in a sense, by the modernist "less is more" philosophy. At its finest, less *is* more, and the finest is limited to a few men, such as Mies van der Rohe. Mies's work is magnificent, with a stripped, subtle, hard-edged and demanding beauty that is going to symbolize the twentieth century for the rest of time. It is also poorly understood and badly knocked off. Even so, the glass box vernacular that grew out of his style is some of the best "background" architecture in history.

But this is an arcane and specialized esthetic—it was undoubtedly easier for the Popes to buy the overt grandeur of Borromini. Business clients rarely understand or want it. They are pursuing sleek space-profit formulas and effective technological solutions that no longer aspire to the kind of moving artistic greatness in the timeless and spiritual sense that architecture, and particularly the big building, has always held a primary concern. (Try standing in front of a Hawksmoor building in London without this visceral hit.) Objectively, the skyscraper's immense, efficient, and impersonal blandness is a perfectly accurate picture of much of the architectural art of our age.

So dull, so prosaic, in fact, are most of today's ambitious big buildings that New Yorkers now value, for their quite accidental esthetics, the staggered shapes of the setback buildings required by law until the early 1960s. The zoning code was changed then to encourage straight-sided towers, something architects had pushed for in the name of both architectural and civic art. Now the "wedding cakes" add the interest of eccentric form, at least, to the speculative norm. Their outlines also define a style and a time and a place, a combination of which art and culture are made.

This ambivalent view of today's construction art is not written in rage or resignation; it is not a cry for impossible change. The needs and responses of big building design today, if not immutable, are certainly justifiable in realistic terms. History is not a process to be short-circuited by dissenters. And there will never be any more great buildings than there are great architects.

Art, however, remains a life instinct from Lascaux to Ronchamps, and it is always going to produce civilization's touchstones. The skyscraper is the miracle and monument of the twentieth century. Its progress, curiously, has linked development and decline. Watching the emergence of the tall building in New York in 1913, the critic Montgomery Schuyler could still write that "hardly any American owner is quite so boeotian as not to show 'a decent respect for the opinion of mankind' in the appearance of his skyscrapers. . . . It is a public malefaction to protrude a shapeless bulk 'above the purple crowd of humbler roofs.' "

Montgomery Schuyler, where are you now?

February 1, 1976

REDISCOVERING CHICAGO ARCHITECTURE

An exhibition called "Chicago Architects" (Cooper Union, 1976) is full of uncelebrated, quirky, sometimes dramatic, and generally unknown buildings. There is only one example of a famous Chicago School "skyscraper"—D. H. Burnham and Co.'s curtain-walled Reliance Building designed by Charles Atwood in 1894–95—and it is paired with the same architect's totally traditional Beaux Arts Hall of Fine Arts for the Columbian Exposition of 1893. Modern critics have lauded the former and ignored the latter.

This is, in fact, the point of the show. The two pictures are a deliberately loaded juxtaposition. The catalogue states immediately that "the organizers of this exhibit of Chicago architecture wish to pay tribute to all those architects who were passed over by the first generation of historians of modern architecture." And the subject matter consists of the work "left out" of orthodox accounts of the Chicago School and its role in the modern movement.

What we are dealing with, then, is revisionist history. As such, the show is both an iconographic feast and an exercise in provocative scholarship. And it is important at a time when serious revisionism is on the rise in assessments of the modern movement and official theory and history are being attacked on all sides.

The aim of the sponsoring Chicago architects—Laurence Booth, Stuart E. Cohen, Stanley Tigerman, and Benjamin Weese—reinforced by Stuart Cohen's knowledgeable catalogue, is to explode and expand the doctrinaire view of the Chicago contribution. That view, canonized by Sigfried Giedion, divides Chicago architecture into two schizophrenic parts: the small-scale, personal, domestic developments of Frank Lloyd Wright and the Prairie School, and the technological development of the structural frame and the tall building, known as the Chicago skyscraper. The palm of modernism was then supposed to be handed to Europe in the early years of the twentieth century for the International Style, while Chicago languished and waited until the 1930s for Mies van der Rohe to revive its progressive structural tradition.

All that happened, if not exactly as recorded. No one disputes or denies Chicago's skyscraper contribution; the confirmed achievements and monuments of modern architecture are not being rejected or downgraded. But a lot of other things apparently happened as well—

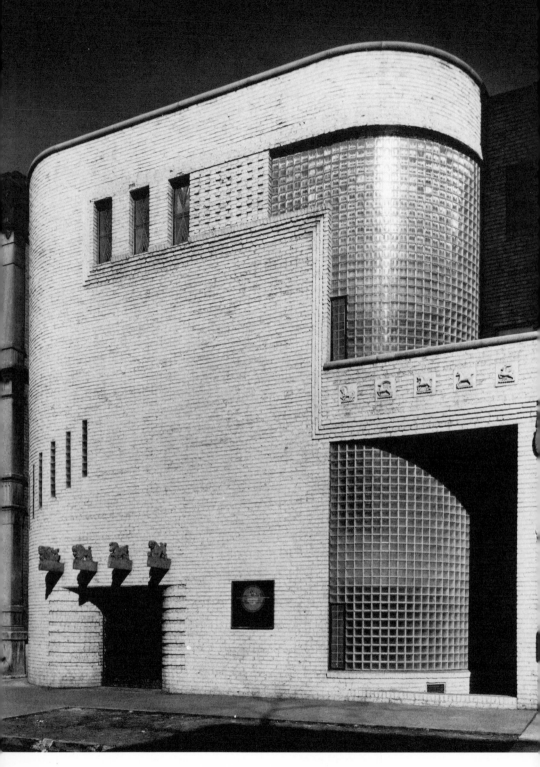

An exercise in provocative scholarship. *Hedrich-Blessing*

particularly in those supposed doldrum years—that have either gone unrecorded or have been consciously suppressed because they did not fit into accepted theories or timetables.

"Chicago Architects" combines rediscovery and reevaluation with irony and a bit of hubris. It is also quite polemical. There is the sound of an axe grinding quietly. But the material contains genuine implications for a broader, more objective understanding of modern architectural history than the hygienically edited standard texts provide of what went on here and abroad. In fact, history and architecture may never be quite the same as this and similar rediscoveries unfold. We are finding a pluralism of ideals and styles that makes twentieth-century architecture far more intricate and dramatic than doctrinaire modernism has allowed, as well as perceiving an American contribution and continuity that may prove to be increasingly significant.

"Chicago Architects" was organized as a response to a larger show of more traditional skyscraper-engineering emphasis, "One Hundred Years of Chicago Architecture," at the Chicago Institute of Contemporary Art. Most of the work in this "countershow" does not begin from engineering considerations. Mr. Cohen, in his text, characterizes it as romantic rather than pragmatic in approach. The buildings are almost all intimate structures closely related to personal experience—houses, schools, and churches, rather than commercial construction, in a galaxy of styles.

Mr. Cohen also points out that it is quite logical for society to want different styles for its churches, museums, libraries, and civic buildings than the style produced commercially by engineering and economic expediency, no matter how elegant that expression may become. This actual variety is a more accurate reflection of American culture than those isolated examples where a structural rationale has been promoted by modernist doctrine as the only "appropriate" solution.

But even the structural rationale can be romantic. George Fred Keck's remarkable "Crystal House"—all-glass with delicate metal trusses—built for the Chicago World's Fair in 1934 and Buckminster Fuller's original (Chicago-born) Dymaxion House of 1927 were both perfectly capable of being produced. They were simply romantic-technological visions whose time had not come. Immediate offshoots appeared in Bertrand Goldberg's mast-hung gas station and ice cream stand—precursors of Marina City's round-towered, world-of-tomorrow look.

There are clearly traced lines presented here of International Style and Art Deco in Chicago in the 1920s and 1930s, from Keck, Holabird and Root, Paul Schweikher, Barry Byrne, and the Bowman brothers.

WHERE THE PAST MEETS THE FUTURE

(I found many of these in the research files of the Museum of Modern Art in New York in the 1940s and they are probably still there.) There are fascinating aberrations, such as the 1930s work of Andrew Rabori, which suggests both the Russian Constructivism of Constantin Melnikoff and the Parisian chic of Art Moderne. Early Shingle Style–Frank Lloyd Wright houses are selected as forerunners of the angular mannerisms of Harry Weese and Walter Netsch.

Specifically, what is dealt with here is ideology, as much as history. There is an increasingly recognized, profound ideological split between the structural-functional esthetic of the orthodox modernists and the "formal, spatial, and consciously symbolic issues" that preoccupy a considerable group of young architects now. This is fueling a revival of eclecticism, not as conventional, academic borrowing, but as a means of image-making—and all is grist for the mill. This urge for style and symbolism has been minimally addressed by the historians of the modern movement.

That is why this kind of history so intrigues the present generation of practitioners; it is with a special eye that the past is being reexamined and, for better or worse, used in their own work. Today's eclecticism is a creative, cannibalistic combination of erudite nostalgia and extremely sophisticated esthetics. It needs revisionist history to feed on. The results are acutely artful exercises in cultural memory and personal value projection—very arch and intriguing—but these are not simple or innocent times.

Nor is this a simple or innocent show; it contains much to debate. Image-makers are not going to supplant problem-solvers and technology can be as elegant as symbols. Right now, history is being revised as a polemic for style, which is where we came in. But in this case the near-past is being raided rather than discarded. In the process, a great deal is being learned, much of value is being restored to the record, and a sound and necessary input is being gained. The rewriting of history is part of the continuing historical process.

March 14, 1976

THROUGH THE ARTIST'S EYE

It was possible, last year, to see *two* Woolworth Buildings in Lower Manhattan. The original is in its accustomed place on Broadway at the foot of City Hall Park, having survived, since 1913, the praise of the distinguished critic Montgomery Schuyler (who hailed it on completion as a shapely, satisfactory, and eye-filling work of art), the scorn of the modernists (who managed to dismiss its 52 Flemish Gothic stories as a deceitful and ludicrous sham), and an impassioned reappreciation by architects and scholars today.

The second Woolworth Building was part of "Ruckus Manhattan," a wry sculptural re-creation—if that word can serve a marvelous mélange of art, wit, social satire, and succinct architectural observation —of the life and landmarks of Lower Manhattan. The reality and its reinterpretation were within walking distance of each other.

"Ruckus Manhattan" is a 6,400-square-foot exhibition by Red Grooms, created with his wife, Mimi Gross Grooms, and 21 helpers (elves?) called the Ruckus Construction Company. This walk-through show of small-scale buildings and full-scale figures was six months in the making in the unoccupied ground-floor space of I. M. Pei's handsome new skyscraper at Pine and Water Streets, courtesy of Orient Overseas Associates and Creative Time, an arts organization dedicated to bringing the creative process to the public. It was co-sponsored by Marlborough Gallery and supported by grants from the New York State Council on the Arts, the National Endowment for the Arts, and numerous individuals and businesses.

The real Woolworth Building is an unparalleled combination of romantic conceit (would you believe Gothic ogival lambrequins, or choir stall canopies, for cornices?) and soaring structural drama. In 1913, the skyscraper was a relatively new achievement, and the steel-framed tower clad in the exquisitely crafted detail of delicate, creamy-white terra-cotta was, briefly, the tallest building in the world. It is still one of the most beautiful and impressive buildings of modern times. Art is alive and well in the Woolworth Building from the brilliant, vaulted mosaics of the richly decorated lobby to the Gothic fancy of the crown at the top. Myth and magic are once again in good architectural repute.

Schuyler, whose judgment was close to impeccable, called the eclectic design a light and suitable way of expressing the thin-walled, powerful metal skeleton that made such height possible, and he praised the building's exotic verticality as a miraculous and appropriate blend of esthetics and technology. Cass Gilbert's masterpiece still "looms in the gray of dawn or haze of twilight, its white spectrality shining over city and river . . . an ornament to the city and a vindication of our artistic sensibility," as Schuyler wrote 62 years ago.

The Woolworth tower of "Ruckus Manhattan," bends forward jauntily. Held firmly in the protective embrace of a dragon, the building rises with a cheerful and total disregard for gravity and the plumb line. The dragon's rainbow wings rise and fall gently; its mouth opens and shuts with mock menace. Its painted scales are made of nickels and dimes. A doll-size Frank Woolworth gazes out out of his tower, and in one of those loony shifts of scale that are a Grooms trademark, a revolving door allows one to enter a small, womblike model of the lobby. Every distorted detail is perfect.

And the building is alive. It glitters and gleams, spoofs and celebrates; it seems inadequate to call it caricature or satire. To this viewer, it is inspired comment. The entire project is carried out with an eye so skilled and sure that it grasps the most salient features of every structure and turns them into a succinct statement on the human and urban condition.

It was a particular delight to have the real buildings just beyond the exhibition space's glass walls. The twin towers of the World Trade Center rise a blandly undistinguished 110 stories. The Grooms Trade Center towers are 30 feet high and a cockeyed triumph, a lighthearted critique of the skyscraper ego. One shaft narrows in fake perspective with a canvas cloud pinned to its top, and the other widens in reverse perspective, with an easy disrespect for architectural overreaching—a perfect so-what response to their size.

After all the words that I have wasted in print to suggest that the buildings' weak pin-stripe design is an inadequate expression of some of the world's most massive construction (the Woolworth Building, with all of its delicate romanticism, never made that misjudgment of basic architectonic relationships), the Ruckus artists have achieved the ultimate putdown. They have simply turned the ribbon-thin mullions into looped and tangled spaghetti.

A few blocks away is One Wall Street, the Irving Trust Company headquarters, an Art Deco masterpiece of 1932 by Voorhees, Gmelin & Walker. The Grooms One Wall Street does a stylish backbend and flies a banner "In Irving We Trust." And around a corner from a Stock Exchange replica with a splendidly disheveled see-through colonnaded facade, a ticker-tape parade plunges down Broadway next to a bone-filled crypt in the Trinity Church graveyard. Figures of loungers on the Federal Hall steps sit beneath the aloof, modeled feet of a George Washington who turns into a painted horizontal flat abruptly at the knees. A crooked West Side Highway, obviously in terminal disrepair, sports bubble-domed cars, a ship in full sail, and a Hertz truck. The Statue of Liberty, endlessly intoning Emma Lazarus's doleful doggerel, wears red platform shoes. Beneath it all, sewer alligators embrace.

Throughout the work, the monumental and the human factors coexist in a marriage of screwball scale and evocative detail, using techniques from full sculpture to the comic strip. But the real technique is visual irony. Both people and buildings are lovingly observed—from the cultural microcosm of the New York newsstand (full size) to a fine jumble of old brick buildings (miniaturized) adjoining the Woolworth Building in a nice demonstration of how the gorgeous and the mundane lie down together in city streets.

Like a tipsy matron with a tiara, a small building with a crowning acanthus cornice makes it clear that a shabby old structure has been robbed of its pretensions to dignity. In the same way, the costumes of bravura and outrage of the human inhabitants—in contrast to the building-costumes of institutional solemnity—are presented knowingly as body speech in the New York idiom.

Someone else will have to deal with this work in the proper art-critical context of the Pop art tradition or satirical realism, or whatever framework is appropriate. For me, it is a cultural-esthetic-architectural document that deserves its own permanent room at the Museum of the City of New York. Because it *is* New York. And it is nonpareil architectural criticism.

In Lower Manhattan, the somber classical facades jostle the cheap plastic luncheonettes in recognizable street scenes that join magnificence and triviality. Life imitates art.

December 21, 1975

Looking Back at
the Future

THE CITY AS DREAM: HUGH FERRISS

After all this harsh reality, it is time to celebrate the city as dream and fantasy. It is time to look back 50 years to the world of tomorrow. Predicting the form of the future was serious business in the 1920s. But it is not a world that the world of today would recognize, based as it was on the perfectability of man and technology for creating noble, shining cities and universal peace. From the state of mind to the state of the city, we live in another world entirely.

The city of the 1920s was hitched to the machine and the stars. Skyscrapers raced to completion. Artists and philosophers dwelt on the miracle and promise of metropolis, of the new architecture and of the new morality that would shape it. The city of the future seemed at hand. It never arrived; what followed were depression and wars and the slide of those dreams and ideals into cynicism and corruption. What came after was bottom-line architectural pragmatism and the city as setting for social tragedy rather than a brave new world.

It is a time waiting now for the historian, begging to be documented while the buildings and records last, before superficial nostalgia drains it of its deeper meanings. There are still those incredible buildings of the New York skyline that grow more strikingly beautiful as the city does its best to diminish them. And there are also the remarkable, almost forgotten drawings of Hugh Ferriss, the extraordinary architectural illustrator who caught the period's substance and spirit and style.

Familiar to all architectural professionals beyond middle age and totally unfamiliar to the young (who are currently engaged in an orgy of rediscovery), Ferriss drawings are undoubtedly due for a revival. His art was catalytic to the twenties. There is scarcely a major structure of that time in an American city, and in New York in particular, that Ferriss did not draw. He continued to be the prestige illustrator of architecture until his death in 1962, but by then neither the art of design nor the hopes of the city were the same and he could no longer synthesize the mood and structure of a special magic moment. In the later years, only sinuous expressways and monumental dams offered equivalent drama.

Trained as an architect, Ferriss chose to be a renderer, to deal in other men's designs and visions. But he had visions of his own. The personal image of the city that he developed in the second decade of

the twentieth century is as much a part of architectural history as the
real and existing buildings that he recorded with such specialized skill.
He drew in pencil, crayon, and charcoal, and the strongly shaded
blacks and grays and soft, rubbed tones that characterize his work
project both poetry and power.

Those studies that went beyond reality to depict "The Imaginary
City" make up a majestic, grisaille world of uncommon seductivity.
It is tempting to say that they are Piranesi updated, but their shadowed
splendors offer an ordered, monumental urban beauty rather than the
dark, disturbing side of grandeur. Like Piranesi, however, Ferriss also
makes the city an awe-inspiring place.

This vision, with hindsight, is full of failed dreams and impossible
predictions and is rich in historic irony. It is as revealing for its in-
accuracies as for its statements of actuality. The cities were unbuildable and the styles of the future enchantingly off base. But the impact
of these drawings on the design of the important buildings of their
own day was extraordinary; it has yet to be fully credited or understood.

In 1930, the historian and critic Sheldon Cheney wrote in *New
World Architecture:* "More than any architect since Sullivan, Ferriss
influenced the imagination of designers, students, and public. Many a
building of 1928–29 looks like a fulfillment of a Ferriss idealistic
sketch of four or five years earlier." These are the buildings that have
become the landmarks of their age.

For Ferriss not only created a conceptual climate for the men who
actually designed the buildings; they even aspired to his version of the
modern style. In those years it was a style in formulation, not yet a
formula, before zoning and speculative economics had set the city in
an immutably pragmatic mold. Functionalism had not yet stripped
beauty bare (and cheap). The poignance of this grand ideal of the
conscious and ambitious pursuit of the largest possible environmental
elegance gives the period its spectacular nostalgia. It is architecture as
ecstasy. In more sedate, art-historical terms, it catches the important
transition between the Beaux Arts and the fully flowered Modern
Movement.

After graduation from the School of Architecture and Engineering
at Washington University in St. Louis, Ferriss came to New York to
work for Cass Gilbert while the Woolworth Building was being designed in the Cass Gilbert office, sometime before 1913. It was a period
when skyscrapers wore historical dress and architects, as he later recalled, wore silk hats. By the 1920s he was filled with doubts about
such elaborate eclecticism and he left to open his own studio.

He soon became the favored renderer of the leading "modernists" of the day. He drew the "seminal" structures—tremendously admired then and ignored now—such as Arthur Loomis Harmon's Shelton Hotel on Lexington Avenue, built in 1922 (now scheduled for demolition). One of the most important of the large "setback" structures under New York's new zoning law of 1916, it was highly praised for the "broad modeling" of its masses, a concept considered an extreme departure from traditional decorative facades. Ferriss wrote of it later, in 1929, "It evokes that undefinable sense of satisfaction which man ever finds on the slope of a pyramid or a mountainside."

He did a series of studies of the "zoning envelope" that purported to show how architects could build within the space defined and restricted by the law. Radically abstract, they challenge Ledoux in their boldly evocative geometry. He referred to these volumetric schemes as the "crude clay" of architecture. ("Crude clay" was later replaced by the computer.)

Sloan and Robertson's Chanin Building and Raymond Hood's American Radiator Building in New York, Hood and Howell's Chicago Tribune Tower, Albert Kahn's Fisher Building in Detroit and William Van Alen's Chrysler Building, recorded during construction, were all among his subjects. Their design ranged from elaborate skyscraper eclectic and rich Art Deco to what was then approvingly called the "stripped style," in which limited ornament of a "modern" persuasion was used to emphasize massed, plain volumes in the new mode.

This mode was characterized by Cheney as "a new massiveness and precision, clean lines, hard edges, sanitary smoothness, restless drive . . . the poetry of daring." These were "buildings grown organically out of machine-age materials and methods of structure, out of modern needs and modern living, out of honest creativeness, free of stolen trappings." Without blushing, he extended the architectural revolution to the promise of cleaner, brighter lives and a new world peace and order. The proselytizers of the new architecture had seen the promised land.

In 1929, Ferriss published his drawings and descriptions of "The Metropolis of Tomorrow." It is a curious and wonderful Elysium. Tied closely to the formal vistas and geometry of the Beaux Arts, with spaced towers organized on straight and radial axes, it also suggests something of Le Corbusier's towers in a park.

But the buildings take a variety of romantic-modern guises, and it is still uncompromisingly the City Beautiful as it grew out of late nineteenth-century classicism and the 1893 Chicago World's Fair. There are visualizations of glass and concrete structures, stripped, streamlined and massed with a hybrid glamour reminiscent of ancient ziggurats and unborn futuramas. There are strong whiffs of European modernism. There are previsions of Carole Lombard.

It is high fantasy and high art. The city is rigidly organized into a Business Zone, an Arts Zone, and a Science Zone, with superblock towers rising at intersections and ranged as vertical, faceted shafts (his gift of prophecy did not include bleak slabs) along wide avenues. Traffic was sorted into multilevel pedestrian and vehicular precincts. There were overhead roads bridging skyscrapers and airplane shelves attached to them. And it was all meant to enhance the health, convenience, and pleasure of the inhabitants.

Ferriss did more than invent city forms; he transfixed the city's special atmosphere. One feels the light and the hour, whether he drew the city at dawn, or in daylight, or with theatrical night illumination. But beyond this lyrical drama, the architectural substance is thoroughly understood, as no conventional illustrator ever grasps it. Awesome and accurate draftsmanship suggests looming mysteries. "These terraced crags, these soaring towers and pylons and piers overwhelm," Cheney said of New York, in prose no more overwrought than that of most of his contemporaries. "This is at once a new Babel and a City Divine."

It is obvious that Ferriss loved it. Sitting in his studio high over Manhattan, he would watch the early morning city emerge. "A single lofty highlight of gold appeared in the mist: the tip of the Metropolitan Tower," he wrote. "A moment later, a second: the gilded apex of the New York Life Building. And then the other architectural principals . . . the eastern facades grow pale with light . . . a Metropolis appears." It was his city, and in his legacy, it is ours.

January 26, 1975

Index

297

INDEX

INDEX

INDEX

INDEX